WORLD TALES

Happy Birthday
Eric

Love,
Eddie

WORLD TALES

The
extraordinary
coincidence of stories
told in all times,
in all places

Collected
by
IDRIES SHAH

NEW YORK · Harcourt Brace Jovanovich · LONDON

Library of Congress Cataloging in Publication Data
Shah, Idries, Sayed, 1924–
World tales.
Summary: An illustrated collection of
65 folktales, each with an introduction outlining
the appearance of the tale in various cultures.
1. Tales [1. Folklore] I. Title.
GR76.S52   398.2   79-1734
ISBN 0-15-199434-X

First edition

B C D E

"That lurking air of hidden meanings and immemorial mythical signs which we find in some fables, recalling a people, wise and childish at once, who had built up a theory of the world ages before Aesop was born."

Ernest Rhys, 1925.

"The content of folklore is metaphysics. Our inability to see this is due primarily to our abysmal ignorance of metaphysics and its technical terms."

A. K. Coomaraswamy.

"The folk-tale is the primer of the picture-language of the soul."

Joseph Campbell.

"They (tales) appeal to our rational and irrational instincts, to our visions and dreams . . . The race is richer in human and cultural values for its splendid heritage of old magic tales."

Dr. Leonard W. Roberts.

Introduction

It is quite usual to find collections of tales arranged according to language or country: *Tales of Belgium, Stories from the German,* or *Legends from the Indian Peoples;* some such titles must have met your eye at one time or another. It all looks very tidy, scientific even; and the study of stories is indeed a part of scholarly research.

But the deeper you go into things, the more mysterious, exciting, baffling they become. How can it be that the same story is found in Scotland and also in pre-Columbian America? Was the story of Aladdin and his Wonderful Lamp really taken from Wales (where it has been found) to the ancient East; and, if so, by whom and when? A classical Japanese narrative is part of the gypsy repertoire in Europe; where shall we pigeonhole it in national terms?

I have selected and place before you a collection of tales of which one at least goes back to the ancient Egyptian of several thousand years ago. It is presented here not to impress the reader with its age, but because it is entertaining, and also because, although the Pharoahs died out many centuries ago, this tale is recited by people all over the world who know nothing of its origins. This form of culture remains when nations, languages and faiths have long since died.

There is an almost uncanny persistence and durability in the tale which cannot be accounted for in the present state of knowledge. Not only does it constantly appear in different incarnations which can be mapped—as the Tar-Baby story carried from Africa to America, and medieval Arabian stories from the Saracens in Sicily to the Italy of today—but from time to time remarkable collections are assembled and enjoy a phenomenal vogue: after which they lapse and are reborn, perhaps in another culture, perhaps centuries later: to delight, attract, thrill, captivate yet another audience.

Such was the great *Panchatantra,* the Far Eastern collection of tales for the education of Indian princes; the Jataka Buddhist birth-stories believed to date back two and a half thousand years; the Thousand and One Nights, known as 'The Mother of Tales'. Later came the collections of Starapola, Boccaccio, Chaucer and Shakespeare, and a dozen others which now form the very basis of the classical literature of Europe and Asia.

This book contains stories from all of these collections, and many more: because there is a certain basic fund of human fictions which recur, again and again, and never seem to lose their compelling attraction. Many traditional tales have a surface meaning (perhaps just a socially uplifting one) and a secondary, inner significance, which is rarely glimpsed consciously, but which nevertheless acts powerfully upon our minds. Tales have always been used, so far as we can judge, for spiritual as well as social purposes: and as

parables with more or less obvious meanings this use is familiar to most people today. But, as Professor Geoffrey Parrinder says of the myth,* "its inner truth was realized when the participant was transported into the realm of the sacred and eternal."

Perhaps above all the tale fulfils the function not of escape but of hope. The suspending of ordinary constraints helps people to reclaim optimism and to fuel the imagination with energy for the attainment of goals: whether moral or material. Maxim Gorky realized this when he wrote: "In tales people fly through the air on a magic carpet, walk in seven-league boots, build castles overnight; the tales opened up for me a new world where some free and all-fearless power reigned and inspired in me a dream of a better life."

When relatively recent collectors of tales, such as Hans Christian Andersen, the Brothers Grimm, Perrault and others made their selections, they both re-established certain powerful tales in our cultures and left out others from the very vast riches of the world reservoir of stories. Paradoxically, by their very success in imprinting Cinderella, Puss-in-Boots and Beauty and the Beast anew for the modern reader (they are all very ancient tales, widely dispersed) they directed attention away from some of the most wonderful and arresting stories which did not feature in their collections. Many of these stories are re-presented here.

Working for thirty-five years among the written and oral sources of our world heritage in tales, one feels a truly living element in them which is startlingly evident when one isolates the 'basic' stories: the ones which tend to have travelled farthest, to have featured in the largest number of classical collections, to have inspired great writers of the past and present.

One becomes aware, by this contact with the fund of tradition which constantly cries out to be projected anew, that the story in some elusive way is the basic form and inspiration. Thought or style, characterization and belief, didactic and nationality, all recede to give place to the tale which feels almost as if it is demanding to be reborn through one's efforts. And yet those efforts themselves, in some strange way, are experienced as no more than the relatively poor expertise of the humblest midwife. It is the tale itself, when it emerges, which is king.

Erskine Caldwell, no less, has felt a similar power in the story, and is well aware of its primacy over mere thought of philosophy: "A writer," he says (Atlantic Monthly, July 1958) "is not a great mind, he's not a great thinker, he's not a great philosopher, he's a story-teller."

Idries Shah
London, March 1979

---

* G. Parrinder, Foreword to *Pears Encyclopaedia of Myths and Legends,* London 1976, p. 10.

Contents

Illustrators of World Tales
Ivan Tyrrell, Art Director

Detail from 'Anpu and Bata' by Ivan Hissey

A Note on the Illustrations

It is fitting that *World Tales,* the first book of its kind to carry such a high quality of illustrations from so many individuals, should be a new work by Idries Shah. For it is he who is currently demonstrating the wealth to be found in the world's heritage of teaching stories, jokes and tales which have been the inspiration for numerous artists down the centuries.

This unusual and entertaining collection has offered to many of our finest illustrators an ideal opportunity to produce their best work to date. To our knowledge, there has never before been a book where so many different artists of such calibre have contributed in this way.

The finest art has almost always been in the service of something other than an artist's own ego, that is to say, it is commissioned for a purpose. Individual artists, working in isolation, rarely achieve anything of interest to anyone but themselves and a small elitist group. The illustrations in this book stand directly in the great tradition of the popular master illustrators, great communicators like Dulac, Arthur Rackham, The Robertson Brothers, Maxfield Parrish and further back to the renowned illuminators of Medieval Europe, Persia, India, China and Japan. This is not a static tradition; it is as alive and fruitful today as never before, with an increasing number of young artists making brilliant contributions that everyone can appreciate.

As well as decoratively complementing the text the illustrations in *World Tales* act as a delightful aid to visualising new possibilities. They help open the door to that part of our minds where anything is possible and prompt us to wander without inhibition, through the many scenes in these stories, come under their spell, and partake as best we can of whatever they impart.

Ivan Tyrrell
Brighton, March 1979

WORLD TALES

An ancient Sanskrit work, now lost, is believed to be the original of the **Parrot Tales,** which have been found in folk-recitals from Indonesia to Italy. The 14th century Persian **Tuti Nama** (Parrot Book) by Nakhshabi is the collection of linked tales best known in the East, and it is still very widely read and recited. There is a derivative Sanskrit version, the **Seventy Parrot Tales.** Many of these stories, told by a parrot to divert his mistress while her husband is away, are found in the medieval **Seven Wise Masters,** which circulated for centuries in Europe with a popularity second only to the Bible. The book is found in Greek, Hebrew, and other languages. The first European version is thought to have been prepared by the monk Johannes, of the French diocese of Nancy, in about 1184 A.D. The tales are thought to have been dispersed among the people of the West by wandering preachers. "By such means," says the eminent scholar Clouston, "Stories, which had their birth in the Far East more than two thousand years ago, spread into the remotest nooks of Europe; and jests, which had long shaken the shoulders and wagged the beards of grave and otiose Orientals, became naturalized from cold Sweden to sunny Italy."

The frame-story of the **Parrot Tales,** split into three tales, was collected by the learned Giuseppe Pitrè, in Sicily, over a century ago, from peasant lips. Several versions have been found in Italy. The interest of this one, apart from its entertainment value, is the fact that, unlike most of the folk tales of similar origins, it stems from the Sanskrit version, and not from an intermediate Islamic source, such as the Turkish, Arabic, or Persian collections. The medium through which a Sanskrit-based tale reached Europe is not known.

The Chester Beatty Library, Dublin.

Illustration from the 14th Century Persian Tuti Nama

Tales of a Parrot

I

Once upon a time there lived a king, who had an only daughter, who was the sun, moon, and stars to him. He gave her everything which she desired, and there was nothing in the world which she was denied.

On the day when this story begins, the King and the Princess went driving out into the countryside, as it was springtime. So many beautiful flowers were in every valley that they drove quite a long way. They stopped the royal coach, walked about for a while, and after picking a few blossoms, drove back to the palace.

Now, no sooner did the Princess return to the palace hall, than she saw with dismay that her favourite toy, a beautiful life-like doll, had been left behind somewhere — on a hedge, maybe. She was out of her mind with grief, for that doll had been hers since ever she could remember, and as she had no brothers or sisters, it was everything to her. The doll was dressed as she was, daily, and had almost as many jewels as the Princess herself possessed.

So she decided that, without telling her father she would slip out at the first possible moment and go to look for the doll.

It was not long before the King went to change his robes, and she found her chance to escape through a secret exit. Not being very used to going about alone, however, the Princess was soon completely lost. Night was falling when she saw a fine palace in front of her.

Knocking on the door, she shouted,"Who is the owner of this magnificent building?" She called out in a most regal way, and the captain of the guard who was at the entrance said,"Lady, this is the palace of the Great and Glorious King of Spain!"

"I am a king's daughter," she said, and she was at once admitted, and taken to a guest chamber. There she was undressed by several maids, and robed for the night with much ceremony. She soon fell asleep, and without any fear, since she was in a royal household, slept as if she were safe at home.

Next morning, she was taken before the King of Spain.

He was very impressed with her appearance, and with her manner and charm.

"Will you remain here with me and administer the palace as if it were your own?" he asked, for he had

no daughter, and his wife had been dead some years.

"Certainly, I shall be happy to do so," said the Princess, and she soon felt that she had never lived anywhere else in the world.

But there was trouble in the palace among the courtiers. Twelve royal maidens who were related to the King of Spain by marriage felt that they had been passed over for a complete stranger.

Gossip and intrigue circulated and soon the courtiers had taken sides. Some were for the royal maidens, others were for the Princess.

"How can we take orders and instructions from one so young and inexperienced in our ways as this girl!" they whispered. "Who indeed is she, though she says she is a true Princess? Let us plot her downfall!" So they went to her, and with smiles and giggles said, "Oh, dear lady, why do you not come with us upon our next outing? There are many things we could show you, far away from the confines of the court!"

"Oh, no," the Princess shook her head, "I am not sure that I can go anywhere without the permission of dear Royal Papa. He never likes me to leave his side."

"But we know a sure method by which you can be spared," said they, "Let us tell you what to say to His Majesty." "What am I to say?" cried the Princess.

"Just say 'By the soul of your daughter you must let me go with the royal maidens!'" they murmured in her ear.

"Very well," said the Princess, "I will try it." But no sooner had she said the fateful words to the devoted King, than the smile left his face, the light of anger came to his eyes, and he shouted, "Ah! Wretched girl! How dare you speak to me like that! To the trapdoor with you!" And the unfortunate Princess felt herself propelled towards a large trapdoor in the floor. She soon was falling through time and space, falling, falling in the most horrible darkness.

Suddenly, she stopped falling, and could feel the wood of another door. She turned the knob, blindly, and it gave way. Then she felt tinder and matches in her hand, and lit a lamp. Another door stood half-open, and slowly advancing, the Princess saw in the light of the lamp a beautiful young girl, as fair as the moon on her fourteenth night. This unfortunate young creature had her hands bound and a silver padlock on her mouth, so that she could not speak. The Princess looked at her questioningly, and the girl indicated that, under the pillow of the bed, was a silver key. The Princess found it, and saw that it was set with a green stone in the top.

The Princess unlocked the girl's lips, and she said, "I am a king's daughter, stolen away by a wicked magician. He had left me here for I do not know how long, and feeds me when he comes. Every night at midnight he arrives, with two slaves carrying bowls of food and fruit."

"But, tell me," said the Princess, "Is there any way in which you might be freed? This imprisonment must be torment for you!"

"I can only find that out by asking the magician," said the other, "so tonight conceal yourself under the bed, and listen to all that passes between us. I shall try to wheedle some sort of information regarding this out of him, so listen well, dear lady, and save me if you can."

"That I shall do, with all my heart and all my strength, if it comes to that," said the Princess, and got under the bed in readiness for the arrival of the magician.

When twelve o'clock came, the door flew open, and a strange-looking man, with a long dark robe, white beard, and fierce, piercingly blue eyes appeared, attended by two coal-black slaves of savage aspect. The magician took the key, unlocked the younger Princess's lips and with every sign of affection, fed her with his own hands from the bowls.

While she was eating, he was paying her extravagant compliments, and she said, "Now, just for argument's sake, if I were ever to escape from here, how could it be done? I pray you tell me, that I might be diverted by the telling of it!"

The magician looked taken aback for a few seconds; then he smiled and said: "Well, since there is no chance that you ever *could* be able to do it, I will tell you."

"It would be necessary for someone to put gunpowder all around the palace; and, at midnight, when I appear, set light to it. Then it would blow a complete circle around the palace, and I would be blown up into the air. But eat these delicacies — you would not get food like this in the world except through my magical agency!"

The young girl laughed, and passed it off as though the idea meant nothing to her. After that, the magician caused one of the slaves to wash her mouth with rosewater, the magician dried it himself with a fine napkin, and he went away, not forgetting to lock her lips again with the padlock.

After a short while, the Princess came out from under the bed and said, "Sister, sister, have no fear, I

will go and summon help from my adoptive father up there in the castle. Somehow you will be rescued, or we shall be blown up together!"

She crept out of the room, climbed through the trapdoor, and began to shout for the King of Spain.

The King of Spain, who had missed her after she had disappeared through the trapdoor at his command, came to her, and she told him the whole story from beginning to end.

He said "I will send for the captain of the guard, even though it be the middle of the night, to make a ring of gunpowder around the castle as soon as he possibly can get the men roused. I myself will light the powder at the very second twelve o'clock strikes. Leave it to me, and go back to your own room, my dear." "No, no, father," cried the Princess, "I have promised that poor girl that I shall rescue her, or we shall both get blown up together."

"So be it," said the King of Spain, and the brave Princess vanished again down the tunnel. She comforted the girl with the silver padlock on her lips, as well as she could, and whispered words of encouragement to help her pass the hours of waiting.

The King's sappers began digging, and worked away with a will to prepare the mine. The day passed very slowly for the two girls. By the time it was nearly midnight, the gunpowder was ready in one large circle all around the castle.

When the clock struck twelve midnight, the magician came as usual through the door of the chamber. The Princess was hidden under the bed, and the girl with the silver padlock on her lips looked as she always did, patiently waiting for him.

The torch set the gunpowder alight, the ring of powder ignited, and the magician was blown into the sky in a thousand pieces. The two girls were severely shocked for a few seconds; but soon began to laugh with joy and relief, though they had singed eyebrows, torn clothes, and blackened faces.

When the King of Spain saw them, climbing out of the tunnel, he exclaimed "Ah, my beautiful daughter! Come to me and be with me here in harmony for the rest of our lives! You my dear," he added to the brave Princess who had effected the rescue, "You shall have the crown after I am dead!"

"No, no, dear King of Spain," cried she, "I am a king's daughter myself, and I, too, have right to a crown!"

So a feast was prepared which took many days and nights of jollity.

This matter spread all over the earth, everyone taking the story to his or her own country, and everybody talked of the great courage and goodness of that beautiful Princess who had saved another King's daughter from certain death and dishonour.

And all the chief actors in this tale (except, of course, the magician) enjoyed life and happiness in all the days of their sojourn in this world.

II

Once there was a king who had an only daughter who was as beautiful as any young girl ever born to humankind.

On her eighteenth birthday news came that the King of the Turks wanted to marry her.

"Oh, what do I want with a Turk for a husband?" she said, and refused to have anything to do with him.

Soon after this affair, she lapsed into a very unhappy state of health — she, who had never had anything wrong with her in her life before.

Her father the King sent for doctors from far and wide, but none could be found to help her, let alone to tell what was actually wrong with the Princess.

She lay on her silken sheets, eyes rolling, body shivering, her limbs twisted under her.

Her poor father was in distress, and called the wise men of his capital city together. "My friends, hear me at this time of my personal distress as you did when the country was in danger from enemies," he said. "Tell me what I am to do!"

"Your Majesty," said they in unison, "Find the Princess of whom we have just heard, who caused the rescue of the daughter of the King of Spain from the dreaded magician who hid her away and locked her lips. Find her, and she will find a way!" For the Princess who wrought the miracle had become the talk of every country in the world, and there was no quarter of the earth where her name was unknown.

The King ordered ships to set out that very hour to search for the lady. "If the King of Spain will not let her leave him and come, then shall we go to war against Spain, though she be the mightiest country of Christendom!" spoke the monarch boldly, with eyes of fire.

The ships set off, and arrived off Spain very soon. All their guns blazed in salute across the bay, the envoy set foot on the earth of Spain, and bent down to kiss it in homage. "A message, a message from a

faraway king to the King of Spain," was the cry.

The sealed letter borne by an envoy dressed in scarlet and gold, was handed to the King of Spain.

He broke the seal, and let his eye wander over the message. But he clenched his fist and shouted, "I will go to war, but I will never send my dearest adopted daughter on such a mission!" and he tore up the letter.

The Princess came from behind the ivory screen and asked, "What is it, Royal Papa? Who was that letter from, and what is this about?"

"Dear daughter, the King of another country has sent his ships to take you away to help in the affair of *his* daughter. You shall not go, I forbid it!"

"What are you afraid about? I will return to you, in time, after I have settled this thing," she said.

So she went, after taking leave of him with great tenderness.

When she arrived, the King went to greet her.

"My daughter, if you cure this child of mine you shall have my crown!" he vowed.

"I am a king's daughter myself, and I already have a crown," she said, as she had said to the other King. "Let us see what the matter is, never mind about crowns or coronets."

She was taken to the Princess's bedchamber and saw her lying there, all wasted away.

Now, after a few moments thought, the Princess who had just arrived turned to the King and said "Your Majesty, have some soup made, and some chickens cooked. Also, cheese and fruit. Have these things brought to me here, and lock me in this room alone with your daughter for the space of three days.

"No matter what you hear, or even if I cry out for you to open up, do not do so. Within three days I will deliver your daughter to you alive or dead.

"Remember, whatever I say to you, do not open the door."

Soon everything was done to her liking, and the great bolts were fastened on each side. But when she went to sit beside the Princess as the light from the windows failed, she discovered that they had forgotten the tinder to light the candles at night. So, she poked about in cupboards, with the unlit candle in her hand, looking for a tinder-box. One of the doors led to a small room; and, looking out of the window, she saw a light in the distance. She could not stand the dark, so she descended from the window with a ladder of silk to try to find the light.

When she got near the light she saw it was a huge black cauldron placed on a fire. There was a tall Turk stirring something in the pot with a stick.

She greeted him with, "What are you doing, O Noble Turk?" And he replied, "My King wanted the daughter of this King, but she did not want him, so he is having this done as a bewitchment."

"Oh, poor Turk," she said, laying her hand on his sleeve, "you must be tired, stirring like that for so long and so bravely."

"Yes," said the Turk, "I am rather tired now, and I wish that someone else would help me."

"Why, I will help you," said she, "You just lie down there, and I will continue stirring for you."

"That is extremely kind," said the Turk, yawning, and he lay down. She took the stick and began to stir.

"Am I doing it correctly?" asked the Princess.

"Yes, indeed, beautiful lady," the Turk replied, "If only I could sleep for a little while . . ."

"Well, you take a sleep now and I will stir," said she, and the Turk fell into a doze.

When he was asleep she bent down; and, with her amazing strength, threw him into the boiling cauldron. When she saw that he was dead, she lit her candle at the fire and returned up the silken ladder to the bedchamber.

She sat beside the sick Princess's bed, and saw that she seemed to be better. For three days and three nights she nursed her and fed her with the delicacies which the King had provided. When the Princess got up on the morning of the third day, perfectly well again, the girls embraced each other, and called through the door for the King to open it. He came in at once, and kissed them both with great joy.

"Ah, my daughter," he said to the Princess who had wrought the miracle, "I owe you my kingdom and my daughter's life! What in the world can I give you to repay you? Tell me, I am at your command."

"Nothing my gifts have brought me are of any value; I only work by the power vested in me by Providence," she replied.

"Stay with us here," pleaded the King, "and you shall be as dear to me as my own daughter."

"No, you threatened my father with war if I did not come, remember," she said, "and my father will declare war upon your country if I do not return at once, so let me go, with your leave."

Sadly, the King agreed, and thanking her again, gave a great feast in her honour. Loaded with costly presents for herself and her father, she soon departed, and returned to the King of Spain's palace.

III

Once upon a time there lived a king and queen, who had a handsome son whose only diversion in life was to go hunting. Morning and noon he hunted, attended by many huntsmen. Now, one day, he was far afield when he saw a most beautiful doll lying on the ground. It was dressed like a real live princess would be attired, and even had real jewels in its ears and round its neck. He looked everywhere to see where the owner of this fabulous doll might be, but there was no one to be seen in any direction. So he took the doll up onto his horse, as if it had been a lady, and declared to the others "We shall return home at once now," and they rode back to his father's kingdom. In his private room the Prince examined the doll, and placed it upon his mantlepiece, looking at it long. "What a beautiful doll," he said again and again to himself. "If the doll is so beautiful, what must its mistress be like? Surely it is made in her image." After he had taken the doll to his room the Prince would not leave it, gazing upon it fondly hour by hour, murmuring "Just think of the mistress, if the doll is so beautiful!"

When he had not seen the Prince for several days, and the court physician told him he had been keeping to his private apartment, the King went to see him. He found the Prince looking at the doll on the mantlepiece, muttering feverishly "If this is the doll, how beautiful must be the mistress!"

"My boy!" cried the King, "Are you completely out of your wits! What are you doing with that image? Have you become an idol-worshipper in the space of a few days since you came back from your last hunt? Tell me the truth of the matter at once."

The Prince turned lack-lustre eyes upon his father and said in a low voice, "If this is the doll, just think how beautiful the mistress of such a doll must be! Just think of the mistress, if this is only the doll!"

Horrified at his son's wasted appearance and strange manner, the King went back to the throne-room and summoned all his courtiers.

He said: "See what has happened to my son, he has become mad! What is to be done? The physician says he has no physical ill, no fever, no broken bones, but his mind has completely gone. Such a man cannot possibly take my place as ruler when I am gone. What is to be done?"

One aged sage stepped forward and bowed before the throne.

"Speak," said the King.

"Your Majesty, people are talking about a miraculous Princess who goes from kingdom to kingdom, curing people. She is said to have found the King of Spain's lost daughter, and to have cured another princess only recently. Send for her, and if she will not come, declare war upon her father!"

"Well said," agreed the King. "Send an envoy for her at once. I will brook no delay. My son must be cured for the sake of the country and the people, if not for mine."

So a suitable courtier was sent with a long retinue and a sealed letter from the King.

When these foreigners arrived, the hall of audience was full of people thronging through it. The Princess looked from behind the carved screen and said to the King, who was reading the letter: "What ails you, father?"

"Nothing, nothing my dear, said the King, frowning and biting his nails, tossing the letter into the corner rolled up into a ball.

"There must be something wrong. Who are all these strangers at court, and what news does that foreign envoy bring in that letter which you have thrown away?" she asked gently.

"It is war," said the King testily, "Unless I allow you to go on yet another of these ridiculous journeys to the far corners of the world!"

"Is someone ill again?" she asked.

"Yes, this time a young prince, who is behaving very strangely and seems to be quite out of his wits. I do not think that I should expose you to these dangers . . ."said the King.

"I must go, I shall soon come back, I promise, dear father," said she, and after he had embraced her, she set off.

With many attendants and soldiers, the Princess's journey took quite a time, but at last she arrived at the Prince's private room. He was looking at a beautiful doll and sighing deeply, murmuring to himself the while, "Oh, what a beautiful doll. If this is the doll, just think how wonderful the mistress of this doll must be!" But as he was now so feeble, he said it all under his breath.

So the Princess said to the King: "Close me up in this room with the Prince for three days. Lock the doors and do not come in until I call you to open them. Leave some food here for me to give him daily, and in three days I will bring him out alive and well, or dead."

They did as she asked, and she sat with him, feeding him chicken broth sip by sip, until she made him stronger.

At last, when he was able he called in quite a loud voice: "Oh, what a beautiful doll! If that is the doll, how much more beautiful must be the mistress!"

"Ah, wretch," cried the Princess, "so it is *you* who have got my doll!"

He raised himself on one elbow and said, "Are *you* the owner of the doll?"

"Yes," she said, "I am. Now drink this chicken broth and get well."

When he was able to get out of the bed, they called through the door to his father that he was cured.

So the King and the courtiers came in, and carried the Prince out to the people, happy and well, looking even more handsome than he had been before.

The Princess took down her doll from the mantle-piece, and hugged it for sheer joy.

Soon the Prince told her he was in love with her, and begged her to marry him. "For though the doll is beautiful," he said, "You are so much more beautiful, as I knew you would be. Will you marry me and become in time the Queen, when I am King?"

And so she answered that she would.

The King, delighted to have such a wonderful daughter-in-law, gave her many jewels, and the people were wild with joy at having the famous Princess for their Prince's bride.

Several letters were written and sent with trusted messengers right away: among them one to the King of Spain to tell him that she would not be returned to him as a daughter, but later, she would go back with her Prince to pay their respects; and another letter to the King whose daughter she had cured.

At the time of the wedding, which was one of great splendour, all the monarchs came together and helped to make the Princess's good fortune complete. And she lived in great peace and happiness till the end of her days. ∎

The thrilling and romantic story of poor Dick Whittington and his rise to fame and fortune through the exploits of a cat which was his only possession, was first published three hundred and fifty years ago in London. It has remained a rags-to-riches epic ever since. Sir Richard Whittington did, in fact, exist; he was indeed three times Lord Mayor of London; he did marry a certain Alice Fitz-Warren. These, however, are the only three true facts of the story, so far as can be ascertained. He was not of humble birth; the son of Sir William Whittington of Gloucestershire, he was born in about 1358, almost two centuries before his highly-coloured adventures first saw the light of day. And yet his biographer, Besant, seems to have believed the tale of the cat. Research has shown that the tale was current in Europe in the century before Whittington's birth. It is to be found attributed to a merchant of Genoa and two citizens of Venice, not to mention its fame in Portugal, Norway, Denmark, Russia, and France. The earliest form is the legend of the foundation of the royal house of Qays, written by Abdallah, son of Fazlullah, of Shiraz, in Persia, sixty years before Dick Whittington's birth. He, in his turn, refers the events to the 11th century. This enthralling grafting of a popular story onto a real-life figure's history is supplied by the famous folklorist Andrew Lang, in this version, from the ancient chap-book version of Gomme and Wheatley.

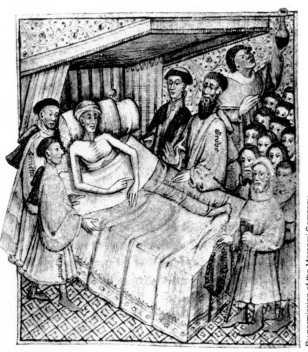

Sir Richard Whittington on his death bed

Dick Whittington and His Cat

Dick Whittington was a very little boy when his father and mother died; so little indeed that he never knew them, nor the place where he was born. He wandered about the country as ragged as a colt, till he met with a waggoner who was going to London, and who let him walk all the way by the side of his waggon without paying anything. This pleased little Whittington very much, as he wanted to see London badly, for he had heard that the streets were paved with gold, and he was willing to get a bushel of it. But how great was his disappointment, poor boy! when he saw the streets covered with dirt instead of gold, and found himself in a strange place, without a friend, without food, and without money.

Though the waggoner was so charitable as to let him walk up by the side of the waggon for nothing, he took good care not to know him when they came to town, and the poor boy was, in a little time, so cold and hungry that he wished himself in a good kitchen and by a warm fire in the country.

In this distress he asked charity of several people and one of them bid him "Go and work, you idle rogue." "That I will," says Whittington, "with all my heart; I will work for you if you will let me."

The man, who thought this was wit and impertinence (though the poor lad intended only to show his readiness to work), gave him a blow with a stick which cut his head so that the blood ran down. In this situation; and fainting for want of food, he laid himself down at the door of one Mr. Fitzwarren, a merchant, where the cook saw him. Being an ill-natured hussy, she said that if he did not go about his business, she would throw boiling water on him. At this time Mr. Fitzwarren came home, and also began to scold the poor boy, telling him to go to work.

Whittington answered that he would be glad to work if anybody would employ him, and that he should be able if he could get some food to eat, for he had had nothing for three days, and he was a poor country boy, and knew nobody, and nobody would employ him.

He then tried to get up, but he was so very weak that he fell down again. The merchant was sorry for him, and he ordered the servants to take him in and give him some meat and drink; and to let him help the cook to do any dirty work that she had to give him. People are too apt to accuse those who beg of being idle, but give themselves no concern to put them in the way of getting something to do, or considering whether they are able to do it, which is not charity.

But we return to Whittington, who would have lived happily in this worthy family had he not been bumped about by the cross cook, who was always roasting or basting, and who, when she had nothing else to do, used to smack poor Whittington! At last Miss Alice, his master's daughter, was told about it and she took pity on the poor boy, and made the servants treat him kindly.

Besides the crossness of the cook, Whittington had another difficulty to get over before he could be happy. He had, by order of his master, a bed placed for him in an attic, where there were a number of rats and mice. They often ran over the poor boy's nose and disturbed him in his sleep. After some time, however, a gentleman who came to his master's house gave Whittington a penny for brushing his shoes. This he put into his pocket, being determined to use it to the best advantage; and the next day, seeing a woman in the street with a cat under her arm, he ran up to know the price of it. As the cat was a good mouser, the woman asked a great deal of money for it. But on Whittington's telling her he had but a penny in the world, and that he wanted a cat badly, she let him have it.

This cat Whittington concealed in his room, for fear she should be beat about by his mortal enemy the cook, and here she soon killed or frightened away the rats and mice, so that the poor boy could now sleep as sound as a top.

Soon after this the merchant, who had a ship ready to sail, called for his servants, as his custom was, so that each of them might venture something to try their luck; and whatever they sent was to pay neither freight nor custom, for he thought justly that God Almighty would bless him the more for his readiness to let the poor partake of his fortune.

All the servants appeared except poor Whittington, who, having neither money nor goods, could not think of sending anything to try his luck; but his good friend Miss Alice, thinking his poverty kept him away, ordered him to be called.

She then offered to lay down something for him, but the merchant told his daughter that would not do, it must be something of his own. Upon which poor Whittington said he had nothing but a cat which he had bought for a penny that was given him. "Fetch the cat, boy," said the merchant, "and send her." Whittington brought poor puss and delivered her to the captain, with tears in his eyes, for he said he should now be disturbed by the rats and mice as much as ever. All the company laughed at the adventure except Miss Alice, who pitied the poor boy, and gave him something to buy another cat.

While puss was beating the billows at sea, poor Whittington was severely beaten at home by his mistress, the cook, who used him so cruelly, and made such fun of him for sending his cat to sea, that at last the poor boy decided to run away and, having packed up the few things he had, he set out very early in the morning on All-Hallows Day. He travelled as far as Holloway, and there sat down on a stone to consider what course he should take; but while he was thinking, Bow bells, of which there were only six, began to ring; and he thought their sounds addressed him in this manner:

"Turn again, Whittington,
Thrice Lord Mayor of London."

"Lord Mayor of London!" said he to himself; "what would one not endure to be Lord Mayor of London, and ride in such a fine coach? Well, I'll go back again, and bear all the pummelling and ill-usage of Cicely rather than miss the opportunity of being Lord Mayor!" So home he went, and happily got into the house and back to his work before Mrs. Cicely made her appearance.

We must now follow Miss Puss to the coast of Africa. How perilous are voyages at sea, how uncertain the winds and the waves, and how many accidents attend a naval life!

The ship which had the cat on board was long beaten at sea, and at last, by contrary winds, driven on a part of the coast of Barbary which was inhabited by Moors unknown to the English. These people received our countrymen with civility; and therefore the captain, in order to trade with them, showed them samples of the goods he had on board, and sent some of them to

the King of the country, who was so well pleased that he sent for the captain and Mr. Fitzwarren's agent to his palace, which was about a mile from the sea. Here they were placed, according to the custom of the country, on rich carpets, flowered with gold and silver. The King and Queen being seated at the upper end of the room, dinner was brought in, which consisted of many dishes. But no sooner were the dishes put down but an amazing number of rats and mice came from all directions and gobbled up all the meat in an instant.

The agent, in surprise, turned round to the nobles and asked if these vermin were not offensive. "Oh, yes," said they, "very offensive; and the King would give half his treasure to be freed of them, for they not only destroy his dinner, as you see, but they attack him in his room, and even in bed, so that he is obliged to be watched while he is sleeping for fear of them."

The agent jumped for joy; he remembered poor Whittington and his cat, and told the King that he had a creature on board ship that would get rid of all these vermin immediately. The King's heart heaved so high at the joy which this news gave him that his turban dropped off his head. "Bring this creature to me," said he; "vermin are dreadful in a court, and if she will perform what you say I will load your ship with gold and jewels in exchange for her." The agent, who knew his business, took this opportunity to set forth the merits of Miss Puss. He told His Majesty that it would be inconvenient to part with her, as when she was gone, the rats and mice might destroy the goods in the ship—but to oblige his Majesty he would fetch her. "Run, run," said the Queen; "I am impatient to see the dear creature."

Away flew the agent, while another dinner was provided, and returned with the cat just as the rats and mice were devouring that also. He immediately put down Miss Puss, who killed a great number of them.

The King rejoiced greatly to see his old enemies destroyed by so small a creature, and the Queen was highly pleased, and desired the cat might be brought near that she might look at her. Upon which the factor called "Pussy, pussy, pussy!" and she came to him. He then presented her to the Queen, who started back, and was afraid to touch a creature who had made such a havoc among the rats and mice; however, when the man stroked the cat and called "Pussy, pussy!" the Queen also touched her and cried "Putty, putty!" for she had not learned English.

He then put the cat down on the Queen's lap, where she, purring, played with her Majesty's hand and then sang herself to sleep.

The King having seen the exploits of Miss Puss, and being informed that her kittens would stock the whole country, bargained with the captain and factor for the whole ship's cargo, and then gave them ten times as much for the cat as all the rest amounted to. On which, taking leave of their Majesties and other great personages at court, they sailed with a fair wind for England—whither we must now attend them.

The morn had scarcely dawned when Mr. Fitzwarren arose to count over the cash and settle the business for that day. He had just entered the counting-house and seated himself at the desk, when somebody came tap, tap, at the door. "Who's there?" said Mr. Fitzwarren. "A friend," answered the other. "What friend can come at this unseasonable time?" "A real friend is never unseasonable," answered the other. "I come to bring you good news of your ship Unicorn." The merchant bustled up in such a hurry that he forgot his gout; instantly opened the door, and who should be seen waiting but the captain and agent, with a cabinet of jewels, and a bill of lading, for which the merchant lifted up his eyes and thanked heaven for sending him such a prosperous voyage. Then they told him the adventures of the cat, and showed him the cabinet of jewels which they had brought for Mr. Whittington. Upon which he cried out with great earnestness, but not in the most poetical manner:

"Go, send him in, and tell him of his fame,
And call him Mr. Whittington by name."

Mr. Fitzwarren was a good man; for when some who were present told him that this treasure was too much for such a poor boy as Whittington, he said: "God forbid that I should deprive him of a penny. It is his own, and he shall have it to a farthing." He then ordered Mr. Whittington in, who was at this time cleaning the kitchen and would have excused himself from going into the counting-house, saying the room was swept and his shoes were dirty and full of hobnails. The merchant, however, made him come in, and ordered a chair to be set for him. Upon which, thinking they intended to make fun of him, as had been too often the case in the kitchen, he begged his master not to mock a poor simple fellow, who intended no harm, but let him go about his business. The merchant, taking him by the hand, said: "Indeed, Mr. Whittington, I sent for you to congratulate you on your great success. Your cat has made you more money than I am worth in the world, and may you long enjoy it and be happy!"

At length, being shown the treasure, and convinced by then that all of it belonged to him, he fell upon his knees and thanked the Almighty for his providential care of such a poor and miserable creature. He then laid all the treasure at his master's feet, who refused to take any part of it, but told him he hoped the wealth would be a comfort to him, and would make him happy. He then applied to his mistress, and to his good friend, Miss Alice, who refused to take any part of the money, but told him she heartily rejoiced at his good success, and wished him all imaginable happiness. He then gave presents to the captain, the agent, and the ship's crew for the care they had taken of his cargo. He likewise distributed presents to all the servants of the house, not forgetting even his old enemy the cook, though she little deserved it.

After this Mr. Fitzwarren advised Mr. Whittington to send for the necessary people and dress himself like a gentleman, and made him the offer of his house to live in till he could provide himself with one better.

Now it came to pass when Mr. Whittington's face was washed, his hair curled, and he was dressed in a rich suit of clothes, that he turned out a genteel young fellow; and as wealth contributes much to give a man confidence, he in a little time dropped that sheepish behaviour which was mainly caused by a depression of spirits, and soon grew a sprightly and good

companion, and Miss Alice, who had formerly pitied him, now fell in love with him.

When her father saw that they had this liking for each other he suggested that they should marry. The Lord Mayor, Court of Aldermen, Sheriffs, the Company of Stationers, the Royal Academy of Arts, and a number of eminent merchants attended the ceremony, and were elegantly treated at an entertainment made for that purpose.

History further relates that they lived very happily, had several children, and died at a good old age. Mr. Whittington served Sheriff of London and was three times Lord Mayor. In the last year of his mayoralty he entertained King Henry V and his Queen, after his conquest of France, upon which occasion the King, in consideration of Whittington's merit, said: "Never had a prince such a subject"; which being told to Whittington at the table, he replied: "Never had a subject such a King." His Majesty out of respect to his good character, conferred the honour of knighthood on him soon after.

Sir Richard many years before his death constantly fed a great number of poor citizens, built a church and a college to it, with a yearly allowance for poor scholars, and near it erected a hospital.

He also built Newgate Prison, and gave liberally to St. Bartholomew's Hospital and other public charities.

■

Don't Count Your Chickens

This tale is the origin of perhaps the best-known proverb in the world — "The Girl and the Pitcher of Milk." Professor Max Muller remarks how the tale has survived the rise and fall of empires and the change of languages, and the perishing of works of art, and stresses the attraction whereby "this simple children's tale should have lived on and maintained its place of honour and its undisputed sway in every schoolroom of the East and every nursery of the West."

In the Eastern versions, it is always a man who is the fantasist and whose hopes come to grief: in the West, it is almost always a woman. The man generally imagines that he will marry and have a son, while the woman tends to think of riches and marriage.

The outline is invariably the same: details change. In the Hindu tale (in the **Hitopadesa***), flour is spilt; in La Fontaine's French fable, milk. Truhana, of the medieval Spanish* **Don Lucanor** *(given here) finds the honey coming to grief; in the Arabic of the* **Kalila***, it is butter and honey. The Turkish* **Forty Vizirs** *collection — and the Greek of Symeon features oil and honey; in Aesop it is eggs which are smashed; in the* **Arabian Nights,** *glass.*

Emphases of the meaning vary. With the Brahmin, it is greed and lack of foresight, with the Persian devotee in the Turkish, undue concentration on one thing; in the Arabian **Kalila** *and elsewhere, there is a hint that violent action is one's undoing. Rabelais, (in his* **Gargantua***) attributes this folly to a shoemaker who struck a pot of milk in his excitement at becoming rich in fantasy: 'Destroying that which may lead to success by the thought of that success itself'.*

Once upon a time there lived a woman called Truhana. Not being very rich, she had to go yearly to the market to sell honey, the precious product of her hive.

Along the road she went, carrying the jar of honey upon her head, calculating as she walked the money she would get for the honey. "First," she thought, "I will sell it, and buy eggs. The eggs I shall set under my fat brown hens, and in time there will be plenty of little chicks. These in turn, will become chickens, and from the sale of these, lambs could be bought."

Truhana then began to imagine how she could become richer than her neighbours, and look forward to marrying well her sons and daughters.

Trudging along, in the hot sun, she could see her fine sons and daughters-in-law, and how the people would say that it was remarkable how rich she had become, who was once so poverty-stricken.

Under the influence of these pleasurable thoughts, she began to laugh heartily, and preen herself, when, suddenly, striking the jar with her hand, it fell from her head, and smashed upon the ground. The honey became a sticky mess upon the ground.

Seeing this, she was as cast down as she had been excited, on seeing all her dreams lost for illusion. ■

The origination of fables has been claimed for the Jews (Solomon is reputed to have composed two or three thousand of them), the Greeks, the Indians, and the Egyptians. Aesop is said to have lived in the 6th century B.C., but there are indications of fables in Egyptian papyri of 800 to 1000 years earlier. Jotham's apologue of the trees who desired a king was for long thought to be the oldest, but the Hebrew Book of Judges, in which it is found, dates in its present form only from about the 3rd century B.C.

'The Hawk and the Nightingale', given here, is from the works of the Greek poet Hesiod, who flourished about 800 B.C. It has been regarded by many as the earliest complete fable traceable to a literary work. It has been attributed to Aesop and others, but Hesiod is the earliest source. It certainly seems like the prototype of 'A bird in the hand is worth two in the bush.'

The Hawk and The Nightingale

A nightingale was sitting alone among the shady branches of an oak tree. She sang with so melodious and trilling a voice that the woods echoed with her song.

A hawk, perched not far away, was searching the woods for something to catch. No sooner had he found the tiny songster than he swooped, caught her in his talons, and told her to prepare for death.

"Oh!" said she, "do not do anything so barbarous and so unbecoming as to kill me. Remember, I never did anything wrong—and I would only be a mouthful for such a one as you. Why do you not attack some larger bird, which would be a braver thing to do and would give you a better meal, and let me go?"

"Yes", said the hawk, "You may try to persuade me if you can. But I had not found any prey today until I saw you. And now you want me to let you go in hope of something better! But if I did, who would be the fool?" ■

Cecino The Tiny

Tom Thumb is the English version of Grimm's 19th century 'Thumblin' and of Perrault's 'Petit Pucet', published almost two hundred years before. The first printed version appeared in London, told by Richard Johnson, in 1621. Tom is supposed to have been the favourite dwarf of King Arthur, but we only hear of this a thousand years after Arthur's supposed date of death. Several cognates and parallels of the tale exist, in Germany, Denmark, South Europe, and India, in which the tiny fellow has many and varied adventures. Like other peasant tales, the one given here ignores morality (Cecino joins a robber band, his father kills all his brothers) and the happy ending—Cecino drowns, and that is that. This kind of structure, in which anything can happen without need for didactic, is perhaps inherent in the fantasy origins of the story: a chick-pea becomes a person, so he really is not anyone at all. The following version was collected from the oral tradition in 19th century Tuscany.

Once there lived a poor ignorant carpenter and his wife, who had always prayed for children, but had never been sent any by the Almighty.

When the husband came back from his daily work at the shop where he was sewing and hammering making tables and cupboards, he did nothing but make his poor wife's life a misery by saying that it was all her fault that they had no children in their long married life.

The woman was very sad about this and tried every way she could think of to conceive. She lit many candles in church, made pilgrimages to special places taken to be sure cures for barren women, ate certain herbs, and also gave her husband many magic philtres.

But to no avail. They could not make children, and each blamed the other, till they made each night a hell upon earth, quarrelling till dawn.

The carpenter began to spend more and more time at his shop, carving and hammering away at more and more cupboards and chests; the wife lit more candles than she could afford, and said her prayers so often that she was mumbling all the time under her breath, until people began to avoid her, thinking her to be a witch.

Life was not happy for either of them, and daily they grew further and further apart, and the carpenter was seriously thinking of leaving her and going away to some other place to start all over again.

One day, a poor-looking old woman knocked at the door of the humble house and asked for charity. The carpenter's wife said: "I cannot give you anything, for I have spent all we can spare on candles, and having masses said so that we may have a child, someday, if God wills," she whimpered.

"Give me something, however mean, and you shall have many sons," promised the old woman, who had nose and chin meeting on her face.

"Good" said the wife, "I will give you all I can find, then." And she went to look in the larder. Coming back a few moments later, she handed the old woman with the nutcracker face a brown loaf. "Will this do?" she asked, "It is all I can spare, honestly. There is nothing else in the house today."

"Wonderful," said the old woman, "You can give me another when you get sons."

"May it be so, in the name of the Almighty!" said the carpenter's wife piously. "Even *one* will do." "You shall have many, my dear. Now I will go home and give my poor old husband something to eat, with this brown loaf," said the crone, and went away, putting the loaf in her bag.

The carpenter's wife went about all day very happily at her daily work, singing, and wondered when she would have her first child.

The old woman went home, fed her old husband, and took a small bag containing a hundred chickpeas back to the carpenter's wife. "For the alms you have given me," she said "You shall have many sons, as I promised. Put these hundred peas in a kneading-trough, and tomorrow they will become as many sons as there are peas."

The carpenter's wife laughed, and thought that the old woman must be mad. "How in the world can peas turn into children?" she screeched, "You said I would have children! Can I not have them in the usual way?"

"No, this is the quickest way for you to have them," said the old woman with nose and chin touching, and went away.

The wife of the carpenter said to herself, "Well, maybe the old creature is a witch, and there may be something in it. I will do as she says; funnier things have happened. If by any chance this is the way to have children quickly, and I miss the opportunity my husband will give me a terrible scolding." So she took the peas, put them in a kneading-trough and waited for the sons the woman had promised her.

That night the husband came home having drunk more wine than usual, and abused his wife, saying; "Move over you barren cow, and let me get some peace and quiet in my own home!" She had never said a word, but under her breath she muttered: "Just you wait until tomorrow, you will see something extraordinary indeed! Just you wait!"

"What are you mumbling about, silly creature?" grumbled the husband, "Mumbling those prayers all night, you get on my nerves. One of these days I'll leave you, just you see if I don't!"

Then he fell into a drunken slumber.

The next morning the hundred peas had turned into one hundred lusty young sons.

"Papa, papa, give me a drink of water!" cried one, "Mama, mama, give me some bread!" screamed another. Another cried: "Pick me up!" Yet another: "I want to go for a walk!" "Papa, papa, make me a paper windmill!" demanded a fifth, and so it went on for about an hour.

The bad-tempered carpenter had had enough of this at such an early hour in the morning, so he took up a stick and began to beat the chick-pea children. Soon he had killed them all, except one, who ran into the bedroom and hid away.

After the carpenter had gone to the shop, the unfortunate wife said to herself, crossly: "Oh, devil take the man, he complained about my not having children, and now I've had them, he has killed them all! Is there no justice in the world? I wish I were dead!"

Then the pea which had escaped called "Mama, don't say that, I am here! I will look after you!"

The carpenter's wife could scarcely believe her eyes and ears, and she cried "How did you manage to escape, my son? What a miracle this is, indeed!"

"Has Papa gone?" asked the child. "Yes," said she, then "How are you named?" and he said "My name is Cecino, Mama."

"What a nice name," she said, "Now, you must go to the shop and take your father's dinner to him, to save me going today, for I feel very tired; I had a sleepless night."

"Yes, you must put the basket on my head," said the boy, "and I will carry it to Papa."

The carpenter's wife, when the meal was ready, put the basket on the child's head and sent him off with

the dinner. When he was near the shop, he began to cry: "Oh, Papa, come and see, I am bringing your dinner." Then the carpenter said to himself, "Drat it, did I not kill them all?" Aloud he said "How did you escape when I killed all your brothers?"

"Oh, I hid under the handle of the pitcher," said the pea child, "and I survived."

"Oh what a clever boy you are!" said the carpenter, "You must go around among the country people and ask at all the houses whether they have anything to mend."

"Very well," said the boy, and the carpenter put him in his pocket. While he walked along the country road, the boy did nothing but chatter, and every person he met said that the carpenter must be mad, because they did not know it was the boy in his pocket who was talking.

When he saw some countrymen he asked "Have you anything which I can mend for you? I am a good carpenter, I can assure you." They answered, "Yes, we have something to be mended, but we cannot let you do it, for you are known to be mad."

"Mad?" said he, "Mad? I have never been taken for mad before, nor have any of my relatives ever been mad! I am wiser than you, I tell you. Why do you say I am mad?"

"Because you do nothing but talk to yourself on the road," said they, "Everybody has noticed it, lately. How do we know you can mend things properly if you are mad?"

"I was talking to my son," said the carpenter, furiously, "It is you who are unjust."

"Where is your son?" they asked.

"In my pocket, of course!" he shouted in reply.

"That's a funny place to keep your son," they said, sneeringly.

"Very well, I will show him to you," said the carpenter and took Cecino with his two fingers, and placed him upon the palm of his hand to show him off to them.

"Oh what an amazing thing," they cried, "You must sell him to us!"

"Sell my son? What are you talking about?" said the carpenter, "I sell you my son, who is so valuable to me?" He put the boy on the horns of an ox, and "Wait for me there, my boy, I will go to that house and ask if

they have any work for me." So the boy said "I will wait here for you, Papa."

Now two thieves passed by, and seeing the ox and its brother standing alone, said "Let us steal these oxen there with no one to look after them. Come!"

Then Cecino called out as loudly as he could "Look out, Papa, two thieves are going to steal the oxen!"

"Where does that voice come from?" the thieves asked each other, and they went near to the oxen and saw the miniature boy on the horn of one of them, as the carpenter hurried back to the cart.

"What have we here?" said one of the thieves, to the carpenter, "You must let us buy him, whoever he is. We have found a rare creature for certain, and one that could be very useful to us!"

"No, no," said the carpenter, "What would his mother say if I sold him? I cannot do it."

"We will give you as much money as you wish," said the thieves, "Just tell his mother that he died on the way home, of some accident. It will be quite easy, just try it."

They tempted him so much that at last he gave the boy to them for a sack of gold.

They took Cecino, put him in a pocket, and went away.

Then they went to the king's stable and wondered if they could steal a fine horse or two from there. "Do not betray us, now," they warned Cecino, "or it will be the worse for you."

"Don't worry," said Cecino, "I will not betray you."

The thieves came back with three fine Arab steeds which they had easily stolen, while there were no royal grooms about. They took them home and put them in their own stable.

Afterwards, they went to Cecino, and said: "Go, feed the horses, give them some oats, we are feeling too tired." So Cecino was soon feeding the horses, but he fell into a bran dish and a black horse swallowed him.

When he did not return, the thieves went to look for him, but there was no sign of the tiny boy. "He must have fallen asleep somewhere in the hay," they said and went to look for him everywhere. "Cecino, Cecino," they called, "where are you?" "Inside the black horse," cried Cecino.

So they killed the black horse, but Cecino was not there. "Cecino, no tricks now, where are you?" they called. "Inside the bay horse!" came the cry, so they killed the bay horse, but he was not in its stomach.

"Cecino, Cecino!" the thieves called out once more, "Where are you?" but this time there was no reply. "A great pity," they said, "That child would have been very useful indeed to us, and think of what we paid for him!"

Then they dragged the two horses which they had cut open into a field.

A ravenously hungry wolf came loping past, and saw the two dead horses. "I *will* have a good meal," said he, his tongue lolling out hungrily, and he ate and ate, managing to swallow Cecino at the same time. The little boy had been in one of the horses all the time, but the thieves had missed seeing him because he was so small. Then the wolf became hungry again, and said to itself, "I shall go and eat a goat this time; all that horsemeat has given me too much wind."

When Cecino heard the wolf talking about eating a goat, circling the field where the goatherd was sitting, he called out at the top of his voice:

"Goatherd, goatherd, the wolf is coming to eat your goats! Beware!"

The goatherd began to throw stones at the wolf, and it ran and ran until it became sick, and Cecino was free once more. He hid under a large rock, beside which some robbers were counting a sum of money.

One of them said: "Now we will divide this bag of money here, as we are far from anywhere, and no one will see us. You others be quiet whilst I am counting, or I shall kill you!"

They kept very still and silent, for they did not want to die, and the robber who was counting had a very sharp knife and a bad reputation for killing without asking questions first.

He began to count: "One, two, three, four, and five." he said. Cecino then started to repeat the robber's words; "One, two, three, four, and five!"

"I told you *not* to speak while I am counting!" shouted the angry robber; "Keep still, or I will kill you!" Once more he began counting. "One, two, three, four,

and five!" and Cecino imitated him again, as loud as he was able.

"All right, then, you have asked for it!" roared the robber and plunged his knife into the heart of the one he thought was imitating him. "Now we shall see if any of you speaks." he said, and wiped his blade on his handkerchief. The counting continued, the robber beginning again: "One, two, three, four, and five!"

As he got to the last number Cecino once more chimed in with "One, two, three, four, and five!" as loud as he was able.

"Take care!" bellowed the killer, "if you say anything again I shall have to finish you off!"

"Do you think I want to be killed?" cried the other robber, "Carry on counting, I swear I will not speak."

But the moment the counting began again, Cecino squeaked out the number of gold coins being counted, and the robber with the knife accounted for the second of his companions.

When he was wiping his knife again on his kerchief, Cecino began to count. "There *is* someone else here, after all!" said the robber to himself, "and I will be apprehended," so he dropped the bag of gold and ran for his life.

When Cecino saw that he was alone, he came out, and saw the two dead robbers, and the bag of gold lying there unattended. He managed to get the bag onto his head, and walked home with it.

When he got near to his parent's house he called out: "Mama, Papa, look what I have brought you! Come out and meet me!"

When the carpenter's wife heard him calling, she went out to meet him, and took the money, saying: "Take care now, that you do not drown in these puddles of rain-water. I will put this gold carefully away for you, my son."

The woman went home, to tell her husband how clever Cecino had been. She looked around for a moment to see if he was following, but could not see him. She got her husband, and they went searching for him everywhere. At last they found poor Cecino drowned in a puddle of rain-water, as his mother had feared would be his fate. ■

If the published record is to be credited, young Mrs. Butler of London was unwittingly fed her lover's heart by her cruel husband, on or about the 6th June, 1707. The public print of the time adds a wealth of circumstantial detail, which may be intended to add plausibility to the account. The lady was, for example, an heiress, from Hackney Boarding School; her admirer was a rich Mr. Perpont (of Fenchurch Street) who had fallen at the Battle of Almanza, in Spain.

Readers of Boccaccio in Britain might well have been surprised that history was repeating itself so near to home: for the Italian writer had reproduced almost exactly the same series of events, from a French troubadour's account dating to six hundred years before the alleged scandal at Hackney. On that occasion, the Lord de Couci's heart had been, equally inadvertently, consumed by the Lady du Fayel, after he had gone off to die in Palestine. He fell at the siege of Acre, in 1191. Thus runs the ninth story of the Fourth Day of the **Decameron.**

But even the gruesome feasts of France and England are startlingly foreshadowed, again in striking detail, by the experience of the hapless Princess Kokla in 78 A.D. She ate the heart of Prince Hodi of the Afghan frontier, according to "every bard of the Punjab"—as General James Abbot discovered when he actually located her memorial statue in 1848. The chief material difference from the other narratives seems to be that the Indian lady ate both the heart and liver, roasted for her by her husband, Raja Rasalu, a traditional hero in North India.

World tales have a habit of appearing again and again in the work of the great writers, almost as if there is something irresistibly archetypal about them.

From the bards of the ancient Punjab to the Troubadours and Crusaders, to Boccaccio and popular eighteenth-century English reading, the "Lover's Heart" theme surfaced again in the words of—Somerset Maugham.

On his 90th birthday, the great writer related a version of the story to his nephew Robin, calling it "a pretty little tale". This was on January 26, 1964: exactly one thousand, eight hundred and eighty-six years after our first tracing of the recital, in the Indian history—or legend—of Prince Hodi and Princess Kokla.

The wise bird negotiates his escape in this Indian painting.

Her Lover's Heart

Many, many years ago, there was a great prince and hunter, whose name is still remembered as a man of skill and cunning, and whose adventures are sung throughout the land of India. He was Raja Rasalu, and he was married to the beautiful Princess, Rani Kokla. They lived in a splendid palace surrounded by beautiful gardens, a true abode for a king.

Rasalu used to go out hunting and, after pursuing the fleet-footed deer on his wonderful steed Fuladi— which means 'steely'—he would shoot one animal and bring back venison for his lady and feed it to her.

One day she said: "If I go with you on the hunt, the deer will come to me, for I have eaten so much of their meat that they will feel an affinity with me."

The Raja agreed to take her along, and, sure enough, when the Rani seated herself in the forest, the deer crowded around, as if fascinated. One of them, their leader, who was a great blue buck named Luddan, was so overcome that, (in spite of his mate's warning), he ran to Kokla and threw himself at her feet.

Now the Raja cut off his ears and his tail as trophies, and let him go, but the buck swore vengeance, and he thought of a plan to punish Kokla the deer-eater.

He made his way to the palace of another prince, the Raja Hodi, and began to wander and cavort in his gardens, eating the fruits and trampling the grass. Raja Hodi came out to kill Luddan, and the buck ran away, luring him by degrees to the palace of Rani Kokla. As he approached, he saw the wonderful gardens and the splendid castle, and then he saw the Princess herself on the flat rooftop, walking arrayed in her finery. He called up to her, and she was attracted to him.

After an exchange of conversation and poems, she invited him into her apartments. The mynah bird which had been left on guard tried to stop him, and told another guard-bird, a parrot, that they should inform their master, Prince Rasalu, that a strange man had been allowed into the castle.

The birds protested to the Rani, but she scolded them, saying that nothing wrong was being done, entertaining a traveller was, after all, quite a normal thing to do. Then, in her rage, Kokla took the mynah and wrung her neck.

The parrot, however, was more crafty. Instead of reproaching the Princess, he said: "Princess, you were right to punish this bird for her insolence! Let me out of my cage, and I shall peck her, just to show my own displeasure!"

The Rani opened the door of the cage. The parrot pecked the mynah, and then flew away. Seeing this, Prince Hodi became afraid. Embracing Kokla hastily, he fled to his own palace and threw himself on his bed, weeping bitterly for the loss of Kokla.

After looking everywhere in the forest, the parrot came upon his master Rasalu, and told him what had happened. Rasalu mounted Fuladi and rode him at top speed to his palace, while a plan formed in his mind.

The Rani was lying asleep when Rasalu arrived home. He at once told Shadi, his parrot: "Fly to the Princess's couch. Take the ring from her finger without waking her. Then speed to Prince Hodi's palace with it and inform him that I, Rasalu, have been killed by a fall in the woods, and that the Princess awaits him. Say that the ring is proof that the message is indeed from her!"

Shadi flew with all haste to Hodi's palace, and told him what he had been instructed to say. Hodi sprang upon his horse and was soon at Rasalu's gate. Rasalu himself came out and asked him what he wanted.

"I was passing by," stuttered Hodi, "and seeing this magnificent place thought I would look at it . . ."

"Pray come in" said Rasalu, "for a guest must be treated as such."

Hodi could not refuse, for fear of arousing suspicion.

As he dismounted, Rasalu called out: "Now die, faithless and dishonourable one!" He drew his sword and sliced right through Hodi, from head to toe. So sharp and thin was his wondrous sword that Hodi did not even feel the impact. In fact, he called out: "You have not touched me, and I shall have my revenge!"

"Just move but one inch," cried Rasalu, "and you will see!" Sure enough, as soon as Hodi moved, he split in two, along the line of the sword-cut.

Now Rasalu took out Hodi's liver and heart, saying, "Kokla shall have venison today such as she has never had before!"

The Princess was still asleep, Rasalu quickly cooked the heart and liver and carried it to her. As she ate it, she said, "I have never tasted anything so delicious as this, my own dear love, which you have killed and cooked for me with your own sweet hands . . ."

"So it should taste to you," answered Raja Rasalu, "for it is the flesh of your lover, eat as much as you will . . ."

Giving an agonised cry of the greatest anguish, the Rani ran to the turret of the castle and prepared to jump. As she looked down, she saw the body of Hodi lying there. Such was her grief that she was dead before she reached the ground, throwing herself from that towering height.

Rasalu, for his part, was staggering with shock. He descended to the bottom of the precipice upon which the castle was built, and kissed the lips of his beloved Kokla for the last time. Then, aware of the affinity which there was between the Princess and Hodi, he placed a cloth over the two of them and buried them, side by side, in the nearby ravine. He was utterly lonely for the rest of his days. ■

This story is very widely dispersed — from southern Europe to Scandinavia, and is also found in Britain and the United States. The 'New Hand' is often taken to be Jesus, who both works miracles and teaches people to avoid pride. It is found among the Gypsies, who may have helped to carry it to Russia, Sicily and elsewhere, from the Middle East. The tale is similar to many unofficial legends of Jesus current in Palestine. The following is adapted from the recital of Dick Brown, a Virginian at Sand Mountain, Alabama, taken down by the American J. P. Suverkrop in 1871. The Brothers Grimm have a famous nineteenth-century version, 'The Old Man Made Young Again', but the tale is certainly centuries old.

The New Hand

There was once a sawmill on the edge of a wood, not far from here in Alabama, with the running river turning the wheel. An old black man, and a very fine man he was, owned the mill. But his son, named Sam, was quite unlike his father, lazy and useless he was. His father had to work hard to keep things going.

One day a stranger came along to the mill, a poor-looking fellow, who said that he would like to learn saw-milling, and that if he could be taught he would work for a year for nothing. The old man was glad to have his help, and young Sam thought that it was all right, too, because then he could shift some of his own work onto the New Hand. So the New Hand started, toting boards and doing chores around the place.

The owner liked the New Hand very much, and always gave him whatever he had himself. But Sam used to push the New Hand around, behind his father's back. When the old man caught Sam bossing and abusing the New Hand — and it happened several times — he punished him properly.

The day came when an old man came to collect a load of planks, and he was groaning with a bad back, and wishing that he was young and spry as he used to be. Then up spoke the New Hand, and he said to Sam and his father:

"If both of you go into the woods where you cannot see what is happening, leaving this man with me, and wait until I call you, I will make him as good as new again. But you must promise not to look, otherwise something bad will happen."

So they promised, and the old man and his son went into the woods until they could not see what was happening at the mill. The New Hand said to the man with the bad back:

"Go and lie down on the saw-frame."

When the man did so, the New Hand took the saw and cut him in two. Then he took the halves of the man and threw them into the stream, and the two pieces joined together. The man came down from the stream alive and well, young and frisky. He started to thank the New Hand, but he told him to say nothing at all.

When the new Hand called them back, Sam and his father came running and they were astonished when they saw this young-looking black in place of the old, limping man. They asked all kinds of questions, but the New Hand would not say anything about it, so they gave up, and things went on the same as usual for a time.

Then the old man got word that his mother was very ill, and that he had better go away to visit her. Before he left, he told Sam not to make any trouble for the New Hand; and, if he did, he would get a beating when his father returned. But Sam forgot this just as soon as the old man had gone, and behaved in a very overbearing way towards the help.

Finally, the New Hand said to Sam:

"If you don't stop behaving like this, I'll quit as soon as my time's up, and that's tomorrow."

But Sam was really insolent, and he said, "Go now, you fool!"

Well, the next day, sure enough, the New Hand was gone, though nobody saw him go, and nobody passed him on the road or in the woods.

And the very next day, along came the black man who had been made young again, and he brought with him his wife: an old woman, carrying a lovely fat possum and a basket of potatoes which fairly made Sam's mouth water. After passing the time of day, the visitor asked after the New Hand, saying that he wanted him to make the old woman well, as he had done for him.

Sam said, "Oh, he'll be here tomorrow. Just leave the possum and come again. I'll give it to him when he gets back."

But the man was too smart for that, and would not leave the things. Sam was afraid that he would lose the possum, so he said:

"The New Hand has gone off to see his sick father, and he told me before he went to carry on and do the

same that he did for you."

So the man told Sam what was wanted, and Sam told the man to go into the woods and shut his eyes. Then Sam sawed the woman in two and threw the pieces into the stream: but there they stayed.

Sam, of course, got very scared, and went down to the water and tried to join the two pieces, but they stayed as they were.

Then the old woman's husband came running and shouting out of the woods, sure that something was wrong. The neighbours collected, and they took Sam away, and he was found guilty of murder.

The judge put on the black cap, and said:

"Hang Sam by the neck until he is dead, and the Lord have mercy on poor Sam."

Now Sam's old father came running, and he rolled in the dust and begged for Sam's life, but the judge would not let him free. Then everyone went towards the gallows, very solemnly. The judge asked Sam if he had anything to say; and Sam suddenly saw the New Hand, standing in the crowd, and laughing; and Sam thought how badly he had treated that poor man.

So Sam said:

"Brothers and sisters, listen to what I am going to say. Never act haughtily to anyone: because if I hadn't acted in that way to a man who is here in this crowd today, I'd have been heaving saw-logs instead of going to be hanged this day."

Then all his friends started to cry and roll about, but the New Hand jumped up alongside Sam and said to him:

"Are you sorry for your actions?"

Sam said:

"Indeed I am, and I ask pardon and hope you'll forgive me when I'm gone."

The New Hand spoke out in a loud voice to the crowd, saying:

"How can you hang this man, when the old woman he is supposed to have killed is standing right over there?"

Sure enough, there she was, standing beside her husband. So they let Sam down, and there were great celebrations. But they have never seen the New Hand, from that day to this, anywhere at all. ■

The Mastermaid

This story, from the Norse is translated by Sir George Webb Dasent, Assistant Editor of the London 'Times' and Professor of Literature at King's College—from the important collection, **Norse Folktales,** *by P. C. Asbjørnsen and S. I. Moe, which contains a wide variety of tales from Scandanavia that are also found throughout the world.*

In addition to its remarkable entertainment value, 'The Mastermaid' has for over a century fascinated scholars, some of whom have found it to resemble the classical myth of Jason and Medea very closely. Others have seen in Shakespeare's **The Tempest** *a reflection of its main theme. The narrative is known from Scotland to the South Seas, in Madagascar and the Buddhist world, in India and—as 'Lady Feather Flight'—in American English tradition. Countless other literary and folktales contain sections or incidents which are to be found in masterly narration in this recension.*

The Aryan and mythological basis of tales was dispersed as a belief by H. Gaidoz (1842—1932). He did this by 'proving' (employing the Muller arguments) that the respected Professor Max Muller was himself only an astronomical myth. For good measure, Gaidoz, editor of the journal Mélusine also 'showed' that both Muller's German home and Oxford itself were imaginary places.

No part of this history of scholarly opinion, fortunately, stands in the way of our enjoyment of this tale.

Once upon a time there was a King who had several sons. The youngest had no rest at home, for nothing else would please him but to go out into the world and try his luck, and after a long time the King was forced to give him leave to go. Now, after he had travelled some days, he came one night to a Giant's house, and there he got a place in the Giant's service. In the morning the Giant went off to herd his goats, and as he left the yard he told the Prince to clean out the stable; "And after you have done that, you needn't do anything else today; for you must know it is an easy master to whom you have come. But what is set you to do, you must do well, and you mustn't think of going into any of the rooms which are beyond that in which you slept, for if you do I'll take your life."

"Sure enough, it is an easy master I have got," said the Prince to himself, as he walked up and down the room, and carolled and sang, for he thought there was plenty of time to clean out the stable.

"But still it would be good fun just to peep into his other rooms, for there must be something in them which he is afraid I should see, since he won't give me leave to go in."

So he went into the first room, and there was a pot boiling on a hook by the wall, but the Prince saw no fire underneath it. "I wonder what is inside it," he thought; and then he dipped a lock of his hair into it, and the hair seemed as if it were turned to copper.

"What a dainty broth," he said; and he went into the next room. There, too, was a pot hanging by a hook, which bubbled and boiled; but there was no fire under that either.

"I may as well try that too," said the Prince, as he put another lock of hair in the pot, and it came out all silvered.

"They haven't such rich broth in my father's house," said the Prince; "but it all depends on how it tastes," and with that he went into the third room. There, too, hung a pot and it boiled just as he had seen in the other two rooms. The Prince had a mind to try this too, so he dipped a lock of hair into it, and it came out gilded so that the light gleamed from it.

"Better and better," said the Prince, "but if he boils gold here, I wonder what he boils in yonder."

He thought he might as well see; so he went through the door into the fourth room. Well, there was no pot in there, but there was a Princess, seated on a bench, so lovely that the Prince had never seen anything like her in his born days.

"Oh, in Heaven's name," she said, "what do you want here?"

"I got a place here yesterday," said the Prince.

"A place indeed! Heaven help you out of it."

"Well, after all, I think I've got an easy master; he hasn't set me much to do to-day, for after I have cleaned out the stable my day's work is over."

"Yes, but how will you do it?" she said, "for if you set to work to clean it, ten pitchforks full will come in for every one you toss out. But I will teach you how to set to work; you must turn the fork upside down, and toss with the handle, and then all the dung will fly out of itself."

"Yes, I will be sure to do that." said the Prince; and so he sat there the whole day, for he and the Princess were soon great friends, and had made up their minds to help one another, and so the first day of his service with the Giant was not long. But when the evening drew on she said it would be as well if he got the stable cleaned out before the Giant came home. When he went to the stable he thought he would just see if what she had said were true, and so he began to work like the grooms in his father's stable. But he soon had enough of that, for he hadn't worked a minute before the stable was so full of dung that he hadn't room to stand. Then he did as the Princess bade him, and turned up the fork and worked with the handle, and in a trice the stable was as clean as if it had been scoured. When he had done his work he went back to the room where the Giant had given him leave to be, and began to walk up and down and to carol and sing. So after a bit, home came the Giant with the goats.

"Have you cleaned the stable?" asked the Giant.

"Yes, now it's all right, master," answered the Prince.

"I'll soon see if it is," growled the Giant, and strode off to the stable, where he found it just as the Prince had said.

"You've been talking to my Mastermaid, I can see," said the Giant; "for you've not got this knowledge out of your own mind!"

"Mastermaid!" said the Prince, who looked as stupid as an owl, "what sort of thing is that, master? I'd be very glad to see it."

"Well, well!" said the Giant; "you'll see her soon enough."

Next day the Giant set off with his goats again, and before he went he told the Prince to fetch home his horse, which was out at grass on the hill-side, and when he had done that he might rest all the day.

"For you must know it is an easy master you have come to," said the Giant; "but if you go into any of the rooms I spoke of yesterday, I'll wring your head off."

So off he went with his flock of goats.

"An easy master you are indeed," said the Prince;

"but for all that, I'll just go and have a chat with your Mastermaid; maybe she'll soon be mine instead of yours." So he went in to her, and she asked him what he had to do that day.

"Oh, nothing to be afraid of," said he; "I've only to go up the hill-side to fetch his horse."

"Very well, and how will you set about it?" said she.

"Well, for that matter, there's no great art in riding a horse home. I've ridden fresher horses before," said the Prince.

"Ah, but this isn't so easy a task as you think," said she, "but I'll teach you how to do it. When you get near it, fire and flame will come out of its nostrils, but look out, and take the bit which hangs behind the door yonder, and throw it right into its jaws and it will grow so tame that you may do what you like."

The Prince said he would do that; and so he sat in there the whole day, talking and chattering with the Mastermaid about one thing and another; but they always came back to how happy they would be if only they could only be with one another and get well away from the Giant. The Prince would have forgotten both the horse and the hill-side, if the Mastermaid hadn't put him in mind of them when evening drew on, telling him he had better set out to fetch the horse before the Giant came home. So he set off, and took the bit which hung in the corner, ran up the hill, and it wasn't long before he met the horse, with fire and flame streaming out of its nostrils. But he watched his time, and as the horse came open-jawed up to him, he threw the bit into its mouth and it stood, quiet as a lamb. After that it was no great matter to ride it home and put it up. Then the Prince went into his room again, and began to carol and sing.

So the Giant came home again at evening with his goats; and the first words he said were:

"Have you brought my horse down from the hill?"

"Yes master, that I have," said the Prince, "and a better horse I never bestrode; I rode him straight home, and put him up safe and sound."

"I'll soon see to that," said the Giant, and ran out to the stable, and there stood the horse just as the Prince had said.

"You've talked to my Mastermaid, I'll be bound, for you haven't got this out of your own mind." said the Giant again.

"Yesterday master talked of this Mastermaid, and today it's the same story," said the Prince, who pretended to be silly and stupid. "Why don't you show me the thing at once? I should like to see it only once in my life."

"Oh, if that's all," said the Giant, "you'll see her soon enough."

The third day at dawn the Giant went off to the wood again with his goats; but before he went he said to the Prince:

"Today you must go to Hell and fetch my fire-tax. When you have done that you can rest yourself all day, for you must know it is an easy master you have come to," and with that off he went.

"Easy master, indeed!" said the Prince. "You may be easy, but you set me hard tasks all the same. But I may as well see if I can find your Mastermaid, as you call her. I daresay she'll tell me what to do," and so in he went to her again.

So when the Mastermaid asked what the Giant had set him to do that day, he told her how he was to go to Hell and fetch the fire-tax.

"And how will you set about it?" asked the Master-maid.

"Oh, that you must tell me," said the Prince. "I have never been to Hell in my life; and even if I knew the

way, I don't know how much I am to ask for."

"Well, I'll soon tell you," said the Mastermaid; "you must go to the steep rock away yonder, under the hillside, and take the club that lies there, and knock on the face of the rock. Then there will come out one all glistening with fire; to him you must tell your errand; and when he asks you how much you will have, mind you say, 'As much as I can carry'."

The Prince sat in there with the Mastermaid all that day too; and though evening drew on, he would have sat there till now, had not the Mastermaid told him that it was high time to be off to Hell to fetch the Giant's fire-tax before he came home. So he went on his way, and did just as the Mastermaid had told him; and when he reached the rock he took up the club and gave a great thump. Then the rock opened, and out came one whose face glistened, and out of whose eyes and nostrils flew sparks of fire.

"What is your will?" said he.

"I have come from the Giant to fetch his fire-tax," said the Prince.

"How much will you have then?" said the other.

"No more than I am able to carry," said the Prince.

"Lucky for you that you did not ask for a whole horse-load," said he who came out of the rock; "but come now into the rock with me, and you shall have it."

So the Prince went in with him, and you may fancy what heaps and heaps of gold and silver he saw lying in there just like stones in a gravel-pit. He got a load just as big as he was able to carry, and set off home with it. Now, when the Giant came home with his goats at even, the Prince went into his room and began to carol and sing as he had done the evenings before.

"Have you been to Hell after my fire-tax?" roared the Giant.

"I have master," answered the Prince.

"Where have you put it?" said the Giant.

"There stands the sack on the bench," said the Prince.

"I'll soon see to that," said the Giant, who strode off to the bench, and there he saw the sack so full that the gold and silver dropped out on the floor as soon as he untied the string.

"You've been talking to my Mastermaid, that I can see," said the Giant. "But if you have, I'll wring your head off."

"Mastermaid!" said the Prince; "yesterday you talked of this Mastermaid, and to-day you talk of her again, and the day before yesterday it was the same story. I only wish I could see what sort of thing she is!"

"Well, well, wait till tomorrow," said the Giant, "and then I'll take you to her myself."

"Thank you kindly, master," said the Prince. "But it's only a joke, I'll be bound."

So next day the Giant took him to the Mastermaid, and said to her:

"Now you must cut his throat, and boil him in the great big pot, and when broth is ready just give me a call."

After that he lay down on the bench to sleep, and began to snore so, that it sounded like thunder over hills.

So the Mastermaid took a knife, and cut the Prince in his little finger, and let three drops of blood fall on a three-legged stool; and after that she took old rags and soles of shoes, and all the rubbish she could lay hands on, and put them into the pot. Then she filled a chest full of ground gold, and took a lump of salt, a flask of water that hung behind the door, and she took, besides, a golden apple, and two golden chickens,

and off she set with the Prince from the Giant's house as fast as they could. When they had gone a little way they came to the sea,and after that they sailed in a ship over the sea.

When the Giant had slumbered a good bit, he began to stretch himself as he lay on the bench, and called out:

"Isn't it done yet?"

"Done to a turn," said the third drop of blood.

Then the Giant rose up, and began to rub his eyes, but he couldn't see who it was that was talking to him, so he searched and called for the Mastermaid, but no-one answered.

"Ah well! I dare say she's just run out of doors for a bit," he thought,and took up a spoon and went up to the pot to taste the broth; but he found nothing but shoe-soles and rags and such stuff; and it was all boiled up together, so that he couldn't tell which was thick and which was thin. As soon as he saw this, he could tell how things had gone, and he got so angry he scarce knew which leg to stand upon. Away he went after the Prince and the Mastermaid, till the wind whistled behind him; but before long he came to the water and couldn't cross it.

"Never mind," he said, "I know a cure for this. I've only got to call on my stream-sucker."

So he called on his stream-sucker, and he came and stooped down, and took one, two, three, gulps; and then the water fell so much in the sea that the Giant could see the Mastermaid and the Prince sailing in their ship.

"Now you must cast out the lump of salt," said the Mastermaid.

So the Prince threw it overboard, and it grew up into a mountain so high, right across the sea, that the Giant couldn't pass it, and the stream-sucker couldn't

help him by swilling any more water.

"Never mind," cried the Giant; "there's a cure for this too." So he called on his hill-borer to come and bore through the mountain, that the stream-sucker might creep through and take another swill; but just as they had made a hole through the hill, and the stream-sucker was about to drink, the Mastermaid told the Prince to throw overboard a drop or two out of the flask. Then the sea was just as full as ever, and before the stream-sucker could take another gulp, they reached the land and were saved from the Giant.

They made up their minds to go home to the Prince's father, but the Prince would not hear of the Mastermaid's walking, for he thought it seemly neither for her nor for him.

"Just wait here ten minutes," he said, "while I go home after the seven horses which stand in my father's stall. It is not far and I shan't be long, but I will not hear of my sweetheart walking to my father's palace."

"Ah!" said the Mastermaid, "don't leave me, for if you once get home to the palace you'll forget me, I know you will."

"Oh!" said he, "how can I forget you; you with whom I have gone through so much, and whom I love so dearly?"

There was no help for it, he went home to fetch the coach and seven horses, and she was to wait for him by the seaside. So at last the Mastermaid was forced to let him have his way; she only said:

"Now, when you get home, don't stop so much as to say good day to any one. Go straight to the stable and put up the horses, and drive back as quick as you can; for they will all come about you, but act as though you did not see them. Above all things, mind you do not taste a morsel of food, for if you do, we shall both come to grief."

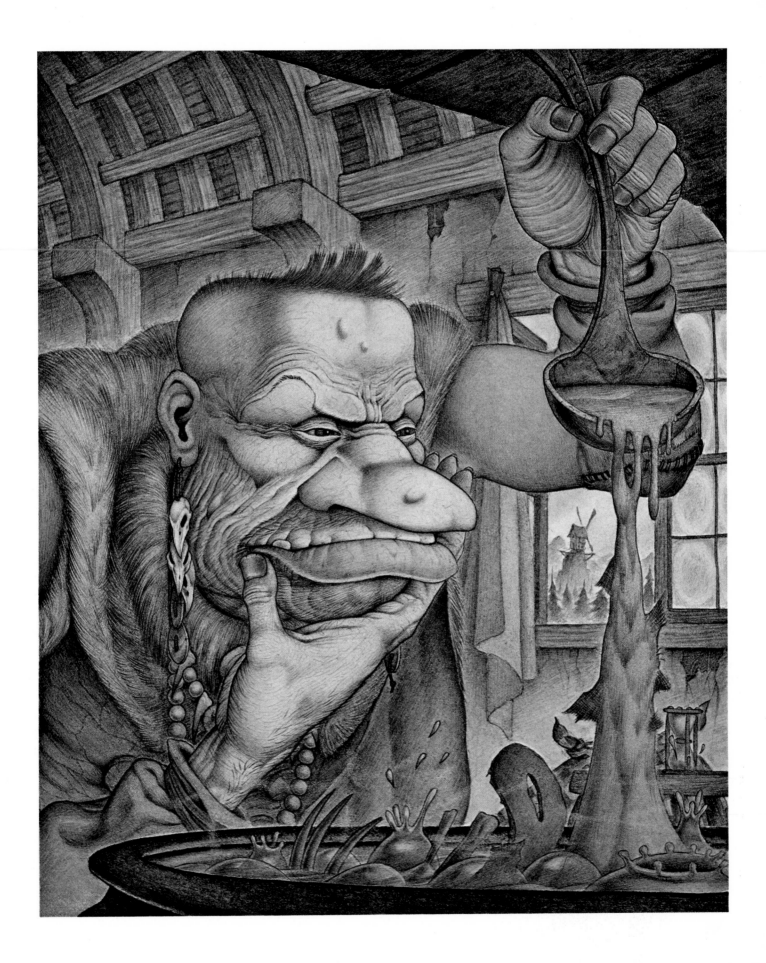

All this the Prince promised; but he thought all the way that there was little fear of his forgetting her.

Now, just as he came home to the palace, one of his brothers was thinking of holding his bridal feast, and the bride and all her kith and kin had just come to the palace. So they all thronged round him, and asked about this thing and that, and wanted him to go in with them; but he made as though he did not see them, and went straight to the stall and got out the horses. And when they saw they could not get him to go in, they came out to him with meat and drink, and the best of everything they had got ready for the feast; but the Prince would not taste so much as a crumb, and got the horses ready as fast as he could. At last the bride's sister rolled an apple across the yard to him, saying:

"Well, if you won't eat anything else, you may as well take a bite of this, for you must be both hungry and thirsty after so long a journey."

So he took up an apple and bit a piece out of it; but he had scarce done so before he forgot the Mastermaid, and how he was to drive back for her.

"Well, I think I must be mad," he said; "what am I to do with this coach and horses?"

So he put the horses up again, and went along with the others into the palace and it was soon settled that he should have as his wife the bride's sister, who had rolled the apple over to him.

There sat the Mastermaid by the sea-shore, and waited and waited for the Prince, but no Prince came; so at last she went up from the shore, and after she had gone a bit she came to a little hut, which lay by itself in a copse close by the King's palace. She went in and asked if she might lodge there. An old dame owned the hut, and a cross-grained scolding hag she was as ever you saw. At first she would not hear of the Mastermaid lodging in her house, but at last, for fair words and high rent, the Mastermaid got leave to be there. Now the hut was as dark and dirty as a pigsty, so the Mastermaid said she would clear it up a little, so that their house might look like other peoples'. The old hag did not like this either, and showed her teeth and was cross; but the Mastermaid did not mind her. She took her chest of gold, and threw a handful or so into the fire, and the gold melted, and bubbled and boiled over out of the grate, and spread itself over the whole hut till it was gilded both outside and in. But as soon as the gold began to bubble and boil, the old hag got so afraid that she tried to run out as if the Evil One were at her heels; and as she ran out of the door, she forgot to stoop, and gave her head such a knock against the lintel, that she broke her neck, and that was the end of her.

Next morning the Constable passed that way, and he could scarce believe his eyes when he saw the golden hut shining and glistening away in the copse; but he was still more astonished when he went in and saw the lovely maiden who sat there. To make a long story short, he fell over head and ears in love with her, and begged and prayed her to become his wife.

"Well, but have you much money?" asked the Mastermaid. He said he was not so badly off, and off he went home to fetch the money, and when he came back he brought a half-bushel sack, and set it down on the bench. So the Mastermaid said she would have him, since he was so rich; but they were scarce in bed before she said she must get up again:

"For I have forgotten to make up the fire."

"Don't stir out of bed," said the Constable; "I'll see to it."

So he jumped out of bed, and stood on the hearth.

"As soon as you have got hold of the shovel, just tell

me," said the Mastermaid.

"Well, I am holding it now," said the Constable.

Then the Mastermaid said:

"God grant that you may hold the shovel, and the shovel you, and may you heap hot burning coals over yourself till morning breaks."

So there stood the Constable all night long, shovelling hot burning coals over himself; and though he begged, and prayed, and wept, the coals were not a bit colder for that; but as soon as day broke, and he had power to cast away the shovel, he did not stay long, but set off as if the Evil One or the bailiff were at his heels. All who met him stared their eyes out at him, for he cut capers as though he were mad, and he could not have looked in worse plight if he had been flayed and tanned, and everyone wondered what had befallen him, but he told no one where he had been, for shame's sake.

Next day the Attorney passed by the place where the Mastermaid lived, and he, too, saw how it shone and glistened in the copse. He turned aside to find out who owned the hut; and when he came in and saw the lovely maiden he fell more in love with her than the Constable, and began to woo her in hot haste.

Well, the Mastermaid asked him, as she had asked the Constable, if he had a good lot of money, and the Attorney said he wasn't so badly off; and as proof he went home to fetch his money. So he came back with a great fat sack of money—a whole bushel sack—and set it down on the bench; and the long and the short of the matter was, that he was to have her, and they went to bed. But all at once the Mastermaid had forgotten to shut the door of the porch, and she must get up and make it fast for the night.

"What, you do that!" said the Attorney, "while I lie here; that can never be; lie still while I go and do it."

So up he jumped like a pea on a drum-head, and ran out into the porch.

"Tell me," said the Mastermaid, "when you have hold of the door-latch."

"I've got hold of it now," said the Attorney.

"God grant then," said the Mastermaid, "that you may hold the door, and the door you, and that you may go from wall to wall till day dawns."

What a dance the Attorney had all night long; such a waltz he never had before, and I don't think he would much care if he never had such a waltz again. Now he pulled the door forward, and then the door pulled him back, and so he went on, now dashed into one corner of the porch, and now into the other, till he was almost battered to death. At first he began to curse and swear, and then to beg and pray, but the door cared for nothing but holding its own till break of day. As soon as it let go its hold, off set the Attorney, leaving behind him his money to pay for his night's lodgings, and forgetting his courtship altogether, for, to tell the truth, he was afraid lest the house-door should come dancing after him. All who met him stared and gaped at him, for he too cut capers like a madman, and he could not have looked in worse plight if he had spent the whole night in butting against a flock of rams.

The third day the Sheriff passed that way, and he also saw the golden hut, and turned aside to find out who lived there; and he had scarce set eyes on the Mastermaid before he began to woo her. So she answered him as she had answered the other two. If he had lots of money she would have him; if not, he might go about his business. Well, the Sheriff said he wasn't badly off, and he would go home and fetch the money; and when he came again he had a bigger sack even than the Attorney—it must have been at least a

bushel and a half, and put it down on the bench. So it was soon settled that he was to have the Mastermaid, but they had scarce gone to bed before the Mastermaid said she had forgotten to bring home the calf from the meadow, so she must get up and drive him into the stall. Then the Sheriff swore by all the powers that should never be, and, stout and fat as he was, up he jumped as nimbly as a kitten.

"Well, only tell me when you've got hold of the calf's tail," said the Mastermaid.

"Now I have hold of it," said the Sheriff.

"God grant," said the Mastermaid, "that you may hold the calf's tail, and the calf's tail you, and that you may make a tour of the world together till day dawns."

Well, you may just fancy how the Sheriff had to stretch his legs; away they went, the calf and he, over high and low, across hill and dale, and the more the Sheriff cursed and swore, the faster the calf ran and jumped. At dawn of day the poor Sheriff was well nigh broken-winded, and so glad was he to let go of the calf's tail that he forgot his sack of money and everything else. As he was a fat man, he went a little slower than the Attorney and the Constable, but the slower he went the more time people had to gape and stare at him; and I must say they made good use of their time, for he was terribly tattered and torn, after his dance with the calf.

Next day was fixed for the wedding at the palace, and the eldest brother was to drive to church with his bride, and the younger, who had lived with the Giant, with the bride's sister. But when they had got into the coach, and were just going to drive off, one of the trace-pins snapped off; and though they made at least three in its place, they all broke, from whatever sort of wood they were made. So time went on and on, and they couldn't get to church, and every one grew very downcast. But all at once the Constable said, for he too was bidden to the wedding, that yonder, away in the copse, lived a maiden:

"And if you can only get her to lend you the handle of her shovel with which she makes up her fire, I know very well it will hold," he said.

They sent a messenger on the spot, with a message to the maiden to know if they couldn't get the loan of her shovel of which the Constable had spoken, and the maiden said "yes" they might have it; so they got a trace-pin which wasn't likely to snap.

But all at once, just as they were driving off, the bottom of the coach tumbled to bits. So they went to work to make a new bottom as they best might; but it mattered not how many nails they put into it, nor of what wood they made it, as soon as ever they got the bottom well into the coach and were driving off, snap it went in two again, and they were even worse off than when they lost the trace-pin. Just then the Attorney said—for if the Constable was there, you may be sure the Attorney was there too—"Away yonder, in the copse, lives a maiden, and if you could only get her to lend you one-half of her porch-door, I know it can hold together."

They sent another message to the maiden, and asked so prettily if they couldn't have the loan of the gilded porch-door which the Attorney had talked of; and they got it on the spot. So they were just setting out; but now the horses were not strong enough to draw the coach, though there were six of them, then they put on eight, and ten, and twelve, but the more they put on, and the more the coachman whipped, the more the coach wouldn't stir an inch. By this time it was far on in the day, and everyone about the palace was in the dumps; for to church they must go, and yet it looked as if they should never get there. So at last

the Sheriff said that yonder, in the gilded hut in the copse, lived a maiden, and if they could only get the loan of her calf . . .

"I know it can drag the coach, though it were as heavy as a mountain," he said.

They all thought it would look silly to be drawn to church by a calf, but there was no help for it, so they had to send a third time, and asked in the King's name if they couldn't get the loan of the calf the Sheriff had spoken of, and the Mastermaid let them have it on the spot, for she was not going to say "no" this time either. So they put the calf on before the horses, and waited to see if it would do any good, and away went the coach over high and low, and stock and stone, so that they could scarce draw their breath. Sometimes they were on the ground and sometimes up in the air, and when they reached the church, the calf began to run round and round it like a spinning jenny, so that they had hard work to get out of the coach, and into the church. When they went back, it was the same story, only they went faster, and they reached the palace almost before they knew they had set out.

Now when they sat down to dinner, the Prince who had served with the Giant said he thought they ought to ask the maiden who had lent them her shovel-handle and porch-door and calf, to come up to the palace.

"For," said he, "if we hadn't got these three things, we should have been sticking here still."

The King thought that only fair, so he sent five of his best men down to the gilded hut to greet the maiden from the King, and to ask her if she would be so good as to come up and dine at the palace.

"Greet the King from me," said the Mastermaid, "and tell him, if he's too good to come to me, so am I too good to go to him."

So the King had to go himself, and then the Mastermaid went up with him without more ado; and as the King thought she was more than she seemed to be, he sat her down in the highest seat by the side of the youngest bridegroom.

Now, when they had sat a little while at table, the Mastermaid took out her golden apple, and the golden cock and hen, which she had carried off from the Giant, and put them down on the table before her, and the cock and hen began at once to peck at one another, and to fight for the golden apple.

"Look," said the Prince; "see how those two strive for the apple."

"Yes!" said the Mastermaid; "so we two strove to get away that time when we were together in the hillside."

Then the spell was broken, and the Prince knew her again, and how glad he was. But as for the witch who had rolled the apple over to him, he had her torn to pieces between twenty-four horses, so that there was not a bit of her left. After that they held the wedding in real earnest; and though they were still stiff and footsore, the Constable, the Attorney, and the Sheriff kept it up with the best of them. ∎

44

The Hermit

The Hermit is one of the favourite tales of the Sufi teachers of the East, illustrating the lack of insight of the ordinary individual. A version of it by the poet Thomas Parnell was published in 1721, and the legend was regarded as his invention until 1773; though it was later thought to have come from Spain and to be an Arabian composition. It had, however, already been printed in the English translation of the medieval monkish tales, the **Gesta Romanorum,** *in 1703, and it was thought to be Voltairean, through that philosopher's use of it in* **Zadig,** *in 1748. It has been found as a popular tale in Sicily and Spain — both formerly Islamic territories — and its first appearance in literature was in the* **Koran,** *nearly fourteen hundred years ago. In Chapter 18 of the Moslem holy book, the account is attributed to Moses' instruction by an unknown mysterious figure, generally believed to be the apparition Khidr, later regarded as the guide of the Sufi mystics. This is Voltaire's presentation.*

'Voltaire', a portrait by Bocourt

In the reign of King Moabdar there lived at Babylon a young man named Zadig. He was handsome, rich, and naturally good-hearted; and at the moment when this story opens, he was travelling on foot to see the world, and to learn philosophy and wisdom. But, hitherto, he had encountered so much misery, and endured so many terrible disasters, that he had become tempted to rebel against the will of Heaven, and to believe that the Providence which rules the world neglects the good, and lets the evil prosper. In this unhappy spirit he was one day walking on the banks of the Euphrates, when he chanced to meet a venerable hermit, whose snowy beard descended to his girdle, and who carried in his hand a scroll which he was reading with attention. Zadig stopped, and made him a low bow. The hermit returned the salutation with an air so kindly, and so noble, that Zadig felt a curiosity to speak to him. He inquired what scroll was that which he was reading.

"It is the Book of Destiny," replied the hermit, "would you like to read it?"

He handed it to Zadig; but the latter, though he knew a dozen languages, could not understand a word of it. His curiosity increased.

"You appear to be in trouble," said the kindly hermit.

"Alas!" said Zadig, "I have cause to be so."

"If you will allow me," said the hermit, "I will accompany you. Perhaps I may be useful to you. I am sometimes able to console the sorrowful."

Zadig felt a deep respect for the appearance, the white beard, and the mysterious scroll of the old hermit, and perceived that his conversation was that of a superior mind. The old man spoke of destiny, of justice, of morality, of the chief good of life, of human frailty, of virtue and of vice, with so much power and eloquence that Zadig felt himself attracted by a kind of charm, and besought the hermit not to leave him until they should return to Babylon.

"I ask you the same favour," said the hermit. "Promise me that, whatever I may do, you will keep me company for several days."

Zadig gave the promise; and they set forth together.

That night the travellers arrived at a grand mansion. The hermit begged for food and lodging for himself and his companion. The porter, who might have been mistaken for a prince, ushered them in with a contemptuous air of welcome. The chief servant showed them the magnificent apartments; and they were then admitted to the bottom of the table, where the master of the mansion did not condescend to cast a glance at them. They were, however, served with delicacies in profusion, and after dinner washed their hands in a golden basin set with emeralds and rubies. They were then conducted for the night into a beautiful apartment; and the next morning, before they left the castle, a servant brought them each a piece of gold.

"The master of the house," said Zadig, as they went their way, "appears to be a generous man, although a trifle haughty. He practises a noble hospitality." As he spoke, he perceived that a kind of large pouch which the hermit carried appeared singularly distended; within it was the golden basin, set with precious stones, which the old man had purloined. Zadig was amazed; but he said nothing.

At noon the hermit stopped before a little house, in which lived a wealthy miser, and once more asked for hospitality. An old valet in a shabby coat received them very rudely, showed them into the stable, and set before them a few rotten olives, some mouldy bread, and beer which had turned sour. The hermit ate and drank with as much content as he had shown the night before; then, addressing the old valet, who had kept his eye upon them to make sure that they stole nothing, he gave him the two gold pieces which they had received that morning, and thanked him for his kind attention. "Be so good," he added, "as to let me see your master."

The astonished valet showed them in.

"Most mighty signor," said the hermit, "I can only render you my humble thanks for the noble manner in which you have received us. I beseech you to accept this golden basin as a token of my gratitude."

The miser almost fell backwards with amazement. The hermit, without waiting for him to recover, set off with speed, with his companion.

"Holy Father," said Zadig, "what does all this mean? You seem to me to resemble other men in nothing. You steal a golden basin set with jewels from a signor who receives you with magnificence, and you give it to a curmudgeon who treats you with indignity."

"My son," replied the hermit, "this mighty lord, who only welcomes travellers through vanity, and to display his riches, will henceforth grow wiser, while the miser will be taught to practise hospitality. Be amazed at

nothing, and follow me."

Zadig knew not whether he was dealing with the most foolish or the wisest of all men. But the hermit spoke with such ascendency that Zadig, who besides was fettered by his promise, had no choice except to follow him.

That night they came to an agreeable house, of simple aspect, and showing signs of neither prodigality nor avarice. The owner was a philosopher, who had left the world, and who studied peacefully the rules of virtue and of wisdom, and who yet was happy and contented. He had built this calm retreat to please himself, and he received the strangers in it with a frankness which displayed no sign of ostentation. He conducted them himself to a comfortable chamber, where he made them rest awhile; then he returned to lead them to a dainty little supper. During their conversation they agreed that the affairs of this world are not always regulated by the opinions of the wisest men. But the hermit still maintained that the ways of Providence are wrapped in mystery, and that men do wrong to pass their judgement on a universe of which they only see the smallest part. Zadig wondered how a person who committed such mad acts could reason so correctly.

At length, after a conversation as agreeable as instructive, the host conducted the two travellers to their apartment, and thanked heaven for sending him two visitors so wise and virtuous. He offered them some money, but so frankly that they could not feel offended. The old man declined, and desired to say farewell, as he intended to depart for Babylon at break of day. They therefore parted on the warmest terms, and Zadig, above all, was filled with kindly feelings towards so amiable a man.

When the hermit and himself were in their chamber, they spent some time in praises of their host. At break of day the old man woke his comrade.

"We must be going," he remarked. "But while everyone is still asleep, I wish to leave this worthy man a pledge of my esteem." With these words, he took a torch and set the house on fire.

Zadig burst forth into cries of horror, and would have stopped the frightful act. But the hermit, by superior strength, drew him away. The house was in a blaze; and the old man, who was now a good way off with his companion, looked back calmly at the burning pile.

"Heaven be praised!" he cried. "Our kind host's house is destroyed from top to bottom!"

At these words Zadig knew not whether he should burst out laughing, call the reverend father an old rascal, knock him down, or run away. But he did none of these things. Still subdued by the superior manner of the hermit, he followed him against his will to their next lodging.

This was the dwelling of a good and charitable widow, who had a nephew of fourteen, her only hope and joy. She did her best to use the travellers well; and the next morning she bade her nephew guide them safely past a certain bridge, which, having recently been broken, had become dangerous to cross over. The youth, eager to oblige them, led the way.

"Come," said the hermit, when they were half across the bridge, "I must show my gratitude towards your aunt;" and as he spoke he seized the young man by the hair and threw him into the river. The youth fell, reappeared for an instant on the surface, and then was swallowed by the torrent.

"Oh, monster!" exclaimed Zadig, "oh, most detestable of men!"

"You promised me more patience," interrupted the old man. "Listen! Beneath the ruins of that house which Providence saw fit to set on fire, the owner will discover an enormous treasure; while this young man, whose existence Providence cut short, would have killed his aunt within a year, and you yourself in two."

"Who told you so, barbarian?" cried Zadig, "and even if you read the issue in your Book of Destiny, who gave you power to drown a youth who never injured you?"

While he spoke, he saw that the old man had a beard no longer, and that his face had become fair and young; his hermit's dress had disappeared: four white wings covered his majestic form, and shone with dazzling lustre.

"Angel of heaven!" cried Zadig, "you are then descended from the skies to teach an erring mortal to submit to the eternal laws?"

"Men," replied the angel Jezrael, "judge all things without knowledge; and you, of all men, most deserved to be enlightened. The world imagines that the youth who has just perished fell by chance into the water, and that by a like chance the rich man's house was set on fire. But there is no such thing as chance; all is trial, or punishment, or foresight. Feeble mortal, cease to argue and rebel against what you ought to adore!"

As he spoke these words the angel took his flight to heaven. And Zadig fell upon his knees. ■

Such a profusion of the traditional stories of the world are to be found in the Balkans that it has even been suggested that this area is one of the original homes of the folk-tale. Hardly a genre — Slavic, Greek, Turkic, Latin, Arabian or Jewish — is unrepresented. Through the Western European connection, the tales most often found in Germany, France, Italy are abundant; from the north are recognizable variants of the lore of the Russian and Scandinavian, as well as Mongolian traditions; and recitals from the ancient classical books are still very much in evidence.

This Serbian story follows the very ancient pattern which has been called 'The Clever Girl', and in contemporary terms it may be regarded as an example of the feminine use of non-linear thinking on which contemporary problem-solving ideas are

The Maiden Wiser Than The Tsar

Once upon a time there was a poor man who had one daughter.

Now, this girl was amazingly wise, seemed to have knowledge far beyond her years, and often said things which surprised her own father.

One day, being without a penny, the poor man went to the Tsar to beg.

The Tsar, astonished at the man's cultivated way of saying things, asked him where he has learned such phrases.

"From my daughter," he replied.

"But where was your daughter taught?" asked the Tsar.

"God and our poverty have made her wise," was the answer.

"Here is some money for your immediate needs,"

increasingly based. The tale is sometimes prefaced by the account of the girl carving a cooked fowl at a dinner where the Prince is present. Nobody can understand why she apportions the pieces in the way in which she does; instead of giving portions to the diners in accordance with their rank, she assigns them symbolically. The Prince overhears her explaining "The head to the head of the family, the wings for me to fly to catch a husband", and falls in love with her. This completes the symbolism of the filling of a need, where the Prince represents linear thinking and needs the other form of wisdom represented by the girl. As an illustration of the respective functions of the two brain hemispheres, recently recorded by scientists, one could hardly expect a better example than this most ancient tale of Serbia.

said the Tsar, "and here are thirty eggs; command your daughter in my name to hatch them for me. If she does this successfully, you shall both have rich presents, but if she does not, you will be put to the torture."

The man went home and took the eggs to his daughter. She examined them, and weighed one or two in her hands. Then she realised that they were hard-boiled. So, she said "Father, wait until tomorrow, maybe I can think what can be done about this."

Next day, she was up early, having thought of a solution, and boiled some beans. She gave her father a small bag of the beans, and said:

"Go with the plough and oxen, father, and start ploughing beside the road where the Tsar will pass on his way to church. When he puts his head out of the carriage window, call out 'Go on, good oxen, plough the land so that these boiled beans will grow well!' "

The father did as she told him, and sure enough, the Tsar put his head out of the window of his carriage to watch the man at work, and, hearing what was being shouted, said "Stupid fellow, how can you expect boiled beans to produce anything?"

Primed by his daughter, the simple man called out, "Just as from boiled eggs chickens can be produced!"

So, laughing, the Tsar went on his way, knowing that the girl had outwitted him.

But it was not to end there.

The next day the Tsar sent a courtier to the poor man with a bundle of flax, saying "This flax must be made into sails for my ship by tomorrow; otherwise, you will be executed."

Weeping, the man went home, but his daughter said "Have no fear, I shall think of something."

In the morning she came to him and gave him a small block of wood, and said "Tell the Tsar that if he can have all the tools necessary for spinning and weaving made out of this piece of wood, I will do the material for his sails out of the bunch of flax."

He did so, and the Tsar was further impressed by the girl's answer. But he put a small glass into the man's hand and said:

"Go, take this to your daughter, and ask her to empty the sea with this so that I may enlarge my dominions with precious new pastures."

The man went home, and gave his daughter the glass, telling her that the ruler had demanded yet another impossibility.

"Go to bed!" she said, "I will think of something by bringing my mind to bear upon it all night."

In the morning she said "Go to the Tsar and tell him that if he can dam up all the rivers of the world with this bundle of tow, then I will empty the sea for him."

The father went back to the Tsar and told him what his daughter had said. The Tsar, seeing that she was wiser than himself, asked that she be brought to court forthwith. When she appeared he asked her:

"What is it that can be heard at the greatest distance?" Without any hesitation she replied at once:

"The thunder and the lie can be heard at the greatest distance, O Tsar." Astonished, the Tsar grasped his beard, and then, turning to his courtiers asked

"What is my beard worth, do you think?" Each of them began to say what they thought the Tsar's beard was worth, making the value higher and higher, hoping

to curry favour with His Majesty. Then, he said to the maiden:

"And what do you think my beard is worth, my child?" Everyone looked on in amazement as she replied:

"Your Majesty's beard is worth every bit as much as three summer rains!" The Tsar, greatly astonished, said:

"You have guessed rightly; I shall marry you and make you my wife this very day." So the girl became the Tsarina. But just when the wedding was over, she said to the Tsar:

"I have one request to make; be graciously pleased to write with your own hand that if you, or anyone in your court be displeased with me, and I had to go away, I should be allowed to take with me any one thing which I liked best." Enamoured of the beautiful maiden, the Tsar asked for pen and parchment, and at once wrote, sealing the document with his own ruby ring, as she had requested.

The years passed most happily for both of them, then one day the Tsar had a heated argument with the Tsarina and said:

"Go, I desire that you leave this palace, never to return!"

"I shall go tomorrow, then," said the young Tsarina dutifully, "Only allow me one more night here to prepare myself for the journey home." The Tsar agreed, and she gave him his bedtime herbal drink with her usual care.

No sooner had the Tsar drunk the potion than he fell asleep. The Tsarina had the Tsar carried to a coach, and they went to her father's cottage.

When the morning came, the Tsar, who had spent a tranquil night, woke, and looked around him in amazement.

"Treason!" he roared, "Where am I, and whose prisoner?"

"Mine, your majesty," said the Tsarina sweetly, "Your parchment, written with your own hand is here," and she showed him where he had written that if she had to leave the palace she could take with her that which she liked best.

Hearing this, the Tsar laughed heartily, and declared that his affection for her had returned. "My great love for you, O Tsar," said she "has made me do this bold thing, but I risked death to do it, so you must see that my love is indeed very great."

Then they were united, and lived happily together for the rest of their lives. ■

A dead man whom one has helped to find rest, as a travelling companion who enables the hero to overcome trials and release a bewitched girl—this is quite as strange a plot as any. It has fired the imagination of the writer of no less a work than the scriptural Book of Tobit, and of Hans Christian Andersen, whose presentation as 'The Travelling Companion' is given here, as an example of the way in which a spare and terse legend was presented in the ficton of his time.

The story's history also involves the ancient English romance, 'Sir Amadas', and Basque, Spanish, and French country tales. It has been reincarnated in Italy as a novel (Messer Danese) and a poem (Brunetto's Constantina). A Scottish Gaelic version has been collected by the celebrated Celtic scholar, Professor Kenneth Jackson, in Nova Scotia. Its enduring attraction is also seen in its appearance in Grimm, in the nineteenth century, and back to Straparola in 1550, as well as in the narrations among the folk-tale reciters of Armenia, Scandinavia, Italy, and Turkey, and among the Gypsies, Slavs, Indians, and Scottish West Highlanders.

The story is here left in the form in which English presenters of Andersen customarily offered it in the heyday of his popularity.

The Travelling Companion

Poor John was sorely troubled, for his father was sick unto death. They two were absolutely alone in the little room. The lamp upon the table was just flickering out, and the night was far gone.

"You have been a good son, John," said the sick father; "God will help you on in the world," and he looked at him with grave, gentle eyes, drew a deep, deep breath, and died: it was just as if he had fallen asleep. But John fell a-weeping. He had now no one left in the whole world, neither father nor mother, sister nor brother.

Poor John! He knelt before the coffin and kissed the hand of his dear father. Many were the tears he wept; but at last his eyes closed, and he fell asleep with his head upon the hard bed-post. Then he dreamed a wondrous dream. He saw the sun and moon bow down before him, and he saw his father fresh and hearty again, and he heard him laugh as he used always to laugh when he was pleased. A lovely girl with a gold crown on her long fair hair held out her hand to him, and his father said, "Look what a nice bride you've got! She is the loveliest bride in the whole world." Then he awoke — and all this bliss was gone. His father lay dead and cold on the bed; there was absolutely no other with them. Poor John!

A week afterwards the dead man was buried. John walked close behind the coffin. He would never see again the kind father who had loved him so much. He heard them throw the earth down on the coffin, he caught sight of the last corner of it, but the next spadeful of earth that was thrown down hid that also. Then his grief overcame him, and his heart was nigh to breaking. Those around the grave sang a hymn; it sounded so pretty, and the tears came into John's eyes: he cried, and it did his heart good. The sun shone beautifully on the green trees, as if it would say, "Don't be distressed John! Can't you see how lovely the blue sky is? Your father is up there now, praying to

From Le Grand Kalendrier Et Compost Des Bergiers

God that things may always go well with you."

"I will always be good," said John; "and then I also shall go to Heaven, and be with my father. Oh, how joyful it will be when we see each other again! What a lot I shall have to tell him, and he too, will show me so many things and teach me so much about the beauty of Heaven, just as he used to teach me here on earth. Oh, how joyful it will be!"

All this passed so vividly before John's mind that he could not but smile at the thought of it, though the tears were all the time running down his cheeks. The little birds were sitting on the chestnut-trees and twittering, "twee-wit, twee-wit!" They were so happy, though they also had been at the funeral. But they knew well enough that the dead man was now in Heaven, and had wings finer and larger than theirs, and that he was now happy, because he had been good on earth, and they were quite delighted at the thought of it. John saw them flit away from the green trees far out into the wide world, and he was minded to follow their example. But first he carved a large wooden cross to place over his father's grave, and when he brought it in the evening, he found the grave nicely trimmed with sand and flowers. Strangers had done this, for they had loved the dead father.

Early next morning John packed up his little bundle, hid in his belt the whole of his patrimony — some fifty rix-dollars and a couple of silver pence — and resolved to seek his fortune in the wide world. But first he went into the churchyard to his father's grave, recited "Our Father", and said "Farewell, dear Dad; I will always be a good man; and oh, pray God that it may be well with me!"

As John went through the fields all the flowers stood so fresh and beautiful in the warm sunlight, and they nodded in the wind as if they would say, "Welcome to the green fields, is it not lovely here?" But John turned himself round once more to look at the church where he, as a little boy, had been christened: and where he had gone every Sunday with his old father and sung hymns; and he saw standing high up in one of the holes of the tower the church-elf in his little red pointed cap, shading his face with both hands, so that the sun might not shine into his eyes. John nodded farewell to him, and the little elf swung his red cap, put

his hand on his heart, and kissed his fingers to him again and again, to show that he wished him well and a right prosperous journey.

John thought of all the fine things that he was going to see in the wide magnificent world, and went farther and farther away, farther than he had ever been before. He knew absolutely nothing of the towns he passed through, or the people he met — he was far away among total strangers. The first night he was obliged to sleep in a haystack in the fields, for he had no other bed. Yet it seemed very cosy to him; the King himself could not have been better off. The whole plain, with the river, the haystack, and the blue sky above it all — what finer bed-chamber could one have? The green grass, with the tiny red and white flowers, was the carpet; the elder-bushes and the hedges of wild roses were the bouquets of flowers on the dressing-table; and for his bath he had the whole river with the clear, fresh water, where the rushes nodded and said both good-morning and good-evening. The moon, high up under the blue ceiling, was a splendid large night-lamp, and it didn't set fire to the curtains, either. John could sleep quite comfortably; and so he did, and he only awoke again when the sun rose, and all the little birds round about sang, "Good morning, good morning! Are you not up yet?"

The bells were ringing for church, it was Sunday. The people went to hear the parson preach, and John went with them and sang a hymn, and heard God's Word; and it was just as if he was in his own church where he had been christened and had sung hymns with his father. There were so many graves in the churchyard, and some of them were overgrown with tall grass. This made John think of his father's grave. It might get to look like these when he was no longer there to trim and weed it. So he sat himself down and plucked off the grass, put up again the wooden crosses that had fallen down, and put back in their proper places the wreaths which the wind had torn away from the graves, thinking to himself all the while, "Perchance someone will do the same to my father's grave, now that I am far away."

Outside the churchyard stood an old beggar leaning on his staff: John gave him all the little silver coins he had, and then went on his way into the wide world so happy and contented. Towards evening a terrible storm arose. John made haste to get under cover, but dark night had fallen upon him before he came at last to a little church which stood all alone on the top of a little hill. Fortunately the door stood ajar, and he crept in, and determined to stay there till the storm had passed away.

"I will lay me down in a corner," said he. "I am quite tired, and feel the need of a little rest." So he sat down, folded his hands, and said his evening prayers; and, before he knew it, he was asleep and dreaming, while outside it was still thundering and lightning. When he awoke again it was midnight, but the storm had passed away, and the moon was shining through the windows upon him. In the middle of the nave stood an open coffin with a dead man in it, for he had not yet been buried. John was not at all afraid, for he had a good conscience; and besides, he knew that the dead hurt no-one; it is living wicked men who do harm. Two such living wicked people stood at that moment beside the dead man who had been placed in the church before being put in his grave; they wanted to do him harm, they would not let him lie in peace in his coffin, but wanted to cast him into the churchyard outside, poor dead man!

"Why do you do that?" asked John; "'tis an evil, wicked deed. Let him sleep in Jesu's name."

"Stuff and nonsense!" said the two horrid men; "he has cheated us! He owes us money which he could not pay, and now he has died into the bargain, and so we shan't get a farthing. That is why we mean to tear him out of his coffin; he shall lie outside the church-door like a dog."

"I have no more than fifty rix-dollars," said John; "it is my whole inheritance; but I will cheerfully give it to you if you will faithfully promise me to leave the poor dead man in peace. I can get on well enough without the money. I have strong healthy limbs, and God will always help me."

"Well," said the horrid men, "if you will pay his debts as you say, you may be quite certain that we shan't do anything to him;" and so they took the money from John, laughed heartily at his softness, and went their way. But John placed the corpse back decently in its coffin, crossed its hands, said farewell, and went with a light heart through a great forest.

Wherever the moon managed to shine in through the trees, he saw on every side of him the prettiest little elves all playing gaily. They did not mind him in the least, for they knew very well that he was good and guileless — and it is only wicked people who cannot see the elves. Some of them were no bigger than your finger, and had their long yellow hair done up with gold combs. They rocked to and fro in couples on the large dewdrops which lay on the leaves and tall grass. Sometimes the dewdrops slipped from under them, and down they fell among the long straw stalks, and then there was such laughter and uproar among the other wee mannikins. It was prodigiously funny! Then they began singing, and John recognized at once all the pretty songs he had learnt as a little boy. Big speckled spiders with silver crowns on their heads weaved long swinging bridges and palaces from one hedge to another, which, when the fine dew fell upon them, looked like shining crystal in the bright moonshine; and thus it went on until the sun rose. Then the little elves crept into the flower blossoms, and the wind dispersed their bridges and palaces, which swung to and fro in the air like big spider webs.

John had just come out of the wood when a strong, manly voice exclaimed behind him, "Hallo, comrade! Whither away?"

"Out into the wide world!" said John. "I am a poor fellow without father or mother, but I am sure God will help me."

"I also am going into the wide world," said the man. "Shall we two go together?"

"With pleasure," said John; so they pursued their way in company, and soon got to like each other very much, for they were both good fellows. But John soon perceived that the stranger was much wiser than he; he had been nearly the whole world over, and there was nothing in existence that he could not tell you something about.

The sun was already high in the sky when they sat them down under a large tree to eat their breakfast, and the same moment an old woman came up. Oh, she was *so* old, quite crooked in fact, and leaned upon a crutch. She had a bundle of firewood on her back, which she had picked up in the wood. Her apron was tucked up and John saw three big bundles of bracken and willow twigs sticking out of it. When she got quite close to them, her foot slipped, she fell down and gave a loud shriek, for the poor old woman had broken her leg. John immediately proposed that they should carry her to her home, but the stranger opened his knapsack, took out a jar, and said he had a salve which would make her leg quite well and sound again in a minute, so that she could go home herself just as if she had never broken her leg at all. In return for this, however, he wanted her to give him the three bundles which she had in her apron.

"You ask a good price," said the old woman, and nodded her head very mysteriously. She would have liked very much to keep her bundles, but it was no joke to lie there with a broken leg. So she gave him the bundles, and no sooner had he rubbed the salve on her leg, than up sprang the old granny, and went on her way much more briskly than before. A wonderful salve, truly, but you could not get it at any apothecary's.

"What do you want with those bundles?" inquired John of his comrade.

"Oh they are three pretty nosegays!" said he. "I have taken rather a fancy to them, for I am a strange sort of fellow." So they went on a bit farther.

"Why, how overcast it is getting!" said John, and pointed ahead of him. "There are some terribly big clouds over there."

"Nay," said his travelling companion. "Those are not clouds, they are mountains, the beautiful big mountains where one can get right above the clouds into the bracing air; and splendid it is, I can tell you! Tomorrow we shall certainly be a good step on our journey into the wide world."

The mountains were nothing like so close as they seemed. It took them a whole day to get to the spot where the black woods grew right up against the sky, and where there were stones as big as a whole town. A stiff pull it would be before they could get right up there, and therefore John and his travelling companion went first of all into an inn to have a good rest and brace themselves up for their journey on the morrow. A crowd of people were assembled in the tap-room, for there was a puppet-show man there. He had just set up his little theatre, and the people sat all round to see the play. But a fat old butcher had taken the front seat, which was by far the best. His big bulldog — ugh! how grim it looked — sat by his side and glared at all the company.

And now the play began, and a very pretty play it was, with a King and Queen who sat upon a velvet throne and had gold crowns on their heads and long trains behind their robes — for they could afford it. The prettiest dolls with glass eyes and large whiskers stood at all the doors, and opened and shut them continually so as to let fresh air into the room. It was quite a pretty play, and not at all sad; but just as the Queen arose and was walking across the stage, then — Heaven only knows what the bulldog was thinking about! But, anyhow, as the fat butcher was not holding him, he made one bound into the middle of the stage, and seized the Queen round the waist, so that it went "Knick! Knack!" It was a horrible sight!

The poor man who was acting the whole play was frightened and distressed about his Queen, for she was the prettiest doll he had; and now the ugly bulldog had bitten her head off. But when all the people had gone away the stranger who had come with John said that he would soon make her all right again, and so he took out his jar and smeared the doll with salve as he had helped the poor old woman when she had broken her leg. As soon as ever the doll was rubbed she became all right again at once — nay! She could now move all her limbs about herself, you had not even to pull the string. The doll became like a living creature, except that it could not talk. The man who had the little puppet theatre was delighted. He now had no need to hold the doll at all. It could dance of its own accord.

Now when it was night, and all the people in the inn had gone to bed, somebody was heard to sigh lamentably, and kept it up so long, that everyone else got up to see what it could be. The man who had acted the play went to his little theatre, for it was from thence that the sighing seemed to come. All the wooden dolls lay higgledy-piggledy; the King and his guards were all mixed up together, and it was they who were sighing so piteously and staring with their big glass eyes, for they wanted so much to be rubbed with the ointment like the Queen, that they also might be able to move about of their own accord. The Queen sank down upon her knees, and held her pretty gold crown up in the air while she seemed to pray, "Oh take it, take it, but anoint my consort and my courtiers!"

Then the poor man who owned the play and all the puppets could not help weeping, for it made him feel so sorry for them all. He promised to give the travelling companion all the money he took for his play next evening if only he would smear four or five of his prettiest dolls with the ointment. But the travelling companion said that all he asked in return was the big sword that hung by the man's side; and, when he had got it, he smeared six dolls with the ointment, and they immediately fell a-dancing so prettily that all the girls — the living, human girls who were looking on — fell a-dancing as well. The coachman and the scullery-maid, the lackey and the parlour maid danced together, and all the strangers followed suit, and the poker and the tongs likewise; but the last two tumbled down at the very first caper. Oh, it was a merry night!

Next morning John left them all and went right away with his comrade up the high mountains and through the large pine forests. They went so high up that the church towers far below looked like small red berries in the midst of all the green, and they could see far, far away many, many a mile, where they had never yet been. John had never in his life seen so much of the beautiful world at one time, and the sun shone so warmly from out of the fresh blue sky. He heard too, the hunters blowing their horns among the mountains, and it was so lovely and blissful that the water came into his eyes for joy and he could not help saying, "O God, how good Thou art! I could kiss Thee, because Thou art so good to us all, and hast given us as our own all the beauty that is in the world."

His companion too, stood with folded hands and gazed away over wood and town in the warm sunshine. At that moment there was a wondrously delightful sound high over their heads. They looked up into the air; a large white swan was sweeping through the sky. It was so beautiful, and it sang as they had never heard a bird sing before; but it gradually grew weaker and weaker, bowed its head, and at last sank quite slowly down at their feet, where it lay dead—the lovely bird!

"Two such beautiful big white wings as that bird has got are worth money," said the travelling companion, "and I mean to take them with me. Now you can see what a good thing it was I took the sword," and with one blow he cut off both the swan's wings, for he meant to keep them.

And now they journeyed many and many a mile across the mountains, till at last they saw before them a large city with many hundreds of towers, which shone like silver in the sunlight. In the midst of the city was a splendid marble palace covered with real gold, and there dwelt the King. John and his travelling companion would not go into the city at once but stopped at an inn outside to smarten themselves up, for they wanted to look nice when they walked about the streets.

The host told them that the King was a good man who never harmed anyone; but his daughter—God preserve us!—she was indeed a wicked Princess. She was beautiful enough, indeed no one could be more pretty and captivating than she; but what was the good of that when she was a vile, wicked witch, through whose fault so many handsome Princes had lost their lives? She had given everyone leave to woo her; anybody might come forward; whether he was Prince or beggar, it was all the same, he had only to guess three things she asked him. If he could give the right answers, she would marry him, and he would reign over the whole land when her father died. But if he could not guess these three things, she had him hanged or beheaded, so evil and wicked was this lovely Princess.

Her father, the old King, was sore afflicted at this state of things, but he could not prevent her from being so wicked, for he had once said that he would have nothing whatever to do with her lovers, and that she could do what she liked in that matter. Hitherto, every Prince who had tried to guess the questions so as to win the Princess had always failed, and so had either been hanged or beheaded, and yet he had always been warned beforehand not to woo her. The old King was so grieved at all the sorrow and misery caused thereby that once a year he knelt down all day with his soldiers and prayed that the Princess might become good; but this she absolutely refused to be, and even the old women who drank brandy dyed it quite black before they drank it, by way of mourning, for what else could they do?

"The nasty Princess!" said John, "she should really have the birch-rod; it would do her good! If only I were the old King, she should bleed for it yet!"

But, of course, a King may not break his word, and this King had promised not to interfere.

At that moment they heard the people outside cry "Hurrah!" The Princess was passing by, and she really was so lovely that all the people forgot for the moment how wicked she was, and so they cried "Hurrah!" Fresh, lovely maidens, all in white silk gowns with golden tulips in their hands, rode on coal-black horses by her side. The Princess herself had a chalk-white horse bedecked with diamonds and rubies; her riding habit was of pure gold, and the whip she had in her hand looked like a sunbeam. The gold crown on her head was as if made of little stars taken from the sky; and her mantle was embroidered with the wings of thousands and thousands of little butterflies. At the same time, she was ever so much lovelier than her raiment.

When John caught sight of her, he turned as red in the face as a drop of blood, and could scarcely utter a single word. The Princess looked exactly like the beautiful girl with the gold crown whom he had dreamed about on the night his father died. He thought her so beautiful, and could not help loving her. It was certainly not true, thought he, that she could be an evil witch who had people hanged or beheaded when they could not guess what she asked them. "Everyone, they say, even the poorest beggar, has leave to woo her; then I, too, will go up to the palace, because I really can't help it!"

Everyone said that he ought not to do so. He would certainly fare as all the others had done. His travelling companion also dissuaded him, but John declared that it would all come right, brushed his shoes and jacket, washed his face and hands, combed his beautiful yellow hair, and so went quite alone into the city and up to the palace.

"Come in!" said the old King when John knocked at the door. John opened the door, and the old King, in a dressing-gown and embroidered slippers, came to meet him. He had his gold crown upon his head, his sceptre in one hand and the orb in the other.

"Wait a bit," said he, and he shoved the orb under one arm, so as to be able to shake hands with John. But as soon as he understood that it was another wooer, he began to weep so violently that the sceptre and orb fell upon the floor, and he had to dry his tears with his dressing-gown. Poor old King!

"Don't do it," said he, "it will go as badly with you as with all the others. Well, you shall see for yourself!" And so he led John into the Princess's pleasure-garden. Oh, what a horrible sight! On every tree hung three or four king's sons who had wooed the Princess, but had been unable to guess the things she had asked them. Every time the wind blew, all their bones rattled so that the small birds were scared away and never dared to come into the garden. All the flowers were tied to dead men's bones instead of sticks, and grinning skulls stood in all the flower-pots. That was a nice garden for a Princess.

"Look there now!" said the old King. "So it will fare with you as with all the others you see here. Give up the idea, do! You make me positively wretched; I take it so much to heart."

John kissed the hand of the good old King, and said that it would all come right in the end, for he was so fond of the lovely Princess. At the same moment the Princess herself came riding into the courtyard with all her ladies, so they went out to meet her, and said good-day. She was lovely indeed, and she held out her hand to John, who loved her more than ever. She surely could never be the evil, wicked witch that all the people said she was! They went up into the drawing-room, and the little pages presented them with sweetmeats and gingerbread-nuts. But the old King was so grieved that he could not eat anything; and, besides, the gingerbread-nuts were too tough for his teeth.

It was now arranged that John was to come up to the palace again next morning, when the judges and the whole Senate would be gathered together to hear how he got on with the guessing. If he got through with it, he was to come twice more, but hitherto there had never been anyone who had guessed the first time, and so they had all lost their lives. John was not a bit anxious as to how he should fare; he was in the best of humours, thought of nothing but the charming Princess, and believed firmly that God would help him somehow but how he had no idea, nor would he even bestow a single thought upon it. He actually danced along the highway as he went back to his inn, where his travelling companion awaited him.

John could not find words to express how nice the Princess had been to him, and how beautiful she was. He longed already for the next day to come that he might go to the palace again and try his luck at guessing. But his travelling companion shook his head and was very sad.

"I am so fond of you," said he, "and we might have been companions together for a long time to come yet. Poor dear John! I could weep my eyes out, but I won't spoil the last evening, perhaps, that we shall ever spend together. We will be merry, right merry. Tomorrow when you are gone I shall have cause to weep!"

All the people in the city had immediately got to know that a new wooer had arrived, and accordingly there was great lamentation. The theatre was closed, all the cake-women tied pieces of crape round their sugar-pigs, the King and the priests knelt in the church. There was such a lamentation, for how could it possibly fare better with John that with all the suitors who had gone before him? Towards evening the travelling companion brewed a large bowl of punch and said to John that they would now be jolly together and drink the Princess's health. But when John had drunk two glasses he became so drowsy that he could not keep his eyes open, so he fell fast asleep. The travelling companion lifted John very softly from the chair and laid him on the bed. And when it was night and quite dark, he took the two large wings which he had cut off the swan, bound them tightly to his shoulders, put in his pocket the largest of the bundles of birches which he had got from the old woman who had fallen and broken her leg, opened the window and flew away over the city straight to the palace, where he crouched down in a corner just under the window which looked into the Princess's bedroom.

The whole city lay in silence when the clock struck a quarter to twelve. Then the window flew open and the Princess flew out in a large white cape, and with long black wings, right across the town to a large mountain.

The travelling companion made himself invisible, so that she could not see him at all, flew behind her, and whipped the Princess with his birches till he drew blood. Ugh! that was something like a flight through the air! The wind caught her cape, so that it bulged out on all sides like a huge sail, and the moon shone through it. "How it hails! How it hails!" said the Princess at every blow she got from the birches, and she had quite enough of it too!

At last she came right up to the mountain-side, and knocked. There was a rolling sound like thunder, while the mountain opened and the Princess went in, the travelling companion following after, for no one could see him—he was invisible. They went through a large, long passage where the walls sparkled most wondrously; there were thousands and thousands of red-hot spiders there that ran up and down the walls and glowed like fire. And now they came to a large room built of gold and silver. Flowers as large as sunflowers, red and blue, gleamed on the walls; but none could pluck these flowers for their stalks were nasty, venomous serpents, and the blossoms were the flames that came out of serpents mouths. The atmosphere was all full of shining glow-worms and sky-blue bats, which flapped their gossamer wings to and fro.

It was indeed a strange sight. In the middle of the floor was a throne supported by four skeleton horses, with a harness of fiery-red spiders. The throne itself was of milk-white glass, and the cushions were small black mice, which bit each other in the heel continually. Above the throne was a canopy of rosy-red spider webs, sewn with the prettiest small green flies, which sparkled like precious stones. In the midst of the throne sat an old Troll, with a crown upon his hideous head and a sceptre in his hand. He kissed the Princess on the forehead, invited her to sit down beside him on the gorgeous throne, and then the music began.

Big black grasshoppers played on the Jew's harp, and the owl beat his stomach with his wings to supply the place of the drum. It was a ridiculous concert. Wee, wee pixies with will-o'-the-wisps in their caps danced round and round the room. No one could see the travelling companion; he had posted himself right behind the throne, and heard and saw everything. The courtiers—for they also now came in—were smart

and distinguished looking; but anyone who had eyes to see could perceive soon enough what sort of people they were. They were neither more nor less than broomsticks with cabbage-heads on, who had come alive by the magic spells of the Troll, and they were dressed up in fine, brocaded garments. But that didn't matter a bit—they were only there for show. So there was a little dancing, and after that the Princess told the Troll that she had got a new wooer, and therefore wanted to know what question she should put to him when he came up to the palace next morning.

"Listen!" said the Troll, "and I'll tell you. You must choose something very easy, and then it will never occur to him. Think of your own slipper; he won't guess that. Then have his head cut off! But don't forget to bring me his eyes, for I want to eat them!"

The Princess curtsied very low, and said she would not forget the eyes; then the Troll opened the mountain, and she flew home again. But the travelling companion followed after and flogged her so vigorously with the birches that she groaned at the violence of the hailstorm, and hastened as fast as she could to her bed-room again through the window. Then the travelling companion flew back to the inn where John was sleeping soundly, unloosed his wings, and laid himself down upon the bed, for he was very tired, to say the least of it.

It was quite early in the morning when John awoke. The travelling companion rose at the same time, and told him that he had dreamed a very strange dream that night, about the Princess and one of her shoes, and bade him therefore ask, when it came to the point, whether the Princess had not thought of one of her own shoes. This indeed was what he had heard from the Troll in the mountain; but he would not tell John anything about that, but simply bade him ask if she had not thought of one of her slippers.

"I may just as well ask about that as about anything else," said John; "you may perhaps have dreamt the right answer after all, for I believe that God helps me at all times. At the same time, however, I will bid you farewell; for if I guess wrong, I shall never see you more." So they kissed each other, and John went off to the city and up to the palace.

The whole of the grand saloon was quite full of people. The judges sat in easy-chairs, and they rested their heads on eider-down cushions because they had so much to think about. The old King stood up and dried his eyes with a white pocket-handkerchief. And now the Princess entered; she was even lovelier than yesterday, and saluted them all so sweetly. To John she gave her hand, and said, "Good morning to you!" And now John had to guess what she was thinking about. Heavens! How kindly she looked; but the instant she heard him say one word "slipper" her face became chalky white, and she trembled in every limb. But it profited her nothing, for he had guessed rightly.

Bless me! how glad the old King was. He cut capers till the boards rocked again, and all the people clapped their hands for him and John, who had thus guessed rightly the first time. The travelling companion beamed with joy when he heard how well it had all gone off; but John clasped his hands and thanked God, Who, he felt sure, would help him the two remaining times. The second guessing was fixed for the following day.

The same thing happened that evening as on yesternight. When John fell asleep, his travelling companion flew after the Princess into the mountain, and flogged her even harder than the first time, for he took two bundles of birches with him on this occasion. Nobody could see him, and he heard everything. The Princess was to think of her glove, and he told this to John just as if he had dreamt it again, so John was able to guess aright—and oh, what joy there was in the Palace! The whole court cut capers just as they had seen the King do the first time, but the Princess lay upon the sofa and would not say a single word.

Now all depended upon whether John would guess rightly the third time. If things went well, he was to have the lovely Princess and inherit the whole kingdom when the old King died; but if he guessed wrongly, he would lose his life and the Troll would eat his beautiful eyes.

The evening before John went early to bed, said his prayers, and then dropped off into a sweet sleep; but the travelling companion bound the wings to his shoulders, fastened his sword by his side, took all three bundles of birches with him and then flew to the palace. It was a pitch-black night.

The storm raged so that the tiles flew from the roofs

of the houses, and the trees in the garden where the skeletons hung swayed to and fro like reeds in the blast. The lightning flashed every moment, and the thunder rolled till it seemed like a single peal lasting through the livelong night. And now the window sprang open and the Princess flew out. She was as pale as death, but she laughed wildly at the bad weather—it didn't seem rough enough for her—and her white cape whirled round in the air like a huge sail. But the travelling companion scourged her with his three bundles of birches till her blood dripped down upon the ground, and she could scarcely fly any farther.

At last however, she came to the mountain. "How it hails and blows!" she cried; "never have I been out in such weather before!"

"Yes," said the Troll. "One may have too much of a good thing!"

And then she told him that John had guessed aright the second time also. If he did so again on the morrow, victory would be his, and she could never come out to the Troll in the mountain again, and would never be able to practise her enchantments as heretofore, whereupon she was sore distressed.

"He will not be able to guess this time," said the Troll. "I will find something the thought of which has never entered his head, unless he be an even greater magician than I am. But now, let us be merry!" and with that he took the Princess by both hands and they danced round and round with all the little pixies and will-o'-the-wisps that were in the room; and the red spiders ran up and down the walls with equal glee; the fire-flowers glowed and sparkled, the owl beat the drum, the crickets piped, and the grasshoppers blew upon their Jew's harps. It was a right merry ball. When the dance had lasted some time, the Princess declared that she must go home or she would be missed at the palace. The Troll said that he would go with her, so that they might have a little more time together.

Away they flew through the bad weather, and the travelling companion beat his birches to shreds on their backs. Never had the Troll been out in such a hailstorm. Outside the palace he bade the Princess farewell, and the same instance he whispered softly to her, "Think of my head!" But the travelling companion heard it all the same, and at the very moment when the Princess glided through the window to her bedroom, and the Troll was about to turn back again, he seized him by his long black beard and hewed off his hideous trollish head close upon his shoulders with his sword before the Troll himself was aware of it. He hurled the body down into the sea for the fishes, but the head he merely dipped once or twice in the water, and then he tied it up in his silk pocket-handkerchief, and took it home with him to the inn, and laid himself down to sleep. Next morning he gave the pocket-handkerchief to John but told him not to unloose it till the Princess herself asked him what it was she was thinking of.

There were so many in the grand saloon in the Palace that they stood as close together as radishes tied up in a bundle. The council sat in their chairs with the soft cushions, and the old King had new clothes on, and his gold crown and sceptre had been well furbished up for the occasion and looked splendid; but the Princess was quite pale, and had on a coal-black dress, just as if she was going to a funeral.

"What have I been thinking of?" said she to John, and straightway he loosed the pocket-handkerchief, and was quite terrified himself when he saw the hideous Troll's head. Everyone shuddered, for it was indeed a terrible sight; but the Princess sat there like a stone statue and could not utter a single word.

At last she got up and gave John her hand because he had guessed aright; and there was no denying it. She looked neither to the right nor to the left, but sighed from the bottom of her heart and said: "You are now my lord and master! This evening we will celebrate our wedding!"

"I don't object," said the old King; "we would have it so!" All the people then cried "Hurrah!" The guards on duty played music in the streets, the bells rang, and the cake-women took the crape off their sugar-pigs, for the joy was universal. Three oxen roasted whole and stuffed full with geese and pullets were placed in the middle of the market-place, and everyone could come and help himself. The fountains were running with wine of the best sort; and everyone who bought a halfpenny roll at the bakers received six large buns into the bargain, and buns with raisins in them too!

In the evening the whole town was illuminated, and the soldiers fired their guns, and the boys let off crackers, and in the palace there was no end of eating, and drinking, and toasting and dancing, and all the fine gentlemen and lovely young ladies danced with each other, and you could hear them singing ever so far off.

But the Princess was still a witch for all that, and cared not an atom for John. The travelling companion did not forget this, and he therefore gave John three feathers from the swan's wings, and a little flask with some drops in it, and he told him to place by the side of the bridal-bed a large vat full of water, and just as the Princess was about to get into bed, he was to give her a little shove so that she should fall into the water, when he was to duck her three times, taking care first of all, however, to throw the feathers and the drops in. In that way the enchantment would be broken, and she would get to be very fond of him.

John did all that his travelling companion had advised him. The Princess shrieked loudly when he ducked her under the water, and wriggled between his hands like a huge coal-black swan with sparkling eyes. When she came up to the surface of the water the second time, the swan was white, with the exception of a single black ring round its neck. John prayed devotedly

to God, and let the water gurgle for the third time over the bird's head, whereupon it immediately changed into the loveliest of Princesses. She was even handsomer than before, and thanked him with tears in her beautiful eyes for breaking her spells. Next morning the old King came in state with his whole court, and the ceremony of congratulation lasted all day.

Last of all came the travelling companion, staff in hand, with his knapsack on his shoulder. John kissed him again and again, and said he must not go away, but must stay with him for all his good fortune was owing to him. But the travelling companion shook his head, and said to him very gently and kindly, "Nay, for my time is now up. I have only paid my debts. Do you recollect the dead man to whom evil-doers would have done a mischief? You gave all you had that he might have rest in his grave. That dead man is myself!" and he straightaway was gone.

The wedding lasted a whole month. John and the Princess loved each other dearly, and the old King lived many happy days and let their wee, wee children ride-a-cockhorse on his knee and play with his sceptre; but John reigned over the whole realm. ■

The Riddles

Over the centuries tales have migrated widely, and have been used by nationalists, followers of creeds and followers of individuals, to support their cause or interest. Hence the same tale is told of Mullah Nasrudin in Iran and of Ivan the Terrible in Russia; of Buddha and of a Christian saint; of William Tell in Switzerland and about Mongol and other heroes. Although the original intention may have been to strengthen the creed or individual, (or even accidental adoption) the price paid has sometimes proved to be rather high. When the tale is shown to have been known before the date of the supposed exploit, great disappointment can set in. Almost the only recourse for those wanting to continue to believe that, for instance, the Arthurian 'sword in the stone' incident was original in Britain was to claim polygenesis: 'multiple and independent invention in different places through coincidence of thought'. The Nordic and Mongolian accounts of wonderful swords could thus be accounted for, as well as the Arabian narrative of Antar the Mighty, and the similarity to the legends of the staff of Moses among the Jews.

Substantially, the following tale—on the Riddle Theme—is found both in the eleventh-century Welsh and also in India of about two thousand years ago. It must be one of the most widespread conceptions, for examples have been collected from every part of Europe, as well as in Arabia, Africa, Mongolia, and the Phillipines. Clever girls, killing demons, and marrying kings, not to speak of magical deaths and the effect of unusual circumstances, are clearly of the greatest intercultural attraction.

This version is found in Turkestan, where the Russian, Turanian, and Iranian ethnic groups meet.

There was a time, and there was not a time, when the sky was green and the earth was a thick stew—there was a King in the mountain fastness of the Pamir Mountains, on the borders of China, India, and the God-Given Kingdom of Afghanistan.   The ruler of that kingdom was very wise, very brave and strong, very chivalrous and very rich. Everyone loved him, and they respected his justice, his mercy and his honesty.

Then, one day, he made a strange announcement; and the heralds cried it through the land:

"One must come to me, neither clothed nor naked, neither afoot nor on a horse, and speak to me neither indoors nor out. If this person comes, the country will be saved. If not, we shall all be destroyed!"

Everyone was amazed by the King's edict, and for long nothing happened, until one day a young girl said quite unexpectedly to her father, a poor firewood-collector:

"Father, I must go to the King. I know how we can be saved; and by this means we shall also be released from our poverty!"

The wood-collector was surprised, and he tried to deter her from her plan, but she would not be gainsaid, and so he reluctantly allowed her to leave their tiny cottage and travel where the King ruled.

When the girl arrived at the King's palace, she lay down at the door and cried:

"Come out, O King—for I am here to save your kingdom!"

The King asked:

"What is that commotion?"

"Your Majesty, there is some peasant girl, shouting that you must see her, for she will save the country!" answered the courtiers.

The King went to the gate, and saw the maiden lying across the threshold:

"I am neither in nor out, and so I have fulfilled one thing you wanted," she said.

"But", said the King, "what about being neither naked nor clothed?" But then he noticed that she was wearing a net, which covered her and yet did not.

"I have been neither riding nor on foot," she explained, "because I came here dragged by a mountain-goat!"

The King told her to enter the palace, and when they were seated in the full court, he said:

"Know, O clever girl, that I am in the power of a terrible Ghoul, a supernatural demon who says he will destroy the country. But he was heard to say in his sleep that only such a person as could do the things which I announced could save the Kingdom."

"I am ready to help," said the girl, "but what do I do next?"

"You must answer the following riddles," said the King; "they have been repeatedly cried out by the Ghoul in its ravings:

"First, how many stars are in the sky?"

"That's easy," said the maiden, "as many as there are hairs in a ghoul's head. This can be confirmed by plucking them out as you tell off each star, one by one."

"Very well," said the King, "I shall tell him. But now to the next question:

"How far is it from here to the end of the earth?"

The girl at once answered:

"Just as far as the return journey from the end of the earth to here!"

"Very well," said the King, "I shall tell the Ghoul. But now to the last question:

"How high is the sky?"

The girl said:

"There is no difficulty with that question. The sky is as high as a Ghoul can kick itself. It is welcome to try, if it does not believe me!"

"Very well," said the King, "I shall tell the Ghoul."

The Ghoul returned from a hunting expedition a few hours later, and it said to the King, in a voice like thunder:

"Stupid King! Have you the answers to the riddles of vulnerability yet?"

The King told him what the maiden had told him.

The Ghoul was furious.

"Those are the right answers; but you still have to pass the final test. This is concerned with the method of killing me! I am to be killed only by someone who is neither man nor beast; by someone who does it neither by day nor night; someone who offers me a present which is not a present; neither by metal nor rope nor poison nor stone nor fire nor water; one who is neither eating nor fasting at the time."

And the Ghoul then went up into a huge tree to sleep, for he was gorged with food from his hunting. He raved away in his sleep in quite an alarming manner.

The King reported the conversation to the wood-collector's daughter.

"Nothing simpler," she said, "I shall start very soon."

Then when it was twilight—neither day nor night—she went to the bottom of the tree where the Ghoul was sleeping and shouted:

"Wake up, Ghoul, for your last moment has come! I am a woman—neither man nor beast. It is neither day nor night. Here is my present which is not a present!"

And she held out a bird. When the Ghoul tried to take it, it flew away. The Ghoul realized that this gift was indeed not one.

"But you *must* be either eating or fasting!" it roared.

"I am doing neither—I am chewing a piece of bark!" the maid shouted back.

And, as she said these words the Ghoul overcome

by rage, toppled to the ground. He was not killed by sword or spear, by rope or arrow, by poison or by anything else other than his own fury which caused him to fall to the ground, where his tremendous weight smashed him to death.

"Now," said the King, as soon as everyone had stopped shaking from the earth-tremor which the impact had caused, "Tell me one last thing, maiden: what am I thinking?"

"That I am so clever and attractive that you will marry me!" said the girl.

And she was right; so they were married and they ruled the land together for the rest of their long and happy lives. ■

This Tibetan tale, taken from Indian sources by Anton von Schiefner, is supposed to inculcate a Buddhist message that animals are reincarnated people. But the underlying idea, that animals are all better than some people, has been seen by some observers as showing this to be a survival of an animal-worship tale, incorporated incompletely into the Buddhist atmosphere. The story travelled westwards through the Indian Panchatantra collection in Sanskrit, of about 750 A.D., into the Syriac 'Kalilag and Damnag' and then into the Arabic version of the same anthology. From there, about 1080 A.D., it was put into Greek by Symeon Seth. The Latin translation, through the Hebrew, was made by Johannes of Capua in the 13th century: and from that book it was diffused into Spanish, German, French, Italian and English. Hence the story has a traceable literary ancestry far more complete than the majority of world tales.

The great King Richard (the Lionhearted) is recorded as having often related a version of this tale after his return from the Crusades. It was certainly current in Palestine when Richard was there; so Matthew Paris, a monk of the Abbey of St. Albans, was probably correct in this assertion, which he wrote in his Chronicle in 1195 A.D., four years before King Richard died.

The Grateful Animals and The Ungrateful Man

In very ancient times, King Brahma-Datta was on the throne of Varanesi, in India. One of his subjects was a man who went into the forest, with his axe, to chop wood; but while he was there he was chased by a lion, and fell into a pit. The lion, who wanted to eat him, fell in as well; and so did a mouse which had been pursued by a snake. A falcon swooped on the mouse, but he got caught in the pit as well, entangled in the undergrowth.

Their natures did not change when they found themselves trapped in this way, and all the predators wanted to kill, while the others were desperately anxious to escape.

The wise lion, however, said to the animals:

"You, honored ones, are all my comrades. As things are at the moment, we are suffering intolerable distress through suffering. Let us not, therefore, expose one another to danger, but sit patiently without disturbance."

Now, fate so decreed that a hunter should be in the area, seeking gazelles, and came across the place where the animals were trapped. As soon as they realized that he was there, they shouted to him to save them.

The hunter understood what had happened, and first of all helped the lion out of captivity. The great beast touched his feet in homage and said:

"I shall show my gratitude to you in due time. But do not draw out the black-headed one"—the man, who of course had black hair—"for he forgets kindnesses done to him."

The hunter set the other creatures free; and they, too, expressed their gratitude to him. And he went on his way.

On another occasion, the hunter came to the place where the lion had killed a gazelle, and the animal touched his feet and gave the game animal to him.

It so happened, some time afterwards, that the King Brahma-Datta had gone into the park with his wives and, after enjoying himself there, fell asleep. The ladies took off their clothes and roamed about the park, put aside their jewels and sat at ease, and generally relaxed. Now, one of the women had put her jewelry down and fell asleep. The falcon, which had been keeping an eye on everything on the ground, swooped down, took up the gems, and flew with them to the hunter, to whom he presented them.

Presently, the King and his womenfolk awoke and returned to Varanesi; but one of the wives said to her husband, "O King! My jewels have been lost in the park."

The King gave orders that the missing objects should be found, and his ministers made the fullest enquiries.

Word reached the black-headed man, who sometimes visited the hunter and knew that he had the ornaments, and how he got them. With ungrateful heart, he went to the King and told him about this.

The King was very angry. His men visited the hunter and said: "We know that you stole the Royal ornaments from the park." The hunter was very frightened, and tried to explain what had happened, telling the whole story. But he was put in chains and thrown into prison.

The mouse, however, came to know of what had happened. He went to the snake and said, "Our benefactor, the hunter, through the evil of the black-headed one, has been cast into prison, what can we do?"

The snake said: "I shall see the hunter." He went to the hunter in his prison and said: "Today I will bite the King. As soon as it is known that this has happened, you will offer to cure him. When he accepts, you will use this special remedy. If you do that, there is no doubt that the King will, as a reward, free you, and make you valuable gifts."

So the snake bit the King, and the hunter cured him, and the King had him released, and made him many presents. ∎

The Value of a Treasure Hoard

"Tales have wings," said Isaac D'Israeli, "whether they come from the East or from the North, and they soon become denizens wherever they alight." The Chinese story which follows, from a Hong Kong collection, is almost literally paralleled in a tale attributed to Laird Braco, an ancestor of the Earls of Fife, in Scotland, who was a miser, and, one day, showed a farmer his hoard. There are many cognates, in as differing settings as the Sufi tales of Persia and a recent one of the American millionaire who paid a colossal sum for a statue which he erected by the roadside.

Once upon a time, in China, there was a priest, who was both avaricious and rich. He loved jewels, which he collected, constantly adding more pieces to his wonderful hoard, which he kept securely locked away, hidden from any eyes but his own.

Now the priest had a friend who visited him one day and who expressed interest in seeing the gems.

"I would be delighted to take them out, so that I, too, could look at them," said the priest.

So the collection was brought, and the two feasted their eyes on the beautiful treasure for a long time, lost in admiration.

When the time came for him to leave, the priest's guest said:

"Thank you for giving me the treasure!"

"Do not thank me for something which you have not got", said the priest, "for I have not given you the jewels, and they are not yours at all."

His friend answered:

"As you know, I have had as much pleasure from looking at the treasures as you, so there is no difference between us, as you yourself only look at them—except that *you* have the trouble and expense of finding, buying, and looking after them." ∎

Over a century ago, a German encyclopaedia entry listed the bibliography of 'Patient Griselda' in no less than fifteen columns. The story appears in Chaucer's **Canterbury Tales** as 'The Clerk's Tale', and Griselda's patience, not her husband's arguable insanity, always seem to be the point noted and stressed. Chaucer took the story from Petrarch's Latin; he in turn got it from the last tale in Boccaccio's **Decameron,** and he from a French tale, 'Parlement des Femmes'. It is found in Afansief's Russian anthology, and was also collected in one form by the Brothers Grimm.

And yet, as **Brewer's Dictionary** has it, Griselda's trials "are almost as unbelievable as the fortitude with which she is credited to have borne them." Griselda's husband seems a monster who took away her children and made her feel, for years, that they had been killed—just to test her. When she had been tested, they lived happily ever after. Strange though Dr. Brewer may understandably find this theme, the Indian cognate, while perhaps explaining the husband's conduct, seems to raise more questions than it answers. According to the ancient **Nidanakatha** of Buddhist birth-stories, Mangala Buddha was involved in a parallel experience. A demon, disguised as a Brahmin, asked him for his two children. He handed them over joyfully. The demon then devoured the children and the Bodhisatta felt no sorrow. On the contrary, he felt rather "a great joy and satisfaction". As a consequence, he was almost instantly transformed into the Buddha.

Both versions are religious; the test is administered in the one case by a husband, standing for the divine testing of humanity, in the other by a demon. In the one case the woman benefits by attaining happiness, so that her husband was really being cruel to be kind; in the other, the father (the Bodhisatta) benefits to the extent of actually becoming Buddha. Although many people of today will have difficulty in understanding the mentality of ancient Eastern and Western audiences—and the promoters of the tale—its tremendously wide currency in ancient and medieval cultures and its frequent literary use give it a place here. This is how it is told by Chaucer.

15th Century illustration of the Canterbury Pilgrims.

Patient Griselda

Once upon a time there was a nobleman called Walter who was both good and powerful, much beloved by his people. After a time, when he had not married, they sent a deputation to him, saying,"Marquis, please marry a wife so that we may have your son to take your place when you are gone from us." And he replied: "I shall marry when I find one whom I can love, and find suitable." So they had to be content.

Now, there was a poor man, living humbly with his daughter, Griselda, near a well of fresh water. Walter was riding by, when he saw the girl, tall and beautiful, carrying a pot of water on her head. He asked her for a drink, and then noticing that she was lovelier than any woman he had ever seen, wished to marry her. In her one simple smock, and barefoot, she arrived at the castle. Women attendants bathed her, dressed her in fine clothes, and prepared her for marriage to their noble lord. After the extravagant wedding and great rejoicing of the people, Walter took Griselda into a private room and said: "Now, wife, you must obey me in all that I wish, and respect my thoughts and commands whatever they may be." So she promised that she would, and for a while they were very happy indeed.

In a year's time a daughter was born to them, a very beautiful child, as fair as her mother. Now came the first great test of Griselda's married life. Her husband came to her and said, "The people who love me are dissatisfied with you. They say that I should not have married someone in such a low station of life as yourself. They do not wish me to have children by you, so the child must be taken away and killed." Griselda was stricken to the heart, but she knew she must do everything her husband required, so she agreed to have the child taken away to be killed in a remote spot. As the huntsman came in to drag the little girl from her arms, she held her for just a moment, and said calmly to him: "Do bury her deep in the earth when it is done, that she will not be torn by wild beasts." Then she kissed her daughter, and sat silently for a while. Not for a moment did she think ill of her husband, or cry out in her pain. Her life with Walter continued as before, with but one difference, that she never mentioned her daughter's name.

Another year passed, and a son of great beauty was born to Griselda. The loss of the other child seemed to have faded from her mind as Griselda cradled her son in her arms, singing to him softly as she fed him. Walter appeared to be satisfied with her, and it seemed that all was well with their life together. But, when the boy was two years old, Griselda had a severe test of her love for her husband. He once more said to her, "Wife, the people are very distressed in case the grandson of a peasant like your father should inherit my land, and rule them. They demand that he too, be taken from you and killed. It is my will that this should be done," and he left her without another word.

Patient Griselda held the child for the last time, and kissed it. Then she said to the same huntsman who had taken away her daughter, "Bury the body deep in the earth, where no beasts or birds of prey can reach him." And without so much as a tear she handed over the infant, wrapped in his warmest clothes against the morning's chill. After that day she did not speak of the baby, yet she treated her husband with the same tenderness and respect as always. She ran the great house with perfect calm and dignity, as if indeed she had been a true noblewoman instead of a poor peasant's daughter, brought up in poverty.

Now, in reality, Walter was not guilty of his children's murder, but had despatched them to his sister's country estate, there to be brought up in luxury and kindness by her. He thought to test Griselda, hoping to find in her character some flaw, some chink in that armour of calm, that goodness of spirit and heart which he could scarcely believe was true and real.

"For," he thought, "she cannot be as good and as true as she appears, devoted to me even after these apparently savage acts of mine. Yet, I will test her further."

So, he said to her,"Griselda, I have some news for you which I must tell you now. For some time past, my life has not been happy, and my love for you has died. My marriage to you was obviously a great mistake, no one was pleased with my marrying a girl of such low degree. My friends will not receive me because of this, and I have now sent for an annulment. You must stop wearing the clothes which should grace a wife of mine, and return to wearing the smock in which you came here. Soon the noble lady whom I am to marry will be coming. Please get the castle in order for her to take over, see to it that everything is replenished and fresh for her. Do you understand what I have said?" he asked, for she did not even change her expression of calm serenity as he was speaking.

"Yes, my lord," said Griselda, smoothing the fine dress she was wearing with her slim hands, "I understand. All will be done as you desire. Just let me remove these fineries and I will take the cleaning of the rooms as my own personal responsibility. I wish you every good fortune in your new happiness." And she went away to remove her clothes. She had preserved in her chest the plain simple smock in which she had arrived, this she took out and put on. Her jewels, furs, silks and fine shoes she returned to Walter, and took up her task as housekeeper with much enthusiasm. What went on in her mind and heart no one knew. It did not appear to her that she was badly done by at all, for she just thought she was making good her promise to Walter when he married her, that she would carry out without question everything required of her. She visited her father in his simple house, and spent a day with him, telling him what had happened. "You must return here," he cried, "I may be a peasant, but you are my beloved daughter, and I will look after you as I did before. I always knew that this would happen, it is not natural that one so highborn as he should take one such as we are for his wife."

"I will have to go back and prepare everything for the wedding feast," said Griselda, with simple dignity, "I have been asked to attend to it, and attend to it I shall. Afterwards, when they are married, I will come back home." So she went back to the castle, walking strongly away in her bare feet, the white smock her only garment.

Now, the noble Walter had sent a letter to his sister, asking her to send with all speed, dressed in fine clothes and jewels, his daughter. The girl was like a princess, tall and fair, and was most excited about the journey upon which she was going, in her aunt's wonderful coach and six horses, but she knew not why. Her younger brother, now a handsome stripling, as good looking as his father had been at the time of the marriage to Griselda, came too. They both were brought swiftly to the castle, and led to the guest chambers.

Griselda was waiting at the door, with fresh flowers for the supposed bride, and gave them to her with charming grace. Walter called Griselda to him and asked: "Is she not beautiful, my new bride?" and

Griselda answered: "Yes, my lord, she is fair. But, and this is the only thing I would like to say to you—I pray you treat this young Princess with greater care than you did me, for as she is so delicate and gently-born, she might not be able to bear what I have done unquestioningly and faithfully, and her heart might break." Then she went away to prepare the wedding feast with the other servants.

The whole castle was decorated with flowers and ribbons, flags and fine carpets were hung from the balconies. Music and singing came from the minstrels' gallery. People arrived from every part of Walter's dominions to do him honour at his wedding. Still patient Griselda attended to every detail, waiting upon the lady and her young brother herself, seeing that everything was to their liking. The nobleman called Griselda to him and said, "Look, does she not have every feature as you once had when you were young, and my wife? Will you not consider her a suitable wife for me, as my people do, and wish her every good fortune?" He looked at her very strangely, waiting to hear her reply.

"Yes, my lord," she answered, "she is indeed very fair, and young, and I wish you all joy with each other." Her eyes were raised to his, and in them he read all that was true, faithful, and honest. His heart smote him, and he seized her hands in his, pulling himself to his feet. "Dearest Griselda!" he cried, "Forgive me, for I have tested you cruelly, but I had to know if you really loved me enough to suffer all these things for my sake. Know, sweet and faithful wife, that this Princess whom I have brought here and her brother are none other than our own dear children, whom you believed dead. Come, let me place this fur robe upon you, and I pray you will take your seat here beside me at the table, so that you will for the rest of our lives be my own beloved wife."

Then at last did Griselda's tears fall, and she wept as she embraced her long-lost daughter and her handsome son, and thanked God that they were returned to her. She swooned twice, and each time her husband raised her up with loving hands.

And Walter, his misgivings about her dispelled, did everything in his power to make her forget the dreadful years of her testing. They lived devoted to each other, and to their children, for the rest of their days, as happy as true and faithful lovers can. Griselda's father, after he understood the tale they told him, was brought to the castle, and he, too, lived the rest of his life in comfort and tranquility, free of all care. ■

In the form of 'The Pardoner's Tale', this allegory is firmly rooted at the very base of English literature, through Geoffrey Chaucer's **The Canterbury Tales** *of nearly six centuries ago. In the records of its transmission through several cultures, however, it enables us to study the preoccupations of each people employing it. In the ancient Indian form, it is presented to inculcate a moral; in its Arabian garb, (and the Italian) the chief figure is Jesus, where the religious aspect is stressed. The old German version is anti-Jewish, and the Florentine recension favours the wisdom of a hermit. The Central Asian writing was by the 13th-century major Sufi mystic—of Chaucerean rank in Persian—Fariduddin Attar; and here the application is that of the gnostic, to the effect that there is an unperceived world beyond normal perceptions. The following version is from the 16th-century Italian; the story is famous, too, as the plot of Hans Sachs' 1547 Meisterleid.*

How Evil Produces Evil

A certain hermit was walking one day in a deserted place, when he came across an enormous cave, the entrance to which was not easily visible. He decided to rest inside, and entered. Soon, however, he noticed the bright reflection of the light upon a large quantity of gold within.

The hermit, as soon as he became aware of what he had seen, took to his heels and fled as fast as he could.

Now in this desert area were three robbers, who spent much time there so that they could steal from travellers. Before long the pious man blundered into them. The thieves were surprised, and even alarmed, at the sight of a man running, with nothing in pursuit; but they came out of their ambush and stopped him, asking him what was the matter.

"I am fleeing, brothers," he said, "from the Devil, who is racing after me."

Now the bandits could not see anything following the devout old man, and they said; "Show us what is after you."

"I will" he said, (for he was afraid of them) and led them to the cave, at the same time begging them not to go near it. By this time, of course, the thieves were greatly interested, and insisted that they should be shown whatever it was that had caused such alarm.

"Here," he said, "is death, which was running after me."

The villains were, of course, delighted. They naturally regarded the recluse as somewhat touched, and sent him on his way, while they revelled in their good fortune.

Now the thieves began to discuss what they should do with the booty; for they were afraid of leaving it alone again. Finally they decided that one of their number should take a little gold to the city and with it buy food and other necessities, and then they would proceed to the division of the spoils.

One of the ruffians volunteered to run the errand. He thought to himself: "When I am in town I can eat all I wish. Then I can poison the rest of the food, so that it kills the other two, and all the treasure will be mine."

While the rogue was away, however, his companions were also thinking. They decided that as soon as he returned, they would kill him, eat the food, and divide the spoils so as to gain the additional third share that would otherwise be his.

The moment the first thief arrived back at the cave with the provisions, the two others fell upon him and stabbed him to death. Then they ate all the food, and expired of the poison which their friend had bought and put into it. So the gold, after all, did indeed spell death, as the hermit predicted, for whoever was influenced by it. And the treasure remained where it had been, in the cave, for a very long time. ■

The Ghoul and the Youth of Ispahan

Episodes from the English 'Jack the Giant-Killer' are found in favourite folktales about encounters with ogres all over the world. In 'Jack', the Giant roars "Fee, fi, fo, fum!" or "Fe, fa, fum!" And, in the Indian version, the Rakshasas say: "Fee, faw, fum!" The Albanian variant of this story is very close to that of the Norse lad and the Troll; and the Sicilian 'Brave Shoemaker and the Giant', is almost identical. Several incidents from Grimm's 'The Brave Little Tailor' appear in this cycle of stories. It is known in South America, where the Chilean adaptation is that of Don Juan Bolondron.

The following is the Persian recital, given by the Shah's personal story-teller to Sir John Malcolm. Parts of it may also be found in the Sanskrit 'Seventy Tales of a Parrot', in the Nordic Edda of Snorro, and varieties have been noted in Cornwall and Kashmir.

Once upon a time there was a clever young lad of the ancient city of Ispahan, in Persia. He was out one day when he came upon a Ghoul, a sort of ogre-giant, terrible in size and horrible in temper. "What can I do?" he asked himself. And well might he ask, for Ghouls love to enslave and destroy people, and even eat them up. All that the young man—Amin the True was his name—had with him was an egg and a lump of salt, both in his pocket.

Now, as everyone knows, the best form of defence is attack, so Amin approached the Ghoul, which was looking at him with frightful fury, and said:

"Ho! Ghoul—let's have a contest of strength."

For a moment the Ghoul was puzzled, because human beings never spoke like that to him, and, like all Ghouls, he was not brilliantly intelligent. Then he said:

"You don't look very strong to me."

"I may not *look* strong," said Amin, "but have you not heard that appearances can be deceptive? Here is a proof of my tremendous strength."

He picked up a stone. "Now I challenge you to squeeze water out of this."

The Ghoul took the stone and tried. Then he said:

"No, it is impossible."

"Not at all—it is easy," replied Amin. While the Ghoul had been squeezing, Amin had placed the egg in his own hand. Now he took the stone in the same hand and squeezed.

There was a crushing sound as the egg broke and the Ghoul saw what he thought to be the liquid from

the stone running between Amin's fingers: and all this was done without Amin showing any sign of strain at all.

Luckily it was not completely light, so the details of what was happening were not entirely visible to the monster.

Then Amin took up another stone and said:

"There is salt in this one, just crumble it between your fingers."

The Ghoul looked at the stone, and saw that it was quite beyond his power to crush it, and he admitted that he could not.

"Oh, give it to me," said Amin. He took it into the hand in which he had already hidden the lump of salt, and crumbled the salt into the hand of the amazed Ghoul.

"Now", said the giant, "you must stay the night with me", and Amin agreed, for he guessed that he would always be able to get the better of him.

When they arrived at the immense cavern which was his host's home, the Ghoul threw Amin an enormous bag made from the hides of no less than six oxen, and said:

"Go and fill this with water, while I make the fire ready to cook."

He went away in search of wood.

Amin wondered what he could do about the water, and then an idea occurred to him. He could hardly drag the bag more than a few feet, so he abandoned it and went down to the stream and started to dig a small channel.

Soon the Ghoul appeared and cried:

"Why are you taking so long? Can't you lift a little bag of water?"

"No, my friend," said Amin, "since you are being so hospitable to me, I have decided to dig a channel to bring the water to you, so that you always have a supply—see, I have started already. There is no point in feats of strength for their own sake; that is just a waste of time and effort."

The Ghoul was hungry, so he said:

"Leave the water; I shall carry it." And he picked up the bag as if it had been a feather and filled it at the river.

"Finish the channel tomorow, if you want to," he said.

The Ghoul ate a huge meal, and, in the darkness of the cave, Amin pretended to eat as well. Then the Ghoul pointed to a sleeping-place, and told Amin to lie down on it for the night.

But there was a crafty look in the Ghoul's eyes, and Amin placed a large pillow in the place where he should be sleeping and hid himself in a corner.

A little before daybreak, the Ghoul woke up. Seizing an immense tree-trunk, he smashed it down on Amin's bed. There was not even a groan, and the Ghoul grinned as he thought that he must have crushed Amin to pulp. Just to make sure, he pounded the bed seven times.

Now the Ghoul went back to sleep, but he had hardly settled himself again when Amin, who had crept back into his own bed, cried out:

"Friend Ghoul, what insect could that be which disturbed me by its flapping? I counted the beat of its wings seven times. Although such things cannot hurt men, they can be disturbing to someone who is sleeping."

The Ghoul was aroused to such heights of fear at hearing that this was a man who felt a shattering blow, seven blows, only as the wings of an insect, that he fled headlong from his cave, leaving Amin its master.

Amin took up a gun which had been left by some victim of the Ghoul, and went out to scout. He had not gone very far when he saw the Ghoul coming back. In his hand he held a large club, and beside him was a fox.

Amin realized that the cunning fox had explained matters to the Ghoul; but he was equal to the challenge. Aiming the gun, he shot it through the head.

"Take that!" he shouted, "for disobedience." To the Ghoul he said:

"That liar," pointing to the fox, "had promised to bring me seven Ghouls, so that I might put them in chains and lead them back to the city of Ispahan: but he brought only you, who are already my slave!"

No sooner were the words out of his mouth than the Ghoul took to his heels. Using the club to help him, he leapt over rocks and precipices, and he was soon far out of sight. ■

The Pilgrim From Paradise

The theme of the crafty adventurer is common to a whole genre of stories; just as the entertainment possibilities in misunderstandings and the working of simpletons' minds are two further well-exploited themes, especially in folklore. These elements are combined in a humorous whole in a tale which is a favourite—and has been such for centuries—in countries as far apart as Norway, Brittany, Italy and Southern India. A distinctive characteristic of this story is that, from the frozen North to the sunbaked South-East of Asia, the essential incidents remain remarkably similar. This version is from the nineteenth-century Bombay collection of Pandit Natesa Sastri.

A kindly and charitable, somewhat simple woman, married to a rich miser, once lived in a village where a certain rogue had made up his mind to fool the woman when he could find an opportunity. One day this man saw the miser ride out to make a tour of his land, and decided that the time to work his trick had arrived. He made his way to the house where the couple lived, and threw himself upon the ground, as if completely exhausted.

The good woman came out at once, asking what his trouble was, and where he was from. "I am a traveller from paradise" he said, "and I have been sent by an ancient couple, to seek news of their son and his wife."

The lady was very much impressed that she had a visitor from the mysterious, inaccessible Mount Kailasa of the Himalayas, and wondered aloud who these lucky people could be whom her guest represented.

The villain gave the names of her husband's parents, whom he knew to be dead, and this of course only increased her interest. "And how are they?" she asked, "Are they well? If only my husband were at home, to hear your news of his dear old father and mother." She asked him to sit down to rest, and plied him with question after question about the departed ones.

She played into the swindler's very hands by asking him whether her parents-in-law had enough to wear and to eat, and if they were really happy.

The thief was anxious to be on his way before the miser returned, so he made short work of his answers. "Lady" he said, "I have no words to describe their miserable state. In the world beyond they have no clothes, no food, only some water to drink. How lucky that you cannot see their sufferings."

"But why should it be so with them?" she asked, "when their son has so much, and when I have everything I need?"

To cut a long story short, she went into the house and brought out a large quantity of clothes and all her own jewels. "Clothes and jewels will not help their hunger" said the confidence-man: and the trusting woman went back into the house and brought as much of her husband's money as she could find.

Collecting up his loot, the villain made off as fast as he could.

Not long afterwards the husband returned, and you can imagine his rage when he heard from the excited lady how a messenger from paradise had brought grave news and taken succour to his mother and father. But there was no time to be lost. Choking back his fury, he merely asked her which way the messenger had gone, and he spurred his horse in hot pursuit.

Before long the miser saw the thief, and started to gain on him minute by minute. The deceiver, realizing that he could not escape, decided to rely on his wits, and climbed up a tall tree with his bundle of booty.

As soon as the miser arrived at the bottom of the tree, he called upon the thief to come down. "Sorry", said the swindler, "I am making my way heavenwards, to Kailasa." He climbed to the very top of the towering peepul tree.

The miser settled himself to wait; but then he became impatient, and started laboriously to climb up after the thief. Waiting until he had almost reached him, the agile thief threw down all the things he had with him and shinned down the tree faster than the miser could follow. Leaping upon the miser's horse, he rode it into the thickest part of the jungle he could find.

The miser, of course, was now completely outwitted. Sorrowfully, he made his limping way back to his home. There was his wife, with radiant face, who called out to him in delight: "Ah, so you have even handed over your horse to be taken to paradise, so that your dear old father can ride."

Unable to admit that he was as much a fool as she had been, the miser could only try to cover his rage and folly by saying: "Yes, that's right . . ." ■

83

Reading the controversies of folklore scholars sometimes feel more like being on a battlefield than strolling in the groves of academe. Edward Clodd (1840-1930), President of the British Folk-Lore Society, insisted that folk traditions represented the 'persistence of barbaric elements' until the present day. 'Rumpelstiltskin' was an example of a primitive name-taboo, found in East Anglia (as 'Tom Tit Tot') quite recently, and so on. Rabbi Moses Gaster of Romania (1856-1934), another President of the same Society, insisted, on the other hand, that tales were 'the last and modern development of folk-lore'. Were these the only possible positions? No. According to a third President of the Folk-Lore Society, Alfred Nutt (1856-1912), 'sometimes it is and sometimes it isn't':

'On the sea shore we may pick up fossils . . . reaching back into a past incalculably remote . . . we may also pick up worn and rounded fragments of ginger beer bottles flung away perhaps only six months before.'

A portrait of Rumi

It all puts one in mind of an anecdote of the Eastern folklore figure Mulla Nasrudin:

Nasrudin entered the Mosque and said to the people: 'Do you know what I am going to tell you?' There were shouts of 'No'; so he said: 'Then I shall not bother with such ignoramuses.' The following day he asked the same question again, from the pulpit. The answer was 'Yes'. 'Then I don't need to tell you!' he said and went out. The third time, when he repeated his question, the people cried: 'Some of us do, some of us do not!' Nasrudin said: 'Then let those who do tell those who do not know!' And he left the building.

The following story, of the unity of all knowledge, from the great 13th century mystic of Balkh (now Afghanistan), Mualana Jalaluddin Rumi, may perhaps get to the heart of the problem.

The Blind Ones and The Matter of The Elephant

Beyond Ghor there was a city. All its inhabitants were blind. A king with his entourage arrived near by; he brought his army and camped in the desert. He had a mighty elephant, which he used in attack and to increase the people's awe.

The populace became anxious to see the elephant, and some sightless ones from among this blind community ran like fools to find it.

As they did not even know the form or shape of the elephant they groped sightlessly, gathering information by touching some part of it.

Each thought that he knew something, because he could feel a part.

When they returned to their fellow-citizens, eager groups clustered around them. Each of these was anxious, misguidedly, to learn the truth from those who were themselves astray.

They asked about the form, the shape of the elephant, and they listened to all that they were told.

The man whose hand had reached an ear was asked about the elephant's nature. He said: "It is a large, rough thing, wide and broad, like a rug."

And the one who had felt the trunk said: "I have the real facts about it. It is like a straight and hollow pipe, awful and destructive."

The one who had felt its feet and legs said:

"It is mighty and firm, like a pillar."

Each had felt one part out of many. Each had perceived it wrongly. No mind knew all: knowledge is not the companion of the blind. All imagined something, something incorrect.

The created is not informed about divinity. There is no Way in this science by means of the ordinary intellect. ■

The Tale of Anpu and Bata, found in an Ancient Egyptian papyrus manuscript, is more than three thousand years old, and is regarded as the oldest story that has come down to us in writing. It may well have been an ancient tradition even then. One of the most interesting things about it is that elements found in tales all over the world ever since are contained in it. The first part has a parallel in the Biblical story of Joseph and the Wife of Potiphar. The core of the story—the life-token indicating death and the 'separable soul'—occurs in over eight hundred versions in Europe alone, and the reciters are unlikely to know that they are part of a line of transmission from the Nineteenth Dynasty of Pharaonic Egypt.

The story is sometimes found, conflated with all or much of the Perseus and Andromeda myth, associated with the exploits of a dragon-slayer, which is encountered in almost every country in the world.

The crumbling papyrus roll, in the British Museum, contains a message from the original scribe, a threat to those who might abuse it, which is similar to those found on Eastern manuscripts even today:

"Excellently finished in peace for the Ka of the scribe of the Treasury Kagabu, of the Treasury of Pahaoh. And for the Scribe Hora, and the Scribe Meramapt. Written by the Scribe Anena, the owner of this roll. He who speaks against this scroll, may Tahui smite him!"

It was the custom of Eastern kings, when pleased with a story related to them, to order it to be written down and placed in the treasury.

'Harvest Scene', from the Tomb of Menna, Thebes. C. 1400 B.C.

Anpu and Bata

Once there lived in Egypt two brothers, and they loved each other greatly. The elder had a beautiful young wife, and a fine pair of oxen for the fields. His name was Anpu, and his younger brother's name was Bata. This young man did everything for his brother, followed him and the oxen to the fields, waited upon him like a servant, harvested the corn, tended the animals. He worked for him day and night; for his brother, in his eyes, had no equal in all the land of Egypt.

Now when the time for ploughing the land arrived, the elder brother said to Bata, "Come with the seeds tomorrow early to the fields, for we must begin sowing, because the Nile flood has retreated from the earth and the day is propitious."

Anpu having gone on ahead, it was left for Bata to bring the seed, so he went to the door of the house, and said to his sister-in-law, Anpu's beautiful young wife, "Let me have the corn from the bin, for my brother and I need it today." The woman replied, "Come in and get it yourself, for I am busy doing my hair and I cannot drop my pins and ribbons and get the corn." So he went in, and helped himself to as much corn as he could carry, for he wanted to start the day of planting well, as the day was propitious.

Seeing him carrying such a load, the wife of his brother said, "You are strong and good-looking, indeed. I had not noticed that you were so presentable before. Come, stay with me a little while here before you go to the fields, for you will both be away all day, and I shall be lonely. Give me something to remember when I am alone."

Bata recoiled at the woman's words, and his face darkened with rage. He said, "You are like a mother to me, for are you not my respected brother's wife? I will forget what you have just spoken. Do you forget it, also." And he went away to the fields, trying to erase her suggestion from his mind, for she was his brother's wife, and though beautiful, now appeared evil in his eyes.

All day they laboured in the fields, and at evening Anpu and Bata returned home. They expected to find food ready as usual, when they came to the house. But there was no fire, no light, no smell of cooking.

Bata went to the stable to attend to the animals, and Anpu went in to see what was the matter with his wife. She was lying huddled under the quilt, crying as if she were in pain.

"What is the matter with you?" he asked, "Has anyone been here in my absence to upset you like this?"

"The only one here in your absence was your wretched brother!" she cried, "Ask him what is the matter with me!"

"But what are you saying? Has he laid hands upon you?" shouted the enraged husband.

"Yes," she replied, "I was here doing my hair when he came in for the seeds, and he said to me 'Be with me a while before I go to the fields and my brother will never know' and he violated me. Oh, I cannot look at you for shame, my husband!" So Anpu sharpened his knife, and stood outside the stable ready to kill his brother as soon as he came to join him for the evening meal.

All unaware of this, the younger brother went about his tasks in the stable, when suddenly his favourite cow spoke to him:

"Beware, Bata, your brother has sharpened his knife and is waiting to kill you behind the door. Run, do not go back to the house, or you will die."

The young man looked out of the stable and saw his brother standing strangely still, with his knife in his hand. Fearing that he could never explain the true state of affairs to his brother, he made a hole in the mud wall of the barn and fled as fast as his feet would carry him. But the elder brother heard him running, and chased after him. The light of murder was in his eyes.

So, in great fear, Bata called out: "Oh Great Ra Harakhiti, Mighty Lord, You are He who divides the Evil from the Good! Save me!" and Ra answered his prayer.

A mighty river sprang up between the two brothers, a river that Anpu could not cross, even if he had had a boat, for it was full of crocodiles. The elder brother was furious that he could not reach Bata to kill him, and cursed him from the other bank.

But Bata called out in a loud voice to him: "O my

brother, do not think ill of me. I cannot prove to you that I did nothing wrong, but my cow warned me, and I fled from you in fear. Why did you come to kill me before you asked me if I had done what you believed I did?"

And his brother said: "Tell me yourself, then, what truly happened?"

Bata answered, "I went to the bin to get the seed myself, for your wife told me she was doing her hair and did not wish to leave her toilette to attend to me. Then, after I had helped myself, she said I looked strong and handsome, and tempted me to stay with her for a short while, saying that you would not know. You see how the truth has been changed."

"Will you swear the oath by Ra Harakhiti that what you have said is true?" cried the elder brother.

"By Ra Harakhiti I swear that it is true," said the younger brother, and he took his knife, and cut a piece of his flesh, and threw it into the water, and the crocodiles ate it. Then the elder brother was satisfied, and he wept for Bata and cursed his wife. He knew that he could not reach his brother, because of the crocodiles, and he stood there, putting away his knife.

"Now we know that you have done a bad thing, trying to kill me, will you now do a good thing for me?" said Bata.

Anpu said he would, so his brother told him, "I am going away to the valley of the acacia. So you go to your house, and look to your cattle. Now this is what you can do for me; my soul shall be drawn out, and put into the flower of the acacia. When the acacia is cut down, as it will be, put the flower in a glass of cold water, for my soul shall be in it. When someone gives you a glass of beer in your hand, and it is agitating in the glass, then do not stay, but go and find the flower, even if you search for seven years, and put it in the water. Farewell."

Then the youth stopped speaking these strange things, and went to the valley of the acacia.

His brother turned away and went back to his house, and he was angered against his wife, so he killed her in the heat of his wrath.

Then he threw his knife away, and looked after his cattle and his fields himself, sorrowing for his brother.

A long time after this had happened, the younger brother was living in the valley of the acacia. He had drawn out his soul, and it lived in the topmost flower of the acacia tree. He had built himself a small house in which he lived, and it was full of good things.

One day, walking in the valley, he met the Nine Gods, who were going forth to look upon the whole land of Egypt. The Nine Gods were talking with each other when Bata came upon them, and they said to him, "O Bata, Bull of the Nine Gods, why are you walking alone? Your brother has slain his wife, and all is level between you. His transgression is forgiven."

Then, as Bata knelt before them, Ra Harakhiti said to Khnumu, "So that he will not be forever alone, make a woman for Bata, a mate for his loneliness." And Khnumu made a wife for him. She was more beautiful than any woman had ever been before. The seven Hathors came to see her when she was created, and they said of one accord: "She will die a sharp death, though the essence of every god is in her!"

All the day Bata hunted and in the evening he came back and placed all his spoils at his wife's feet, for he loved her very much. He said to her one day "Now, I must warn you, never go too near the sea, for if it should seize you, and want to carry you away, I cannot save you, for my soul is in the flower at the top of the acacia, and I have no power, other than in that flower."

When she heard his secret she smiled, and thought about it much.

Next day she went to walk beside the sea, and the sea saw her, and began to cast its waves up towards her. She took to her heels and, being frightened by the passion of the sea, ran away from it. She entered her house, and the sea called to the acacia: "I want to have that woman, I wish that I could take her!" Then the acacia brought a curl from her hair which the woman had cut off while sitting under the tree, and dropped it into the water. The sea carried it to the place where the fullers washed the clothes of the Pharaoh.

One of the washermen who was standing on the sand picked up the curl of hair, and it smelt so sweet that it almost took his senses away. He put it into the clothing which was being taken to the Pharaoh, and when Pharaoh smelt it he was enraptured.

"Where did this rare and wonderful scent come from?" cried Pharaoh. "Bring the wise men, so that they too may smell it and tell me."

The wise men came, with their signs and portents, and told the Pharaoh, "The scent comes from the curl from the hair of a daughter of Ra Harakhiti; the essence of every god is in her. Send messengers to the borders of the sea, and in the valley of the acacia she will be found."

So the Pharaoh sent many men to the valley of the

acacia, and they tried to take the wife of Bata, but he killed them all. None of these men returned to the Pharaoh, and so he sent more, this time men on horseback and strong soldiers, to bring her to him.

Bata had to let her go, but they did not kill him. He remained behind, under the acacia, feeling very distressed. Somehow, from his mind he tried to send a message to his brother, reminding him of what he had said to Anpu across the river of the crocodiles, the last time that he had seen him.

The beautiful woman pleased the Pharaoh very much, and he gave her everything in his power.

"Pharaoh," said she, after he had presented her with gold and jewels and rarest rings, "Send men to cut down the acacia, for my husband's soul is in the topmost flower, and I would that he were dead." So the men went and chopped the tree in the valley so that the topmost flower, in which was the soul of Bata, fell to the ground, and he too, fell dead.

At that very moment, someone handed Anpu, the elder brother, a glass of beer, and the liquid became agitated as he was about to drink it. He remembered what his brother had told him, all that long time ago. He got his stick and his sandals, his clothes for travelling, and set off.

He travelled all day and all night, and arrived at the valley of the acacia. Then he saw that the tree had been cut down, and saw the body of his brother lying dead. He wept bitterly, and looked everywhere for the flower which contained the soul of his brother. But he could not find it. He lay down to sleep under the tree, and said to himself—"Tomorrow, and tomorrow, and tomorrow I will seek it; for I will spend all the days of my life, if necessary, to find the flower."

Next day he did not find it, but he discovered, in a crack in the earth, a seed. He put the seed in a glass of water, and it sprouted. It was soon the flower containing his brother's soul. Within a few minutes the body of Bata shuddered under the cloth which covered it, and soon he was standing well and strong before Anpu. They embraced each other joyfully, and sat talking together for many hours.

Then Bata said to his brother, "I am to become a great bull, by favour of the gods, and you are to get on my back. By the time the sun has risen thrice I shall be in the place where my wife makes a fool of the Pharaoh. And, when I am before the Pharaoh, you shall be taken to him, and he will give you gold and silver, and good things in return. I will be thought of by all as a great marvel, and you will return to our old

village home a rich man." Before Anpu's eyes he turned into a huge bull. So, the elder brother got onto his back, and within three days they were before the Pharaoh.

The Pharaoh had never before seen such a fine creature, in all dominions of the Upper and the Lower Nile, so he gave many presents to the elder brother, and took Bata in his bull form to the royal stables to be looked after in great style. The gigantic bull was so tame that it was often garlanded with flowers by the royal ladies. One day when his wife, now a Princess by command of the Pharaoh, came near to him, the bull said in his human voice, "I am alive, and now the gods have in their wisdom, caused me to be in this marvellous bull's body."

She was greatly affrighted, and wondered how she could get rid of her husband yet again. So she went to the Pharaoh and said, "My lord, I will never be happy unless I have for my illness the liver of that creature, which I am sure is fit for nothing else but to be eaten!" So at once the Pharaoh gave orders for the animal to be slaughtered, and said, "Let the liver be given to the Princess, so that she will soon be well again."

A tremendous feast was planned, and the bull was to be sacrificed to the gods. As he was being slaughtered, the bull shook two drops of blood from his shoulder wound onto the walls of the royal palace. The blood dripped from each side of the gigantic door, and where the blood soaked into the ground two Persea trees grew. They grew and grew, each day taller, and each of them was perfect in every way.

A courtier went to tell the Pharaoh, "Lo, there are two giant trees growing, one on each side of the great door of the palace, these are propitious signs, oh Pharaoh!" And there was much rejoicing because of these trees, and many people made offerings to them, because of their miraculous growth from the bull's blood.

The ladies of the court went out, and placed garlands of flowers around the trees, and prayed to them.

When his wife came, Bata said to her from the trees, in his own voice, which she knew so well, "Deceitful woman, I am Bata, who you have thrice betrayed. First you went to the Pharaoh, then you had my soul-tree cut down, then you had the ox slain. Now I am in the strength of these trees. I shall never die!"

So the Princess went to the Pharaoh and said, "As you love me, will you do me a small favour? I do not like the sight of those two grotesque Persea trees, one on each side of the great door of the palace. Do you please give orders that they be cut down, for they grow even uglier every day, and one day they will bring the palace down, I am sure!"

The Pharaoh, besotted with his love for her, consented, and the next day woodcutters were chopping with might and main at the beautiful Persea trees. The Princess was standing not far away, looking at this activity, rejoicing in her heart, when a tiny chip of wood flew into her mouth. She was so startled that she swallowed it. The trees were at that moment completely cut down, and fell outside the Palace gates.

When nine months had passed, a son was born to the Princess, and there was rejoicing all through the land, for the Pharaoh thought that the child was his son. As the months went by, the Pharaoh loved the baby even more, and raised him to be the royal son of Kush, heir of all the lands of the Upper and Lower Nile.

Not many days after that, the Pharaoh died.

Then the Prince, the heir of the lands, said:

"Let all my nobles come before me, that I may tell them all that has happened to me."

They came, and he told them everything. His elder brother was brought from the village, to be made a minister at his court. Then they brought his wife, and they judged her and she received her punishment.

He was thirty years King of Egypt, and so endeared himself to the people that his brother took his place when he died. ■

God is Stronger

A Hebrew hymn relating to the Holy Land (beginning "A kid, a kid my father bought") is closely similar to the English rhymed tale, **The House that Jack Built.** Varieties of this cumulative tale are found in Norse and in Punjabi, and in Sri Lanka; similar stories have been noted in Scotland and Kashmir. This is the version found in traditional Malagasy folklore, recorded in Madagascar (Malagasy Republic).

Ibotity had climbed a tree when the wind blew, the tree split, Ibotity fell, and his leg was broken. "The tree is strong, for it broke my leg," he said.

"It is the wind which is stronger than the tree" said the tree.

But the wind said that the hill was stronger, since it could stop the wind. Ibotity, of course, thought that strength was of the hill, to be able to stop the wind, which split the tree, which broke his leg.

"No" said the hill, explaining that the mouse was strong for it could burrow into the hill. But the mouse denied this: "For I can be killed by the cat" — and so Ibotity thought that the cat must be strongest of all.

Not so; the cat explained that it could be caught by a rope, and Ibotity thought that this, then, must be the strongest thing.

The rope, however, explained that it could be cut by iron, which was therefore stronger. The iron, in its turn, denied being strongest, since it could be made soft by fire.

Ibotity now thought that the fire must be strongest, to soften the iron: which cut the rope, which bound the cat, which caught the mouse, which undermined the hill, which stopped the wind, which split the tree—which broke the leg of Ibotity.

The fire then said that water was stronger; and the water claimed that the canoe was yet stronger, for it cleft the water. But the canoe was overcome by the rock, and the rock by man, and man by the magician, and the magician by the ordeal by poison, and the ordeal by God, so God is the strongest of all:

"Then Ibotity knew that God could beat the ordeal, which stopped the magician, who overwhelms man, who breaks the rock, which overcomes the canoe, which cleaves the water, which puts out fire, which softens iron, which severs the rope, which binds the cat, which kills the mouse, which undermines the hill, which stops the wind, which splits the tree, which breaks the leg of Ibotity." ∎

Although this tale is found in the story-books of both the East and West, it is far less often represented there than most traditional tales. Taoist and Sufi masters are reputed to have used it to illustrate the theme that "the quest is what teaches you that only the end has meaning, not the assumption of what the end might be."

This is the only story in this collection which seems to be increasing in currency, particularly in the oral transmission. When I was collecting tales in Europe, Asia and Africa a quarter of a century ago, I did not find a single example. Between 1960 and 1978, however, no less than ten story-tellers, in six different countries, provided versions.

The particular shape given here is a current one from Uzbekistan. The tale is more usually found as a two-liner, something like this:

"A man once heard that he would attain to wisdom if he could meet the Happiest Man in the World, and obtain his shirt.

It took him nearly all his life to find him. And then he noticed that the Happiest Man did not own a shirt."

The Happiest Man in The World

A man who was living in comfortable enough circumstances went one day to see a certain sage, reputed to have all knowledge. He said to him:

"Great Sage, I have no material problems, and yet I am always unsettled. For years I have tried to be happy, to find an answer to my inner thoughts, to come to terms with the world. Please advise me as to how I can be cured of this malaise."

The sage answered:

"My friend, what is hidden to some is apparent to others. Again, what is apparent to some is hidden to others. I have the answer to your ailment, though it is no ordinary medication. You must set out on your travels, seeking the happiest man in the world. As soon as you find him, you must ask him for his shirt, and put it on."

This seeker thereupon restlessly started looking for happy men. One after another he found them and questioned them. Again and again they said: "Yes, I am happy, but there is one happier than me."

After travelling through one country after another for many, many days, he found the wood in which everyone said lived the happiest man in the world.

He heard the sound of laughter coming from among the trees, and quickened his step until he came upon a man sitting in a glade.

"Are you the happiest man in the world, as people say?" he asked.

"Certainly I am," said the other man.

"My name is so-and-so, my condition is such-and-such, and my remedy, ordered by the greatest sage, is to wear your shirt. Please give it to me; I will give you anything I have in exchange."

The happiest man looked at him closely, and he laughed. He laughed and he laughed and he laughed. When he had quietened down a little, the restless man, rather annoyed at this reaction, said:

"Are you unhinged, that you laugh at such a serious request?"

"Perhaps," said the happiest man, "but if you had only taken the trouble to look, you would have seen that I do not possess a shirt."

"What, then am I to do now?"

"You will now be cured. Striving for something unattainable provides the exercise to achieve that which is needed: as when a man gathers all his strength to jump across a stream as if it were far wider than it is. He gets across the stream."

The happiest man in the world then took off the turban whose end had concealed his face. The restless man saw that he was none other than the great sage who had originally advised him.

"But why did you not tell me all this years ago, when I came to see you?" the restless man asked in puzzlement.

"Because you were not ready then to understand. You needed certain experiences, and they had to be given to you in a manner which would ensure that you went through them." ■

The Greek idea of the head of a Gorgon, one look at which can turn one into stone, is so arresting as never to be forgotten when once heard. The myth of the adventures of Perseus (told by Kingsley in **The Heroes***) has all the elements of folk tales: the magical apparatus; the perilous voyage; the beautiful maiden, daughter of a King; the threat of death, and the killing of a monster all figure prominently. The legend of St. George has been seen as but a re-telling of the 'killing of the monster and rescue of the maiden' episodes from this narrative. According to early commentators, the theme is a portrayal of the victory of the Christian hero over evil, though later analysts saw it as a solar myth. More recently a psychoanalytical explanation has been preferred: and no doubt reinterpretations will continue, according to the opinions of the experts from time to time. Andrew Lang, the distinguished folklorist, reconstituted the myth in a fairy-tale book from Apollodorus, Simonides, and Pindar as 'The Terrible Head', thus giving us an opportunity of comparing a version for popular consumption with the classical texts available in standard books.*

This may represent the first stage of popularization through which other literary presentations have gone in their transition into fireside telling.

The Gorgon's Head

Once upon a time there was a King whose only child was a girl. Now the King had been very anxious to have a son, or at least a grandson, to come after him, but he was told by a prophet that his own daughter's son should kill him. This news terrified him so much that he determined never to let his daughter be married; for he thought it was better to have no grandson at all than to be killed by his grandson. He therefore called his workmen together, and bade them dig a deep round hole in the earth, and then he had a prison of brass built in the hole, and then, when it was finished, he locked up his daughter. No man ever saw her, and she never saw even the fields and the sea, but only the sky and the sun—for there was a wide open window in the roof of the house of brass. So the Princess would sit looking up at the sky, and watching the clouds float across, and wondering whether she should ever get out of her prison. Now one day it seemed to her that the sky opened above her and a great shower of shining gold fell through the window in the roof and lay glittering in her room. Not very long after, the Princess had a baby, a little boy, but when the King heard of it he was very angry and afraid, for now the child was born that should be his death. Yet, cowardly as he was, he had not quite the heart to kill the Princess and her baby outright, but he had them put in a huge brass-bound chest and thrust out to sea, so that they might either be drowned or starved, or perhaps come to a country where they would be out of his way.

So the Princess and the baby floated and drifted in the chest on the sea all day and all night, but the baby was not afraid of the waves nor of the wind; for he did not know that they could hurt him, and he slept quite soundly. And the Princess sang a song over him, and this was her song:

A Gorgon Head Shield

Child, my child, how sound you sleep
Though your mother's care is deep
You can lie with heart at rest
In the narrow brass-bound chest
In the starless night and drear
You can sleep, and never hear
Billows breaking, and the cry
Of the night-wind wandering by;
In soft purple mantle sleeping
With your little face on mine,
Hearing not your mother weeping
And the breaking of the brine.

Well, the daylight came at last, and the great chest was driven by the waves against the shore of an island. There it lay, with the Princess and her baby in it, till a man of that country came past, and saw it, and dragged it on to the beach, and when he had broken it open, behold! there was a beautiful lady and a little boy. So he took them home, and was very kind to them, and brought up the boy till he was a young man.

Now when the boy had come to his full strength, the King of that country fell in love with the mother and wanted to marry her; but he knew that she would never part from her boy. So he thought of a plan to get rid of the boy, and this was his plan.

A great Queen of a country not far off was going to be married, and this King said that all his subjects must bring him wedding presents to give her. And he made a feast to which he invited them all, and they all brought their presents; some brought gold cups, and some brought necklaces of gold and amber, and some brought beautiful horses. But the boy had nothing, though he was the son of a princess, for his mother had nothing to give him. Then the rest of the company began to laugh at him, and the King said: "If you have nothing else to give, at least you might go and fetch the Terrible Head."

The boy was proud and spoke without thinking;
"Then I swear that I *will* bring the Terrible Head, if it

may be brought by a living man. But of what head you speak I know not."

Then they told him that somewhere, a long way off, there dwelt three dreadful sisters, monstrous, ogrish women, with golden wings and claws of brass, and with serpents growing on their heads instead of hair. Now these women were so awful to look on that whoever saw them was at once turned into stone. And two of them could not be put to death, but the youngest, whose face was very beautiful, could be killed, and it was her head that the boy had promised to bring. You may imagine it was no easy adventure.

When he had heard all this he was pretty sorry that he had sworn to bring the Terrible Head, but he was determined to keep his oath. So he went out from the feast, where they all sat drinking and making merry; and he walked alone beside the sea in the dusk of the evening, at the place where the great chest, with himself and his mother in it, had been cast ashore.

There he went and sat down on a rock, looking towards the sea, and wondering how he should begin to fulfil his vow. Then he felt someone touch him on the shoulder; and he turned and saw a young man like a King's son, having with him a tall and beautiful lady, whose blue eyes shone like stars. They were taller than mortal men, and the young man had a staff in his hand with golden wings on it, and two golden serpents twisted around it, and he had wings on his cap and on his shoes. He spoke to the boy, and asked him why he was so unhappy; and the boy told him he had sworn to bring the Terrible Head, and knew not how to begin to set about the adventure.

Then the beautiful lady also spoke, and said that it was a foolish oath and hasty, but that it might be kept if a brave man had sworn it. Then the boy answered that he was not afraid, if only he knew the way.

Then the lady said that to kill the dreadful woman with the golden wings and the brass claws and to cut off her head, he needed three things: first a Cap of Darkness, which would make him invisible when he wore it; next, a Sword of Sharpness, which would cleave iron with one blow; and last, the Shoes of Swiftness, with which he might fly in the air.

The boy answered that he knew not where such things were to be procured, and that, lacking them, he could only try and fail. Then the young man, taking off his own shoes, said: "First, you shall use these shoes till you have taken the Terrible Head, and then you must give them back to me. And with these shoes you will fly as fleet as a bird, or a thought, over the land and over the waves of the sea, wherever the shoes know the way. But there are ways which they do not know, roads beyond the borders of the world. And these roads must you travel. Now first, you must go to the Three Grey Sisters who live far off in the north, and are so very old that they have only one eye and one tooth among the three. You must creep up close to them and as one of them passes the eye to the other you must seize it, and refuse to give it up till they have told you the way to the Three Fairies of the Garden. They will give you the Cap of Darkness and the Sword of Sharpness, and show you how to wing beyond this world to the land of the Terrible Head."

Then the beautiful lady said, "Go forth at once, and do not return to say good-bye to your mother, for these things must be done quickly, and the Shoes of Swiftness themselves will carry you to the land of the Three Grey Sisters— for they know the measure of that way."

So the boy thanked her, and he fastened on the Shoes of Swiftness, and turned to say goodbye to the young man and the lady. But behold! they had vanished, he knew not how or where! Then he leaped in the air to try the Shoes of Swiftness and they carried him more swiftly than the wind, over the warm blue sea, over the happy lands of the south, over the northern peoples who drank mare's milk and lived in great waggons, wandering after their flocks. Across the wide rivers, where the wild fowl rose and fled before him, and over the plains and the cold North Sea he went, over the fields of snow and the hills of ice, to a place where the world ends, and all water is frozen and there are no men, nor beasts, nor any green grass.

There in a blue cave of the ice he found the Three Grey Sisters, the oldest of living things. Their hair was as white as snow, and their flesh of an icy blue, and they mumbled and nodded in a kind of dream, and their frozen breath hung around them like a cloud. Now the opening of the cave in the ice was narrow, and it was not easy to pass in without touching one of the Grey Sisters. But, floating on the Shoes of Swiftness, the boy just managed to steal in, and waited till one of the sisters said to another, who had their one eye:

"Sister, what do you see? Do you see old times coming back?"

"No, sister."

"Then give me the eye, for perhaps I can see farther than you."

Then the first sister passed the eye to the second, but as the second groped for it the boy took it cleverly out of her hand.

"Where is the eye, sister?" said the second grey woman.

"You have taken it yourself, sister," said the first grey woman.

"Have you lost the eye, sister? Have you lost the eye?" said the third grey sister. "Shall we never find it again, and see old times coming back?"

Then the boy slipped from behind them out of the cave into the air, and he laughed aloud.

When the old women heard that laugh they began to weep for now they knew that a stranger had robbed them, and that they could not help themselves. Their tears froze as they fell from the hollows where no eyes were, and rattled on the icy ground of the cave. Then they began to implore the boy to give them their eye back again, and he could not help feeling sorry for them, they were so pitiful. But he said he would never give them the eye till they told him the way to the Fairies of the Garden.

They wrung their hands miserably, for they guessed why he had come, and how he was going to try to win the Terrible Head. Now the Three Grey Sisters were

100

akin to the Dreadful Women and it was hard for them to tell the boy the way. But at last they told him to keep always south, and with the land on his left and the sea on his right, till he reached the Island of the Faries of the Garden. Then he gave them back the eye, and they began to look out once more for the old times coming back again. The boy flew south between sea and land, keeping the land always on his left hand, till he saw a beautiful island crowned with flowering trees. There he alighted, and there he found the Three Faries of the Garden. They were like three very beautiful young women, dressed one in green, one in white, and one in red, and they were singing and dancing around an apple tree with fruit of gold, and this was their song:

The Song of the Western Fairies

Round and round the apples of gold,
    Round and round dance we;
Thus do we dance from the days of old
    About the enchanted tree;
Round, and round, and round we go.
    While the spring is green, or the stream
      shall flow,
Or the wind shall stir the sea!

There is none may taste of the golden
    fruit
    Till the golden new times come;
Many a tree shall spring from shoot,
Many a blossom be withered at root,
    Many a song be dumb;
Broken and still shall be many a lute
    Or ever the new times come!

Round and round the tree of gold,
    Round and round dance we,
So doth the great world spin from of old
Summer and winter, and fire and cold,
Song that is sung and tale that is told,
Even as we dance, that fold and unfold
    Round the stem of the fairy tree!

These grave dancing fairies were very unlike the Grey Women, and they were glad to see the boy, and treated him kindly. Then they asked him why he had come; and he told them how he was sent to find the Sword of Sharpness and the Cap of Darkness. And the fairies gave him these, and a wallet, and a shield, and belted the sword, which had a diamond blade, around his waist, and the cap they set on his head, and told him that now even *they* could not see him, though they were fairies. Then he took it off, and they each kissed him and wished him good fortune, and then they began again their eternal dance around the golden tree, for it is their business to guard it till the new times come, or till the world's ending.

The boy put the cap on his head, and hung the wallet around his waist, and the shining shield on his shoulders, and he flew beyond the great river that lies coiled like a serpent around the whole world. And by the banks of that river, there he found the three Terrible Women all asleep beneath a poplar tree, with the dead poplar leaves lying all about them. Their golden wings were folded and their brass claws were crossed, and two of them slept with their hideous heads beneath their wings like birds, and the serpents in their hair writhed out from under the feathers of gold. But the youngest slept between her two sisters, and she lay on her back, with her beautiful sad face turned to the sky; and though she slept her eyes were wide open. If the boy had seen her, he would have been changed into stone by the terror and the pity of it, she was so awful; but he had thought of a plan for killing her without looking at her face.

As soon as he caught sight of the three from far off, he took his shining shield from his shoulders, and held it up like a mirror, so that he saw the Dreadful Women reflected in it, and did not see the Terrible Head itself. Then he came nearer and nearer, till he reckoned that he was within a sword's stroke of the youngest, and he guessed where he should strike a back blow behind him. Then he drew the Sword of Sharpness and struck once, and the Terrible Head was cut from the

shoulders of the creature, and the blood leaped out and struck him like a blow. But he thrust the Terrible Head into his wallet, and flew away without looking behind.

The two Dreadful Sisters who were left wakened, and rose in the air like great birds; and though they could not see him because of his Cap of Darkness, they flew after him up the wind, following by the scent through the clouds, like hounds hunting in a wood. They came so close that he could hear the clattering of their golden wings, and their shrieks to each other: "Here, here." "No, there; this way he went," as they chased him. But the Shoes of Swiftness flew too fast for them, and at last their cries and the rattle of their wings died away as he crossed the great river that runs around the world.

When the horrible creatures were far in the distance, and the boy found himself on the right side of the river, he flew straight eastward, seeking his own country. But, as he looked down from the air, he saw a very strange sight—a beautiful girl chained to a stake at the high-water mark of the sea. The girl was so frightened or so tired that she was only prevented from falling by the iron chain around her waist, and there she hung, as if she were dead. The boy was very sorry for her, and flew down and stood beside her. When he spoke she raised her head but his voice only seemed to frighten her. Then he remembered that he was wearing the Cap of Darkness, and that she could only hear him, not see him. So he took it off, and there he stood before her, the handsomest young man she had ever seen in all her life, with short curly yellow hair, and blue eyes, and a laughing face. And he thought her the most beautiful girl in the world. With one blow of the Sword of Sharpness he cut the iron chain that bound her, and then he asked her why she was here, and why men treated her so cruelly.

She told him that she was the daughter of the King of that country, and that she was tied there to be eaten by a monstrous beast out of the sea; for the beast came and devoured a girl every day. Now the lot had

fallen on her; and, as she was just saying this, a long fierce head of a cruel sea-creature rose out of the waves and snapped at her. But the beast had been too greedy and too hurried, so he missed his aim the first time. Before he could rise and bite again, the boy had whipped the Terrible Head out of his wallet and held it up. And when the sea beast leaped out once more its eyes fell on the head, and instantly it was turned into a stone. And the stone beast is there on the sea-coast to this day.

Then the boy and the girl went to the palace of the King, her father, where everyone was weeping for her death, and they could hardly believe their eyes when they saw her come back well. And the King and Queen made much of the boy, and could not contain themselves for delight when they found he wanted to marry their daughter. So the two were married with the most splendid rejoicings, and when they had passed some time at court they went home in a ship to the boy's own country. He could not carry his bride through the air, so he took the Shoes of Swiftness, and the Cap of Darkness and the Sword of Sharpness up to a lonely place in the hills. There he left them, and there they were found by the man and woman who had met him at home beside the sea, and had helped him to start on his journey.

When this had been done, the boy and his bride set forth for home, and landed at the harbour of his native land. But whom should he meet in the very street of the town but his own mother, flying for her life from the wicked King, who now wished to kill her because he found that she would never marry him! For if she had liked the King little before, she liked him far worse now that he had caused her son to disappear so suddenly. She did not know, of course, where the boy had gone, but thought the King had slain him secretly. So now she was running for her very life, and the wicked King was following her with a sword in his hand. Then, behold! She ran into her son's very arms, but he only had time to kiss her and step in front of her, when the King struck at him with his sword. The boy caught the blow on his shield, and cried to the King:

"I swore to bring you the Terrible Head, and see how I keep my oath!"

Then he drew forth the head from his wallet, and when the King's eyes fell on it, instantly he was turned to stone, just as he stood there with his sword lifted!

Now all the people rejoiced, because the wicked King should rule them no longer. And they asked the boy to be their king, but he said no, he must take his mother home to her father's house. So the people chose for King the man who had been kind to the boy's mother when first she was cast on the island in the great chest.

Presently the boy and his mother and his wife set sail for his mother's own country, from which she had been driven so unkindly. But on the way they stayed at the court of a King, and it happened that he was holding games, and giving prizes to the best runners, boxers, and quoit-throwers. Then the boy would try his strength with the rest, but he threw the quoit so far that it went beyond what had ever been thrown before, and fell in the crowd, striking a man so that he died. Now this man was no other than the father of the boy's mother, who had fled away from his own kingdom for fear his grandson should find him and kill him after all. Thus he was destroyed by his own cowardice and by chance, and thus the prophecy was fulfilled. But the boy and his wife and his mother went back to the kingdom that was theirs, and lived long and happily after all their troubles. ■

This story must be one of the most popular in history. It is found in a Chinese collection dated to 412 A.D., reputed to originate from the era of the great Indian emperor Ashoka—about 230 B.C. It is still alive in the story-teller's repertoire in India, and was for centuries a favourite tale in Europe. It is found in the Greek translation of the Eastern Book of **Sindibad,** *and also in Latin, almost a hundred years before it was claimed to be an historical incident in the life of the Welsh Prince Llewellyn and his faithful hound Gellert, a greyhound presented to him in 1205 A.D. There is, indeed, a Welsh proverb: "I am as sorry as the man who killed his greyhound". In some versions the mongoose becomes a wolf, or a snake, or even an eagle. In France, where the event was also believed to have occurred as an historical fact, the dog was, in the Middle Ages, regarded as a miracle-working martyr, and sick children were taken to his reputed grave. In Persian it is related as a Chinese tale; and it is also extant in Hebrew, Spanish, and Syriac versions.*

The Brahmin's Wife and The Mongoose

Another Indian version has a man kill the mongoose.

In India there flows a most holy river called the Ganges (named for the Goddess Ganga, Hindu divinity of the rivers), near the ancient city of Banaras. Near this city was a town called Mithila, where there dwelt a poor man, of the Brahmin faith and tradition, called Vidyadhara. He had no children, and he and his wife greatly loved, instead of a son or daughter, a tame mongoose.

For a long time the god Visvesvara and his wife Visalakshi observed this kindly pair, and so by divine power they blessed them with a son.

The child and the mongoose were brought up together, as twin brothers in the same cradle, for the Brahmin believed that the gods had given them a child because of their good behaviour towards the animal.

One day, in the morning, when the Brahmin had gone out to beg alms of the pious and charitable, and his wife was busy over her herb-pots, a snake glided through a hole in the garden wall.

The mongoose kept watch beside its young master, as usual, and saw its ancient enemy. The snake came towards the cradle, and hissed, fixing its glittering eyes upon the child.

Without a moments hesitation, the brave little animal attacked the snake, and a fierce fight ensued. Soon the venomous cobra was dead, torn to pieces by the faithful mongoose.

Covered with blood, the mongoose ran to the child's mother with great excitement to show her what had been done.

"Oh, wretched mongoose!" cried she, following it to the room where the upturned cradle and blood-stained bedcovering showed no sign of the child. "You have in your dreadful jealousy killed my son, the light of my eyes!" and with several strokes of the knife in her hand, she killed the creature.

But, crawling from a darkened corner of the room, the child laughed for joy, and the unhappy mother saw the mangled portions of the snake beside the cradle.

The mongoose had paid for the kindness which the Brahmin and his wife had shown it with its life. ■

The Magic Bag

This tale, told by a Berber tribesman in Morocco, has been said to date from the time when Christian priests and monks were still being challenged by local magicians who would not readily accept the new religion. North Africa certainly was Christianized before the Islamic conquest, and there is no way of telling whether this is the reason. On the other hand, the tale appears in similar form, with some of the same elements, both in Germany, ('Brother Lustig') and in Italy ('Brother Giovannone') in which the hero is a monk and the bag is a gift from St. Peter, who is eventually blackmailed into letting him into Paradise with the threat of its use. In the Sicilian version the monk actually imprisons Death in the bag, preventing people from dying as in the tale 'Occasion' in this collection.

There is a similarity, though not an identity, of this kind of tale with Central Asian ones where people with unusual powers are able to combat the normal reward-and-punishment routine laid down by local religion. Some versions, as in the case of a version from Tuscany, have the hero suspending his own demise (through trapping Death); he is hence called Godfather Misery, because 'Misery never ends'. In the telling of the same tale from Venice, where he is called Beppo Pipetta, he gets into Heaven by a trick. Refused admittance, he throws his cap in and then slips in and sits on it "because I am sitting on my own property, and on my own property I do not take anyone's orders!"

There was once a priest and a magician. The Priest said, "It is only through me that you will get to Heaven."

The Magician said, "Is there no other way to achieve seemingly impossible things?"

"No," said the Priest, "We priests have the monopoly apart from some saints, but they are few and far between. As you know, they are almost all in the distant past."

Now the Magician had a magical bag, and it could swallow anything its owner wanted. The Priest did not know that, but he was new in those parts, so that explained his confident manner.

The Magician said, "If you have all the power, then you will not mind if I say to this bag, 'Swallow the Priest!'"

"Not at all" said the Priest, "though it is a proof of your barbarian state, may your soul be saved!"

The Magician took up his bag and said to it, "Swallow the Priest!"

The bag drew the Priest into itself, and he was never seen again.

Now the Magician decided that there was no need to allow priests, and others for that matter, to have all the dealings with the invisible world. So he always put into the bag any priests or monks who would not accept his claim to equal rights of intervention in matters such as these. In the end, most of the priests concentrated on exhorting people to do good, while the Magician used his bag to swallow people and things which were bad.

Finally a whole swarm of devils, voraciously hungry, because so much bad was disappearing without trace, tracked down the Magician. He told the bag to swallow them, and it did. But they were too tough for it to digest; the time for the total dissolution of demons had not yet arrived. So the Magician took the bag to a blacksmith. "How much to hammer this bag completely flat, as slim as a knife-blade?" The smith said that he would do it for ten silver pieces. So he hammered day and night, but he could not get the bag flat. The demons, as is their habit, could always inflate themselves slightly after a blow had made them flat for a moment or two.

"You must have the devil in this bag!" shouted the furious and baffled smith. "Yes, indeed I have" said the Magician. Giving the smith only one silver piece for his trouble, he opened the bag and all the devils streamed out, back to Hell, feeling very battered.

Now the Magician carried on his life in much the same way, avoiding anything unpleasant by making it go into the magical bag, until it was nearly his time to die.

He went to see a wise Hermit about it. The Hermit said, "If you have not been honed by pleasant and unpleasant things, you may get neither to Heaven nor to Hell, and you may cease to exist. But that is what

some people want, anyway!"

When he died, the Magician found himself at the gates of Hell. "Why am I here since I got rid of so much evil in my life?" he asked the demon at the gate. The demon looked in his book. "Because you spent so much time concentrating on bad things that you have a natural affinity for us—come in," he said.

The Magician did not like the sound of this at all, so he said to the bag, which was over his shoulder, "Swallow all this!" In a twinkling of an eye there was no Hell to be seen.

The Magician made his way to Heaven. At the gate he was stopped. "I have to come in!" he said.

"Why?" asked the angel on duty.

"Because Hell has ceased to exist, and there is no other place to go."

"I can get Heaven into this bag in a twinkling of an eye, and you, too, if you don't let me in!"

And that, they say, is how he got into Heaven.

But there are some who say that the places he visited were not Heaven or Hell at all.

But you just decide, as I have given you all the help I can, and it is nearly time for me to jump into my magical bag. ■

Catherine's Fate

If it were to be asked "What are world tales actually about?" — the answer would have to be "They are about fate or destiny." Some cover a long life, some only a few incidents from a career. Some are supposed to be about the lives of real people, others purport to cover happenings—which can still be called 'fate'—in the lives of mythical creatures. Fairies and superstitions are instruments of fate, too: the fairy godmother alters fate, and the rabbit's-foot is carried in the hope that it will cause a favourable fate.

Fairy tales are often imagined to be so named because they feature gentle feminine apparitions with gauzy wings. This is only a recent idea. The word fairy comes from the Latin fata (fate), which became 'enchantment' in French. So fate and magic are always associated in traditional tales: and the kind of 'fairy' found in modern Western story-books, usually for children, is only one form of this concretized Fate.

In this tale, found in Sicily and known in the Far East as well, Catherine's Fate takes a more direct and positive form, as an imposing woman.

In Greek and Roman times, there were believed to be three Fates, which arbitrarily controlled every person's life. Of these, Lachesis measured the Thread of Life; and the special thread which features in this story may indicate an improvement in life, and eventual happiness, bestowed by Lachesis.

There once lived a very rich and generous merchant who had a gorgeous palace. The pride of his life was his daughter, a beautiful creature called Catherine. Catherine was tall and slim, with black hair and large, lustrous eyes. Her hands and feet were small and delicate, her skin as soft as the petals of a rose.

In the palace there were thrones of gold, chairs of silver set with precious turquoises, picture-frames set with rubies, water-jugs set with diamonds. All around her was luxury and beauty. Peacocks strolled in the gardens, flowers bloomed in pots hanging from the trees; all was the best that money could buy.

One day, when Catherine was walking in the garden, dressed in long silken robes sewn with the finest pearls and a cap with tassels of pearls, a very elegant-looking lady appeared before her.

There was an extraordinary look about this lady, her eyes were very penetrating and dark, her clothes did not seem to be anything but luminous draperies.

"Catherine, my dear child," said the lady, "what would you rather have: would you like to enjoy your life in your youth, or would you like to enjoy it in your old age? You have only these two choices."

Catherine thought for a moment, and then she said: "If I have my enjoyment now, will I suffer for it in my last years?"

And the tall lady said "Yes".

"But how do you know?" asked Catherine, still pondering the question. "I am your Fate," answered the apparition. "Oh, then I will have my good fortune in my old age," said Catherine.

"Very well, so be it," said her Fate, and vanished.

Catherine thought nothing of this encounter, and returned to the house to change her clothes for something even finer. But a few days later, terrible things began to happen.

There was a great storm at sea. Catherine's father had expected his ships to return from a foreign country, loaded with rich cargoes, and they were all sent, by the tempest, to the bottom of the sea.

His warehouses were gutted by a mysterious fire, so when he decided to refit new ships, there was nothing

to put in them. He hired his ships to a duke who wanted to go to war with another prince, and all the ships were sunk in an engagement with pirates. The duke's men were put to the sword, and he, too, was penniless.

Thieves broke in and stole all Catherine's jewels, her clothes had to be sold to keep them in food a little longer. At last, wretched and ill, Catherine's father died, leaving her alone in the world. Penniless and in very simple garments, Catherine decided to leave this unlucky city and find some work, if possible, in another place. So she said farewell to the city of her birth, and trudged off.

She eventually reached a noble city far from her own country, and was standing in the street, wondering which way to go. She only had a little money, given to her by an old nurse, and was wondering where she could buy a piece of bread.

A lady of quality, looking out of her window, saw her and called out: "Who are you, my dear, and where do you come from? You are not from this part of the land."

"Lady, I am all alone in the world, as my father, who was once a rich merchant, has died, and I am looking for somewhere to buy a piece of bread," she said.

"Come into my house, I need a servant, and you will do very well," said the noblewoman, and Catherine went gratefully inside the big house.

The lady became very fond of Catherine, and trusted her with all the things she possessed. One day the mistress said to her:

"I have to go out for a little while; lock the door behind me, and let no one either in or out until I return." So Catherine locked the door, and sat down by the fire. No sooner had the noblewoman gone, than the door flew open and her Fate entered.

"So, here you are, Catherine!" cried her Fate harshly. "You have found yourself a very nice place here, haven't you? Well, you can't escape me like that you know!" and she began to throw the mistress's valuables all over the floor, breaking glass and china, and tearing priceless linen to pieces.

"Oh, no, no, no," cried Catherine, "I shall get into the most dreadful trouble! The lady trusts me!"

"Oh, does she?" sneered her Fate, "well, explain this to her when she comes back then!" and she ripped the long silken curtains to tatters.

Catherine put her hands to her face and ran from the house, never looking back in case her Fate was following.

No sooner had she gone, than her Fate put everything back exactly as it had been before, and disappeared.

When the lady came back the house was perfectly tidy, but Catherine was gone. The mistress called and called, but of course the poor girl did not hear, for she was far away.

The lady looked everywhere, and thought perhaps Catherine had robbed her, but nothing was missing. She could not understand what could have happened, the girl had seemed to be perfectly reliable.

Now poor Catherine ran on until she reached another city, and when looking for somewhere to buy a piece of bread, was noticed by another lady standing at her window.

The lady opened the window and said to her: "Where are you from, and what are you doing in this place, when so obviously you seem to be lost?"

"I am a poor girl from far away, and I am looking for something to eat, as I am very hungry," said Catherine.

"Well, come into my house," said the lady, "I will feed you and clothe you, and you may have a position in my household." So Catherine went in.

But the very same thing happened as before.

No sooner was she settled in the house, and trusted with all the valuables, than her Fate appeared, and created chaos in a few seconds.

"Do you think that there was anywhere in this world I would not be able to find you?" cried her Fate harshly, sweeping a line of priceless scent-bottles to the ground and smashing them to smithereens. Catherine put her hands to her face and ran.

And so it went on for the space of seven years. Each time Catherine was taken on by some nice lady, the appearance of her Fate caused her to travel on and on, endlessly, it seemed to her. But she never escaped for long.

But, and this Catherine did not know, her Fate always restored everything to its former state the minute Catherine had disappeared.

Now seven years passed in this manner, and when Catherine was working for a very noble lady with a very kind heart, it was almost as if Catherine's Fate had forgotten about her. Day after day, Catherine looked after the house, and things were always right for her. The tension was very great, though, for every hour she expected the door to fly open and her Fate to appear.

Each day, she had to go up the mountain with a basket of the finest bread and cheese for her mistress.

A tall, dignified personage took the bread from her gracefully each day, and after bowing, disappeared into a cave.

One day her mistress told her: "I always have to propitiate my Fate in this way. If that fresh bread and cheese were not sent to her, I shudder to think what she might cause to happen to me."

At this Catherine began to weep, unable to hide her grief, for she had suffered so much in the last seven years that she could no longer hide her sadness.

"My dear child, what is the matter with you? Tell me at once!" cried the kind-hearted mistress, placing her hand on Catherine's shoulder.

So Catherine told her the story of her Fate's cruelty, and continued, "I do not think that I can stand any more of this anguish, expecting her to appear any moment and to tear everything to pieces, as she has done so often. In fact, I would like to go away from here, soon, so that I do not bring my Fate's destruction upon this house."

"Now, let me think of a plan," said the noble-woman, striking her forehead, "Yes, I have it. When you go up the mountain with my Fate's bread, tell her your story, and appeal to her to have a word with *your* Fate, that she leaves off tormenting you like this. I am sure my Fate, who is kind, will help."

So, next day, when Catherine went up to the mountain with the bread for her mistress's Fate, she asked her to intercede with her own Fate. "Well, your Fate is asleep under seven quilts, just now," said the lady's Fate, "but when you come tomorrow she might be awake and I will take you to her."

Catherine went away full of hope, and slept that night quite peacefully.

When she took the bread up the mountain next morning, her mistress's Fate took her to her own Fate, who lay in a large bed, covered to the eyes with seven feather quilts.

"Now sister, here is Catherine," said the Fate of the noblewoman. "Leave off tormenting her so; I beg you to give her a little rest now."

Her Fate said nothing but, "Here is a skein of silk, look after it carefully, it will be of great use to you, now leave me to rest." And she pulled the quilts over her head.

Puzzled by this, Catherine went home. Her mistress was all agog to know what had happened, but could not make head nor tail of the story Catherine told her. "The silk is worth scarcely anything," she said, "but you had better keep it. It might be of some use, as

your Fate said."

The King of that country, who was young and extremely handsome, was to marry, and there was much consternation at the royal tailor's, when it was discovered that no silk of the right colour to sew the King's wedding robe together was to be found in the entire kingdom.

"Issue a proclamation," said the King, "I must have my robes done in time! Send to the four countries bordering my land, send to every quarter of my dominions! Whoever has silk of this colour must bring it to the court, and I shall reward the owner of the silk generously."

The noblewoman heard the proclamation and came to tell Catherine, "Catherine, my child, put on this dress and take your skein to the court. It is exactly the colour the King's tailor is looking for," she cried excitedly. "You will be rewarded most generously, I am sure."

When Catherine appeared at the Court before the throne, the young King found her so beautiful to look upon that he could not take his eyes off her face.

"Your Majesty," said she, "will this silk be suitable for your wedding robe?"

"You shall be paid in pure gold for it," said the King. "Bring the scales, and we will weigh the skein; whatever it weighs, you shall have the equivalent in the finest gold of my realm."

They brought the scales, but no matter how much gold was put upon the scales, the skein was always heavier.

Then the King had larger scales brought, and threw all his treasure on to the scales, and still the skein weighed more.

Then, in extreme exasperation, the King took the crown from his head and put it on the scales. At that very second the scales balanced and the King laughed.

"Where did you get this silk, my dear?" he asked Catherine.

"From my mistress," said Catherine, and the King shouted "Impossible! What sort of lady is your mistress that she has magic silk like this?"

Then Catherine told all that had happened to her to the King, and he took her hand in his. "I will marry you instead of the girl to whom I have been betrothed," he said, and so it happened.

Afterwards, Catherine, who had suffered so much in her youth, lived to be a very old woman, and was happy until the moment of her death as Queen of that far country. ■

About the first half of the seventh century was written a spiritual romance, supposedly about Barlaam and Josaphat, by a monk named John of Damascus. It was not until many centuries later that it was realized that most of the material in this book related to the life of the Buddha, and not to any Christian saint. The tenth parable in the work is also found in the Talmud, and employed there to encourage good and thoughtful deeds. Its substance was widely used by medieval monks to warn their hearers to prepare for the world to come, and it is also found in the oldest Spanish storybook, **Count Lucanor,** *of the 14th century. This is the Talmudic Parable of the* **Desolate Island:** *where the rich man is God, the slave is man, the island the world, the year of reign his lifespan, and the desolate island the future world.*

Scholars are of the opinion that the myth based on the Buddhist sources (which are still extant) was composed in pre-Islamic Egypt. There is also a literary and oral legend that the Caliph Haroun Al Rashid carried out an experiment, placing a stranger, after drugging him, on the throne to test his worth; then drugging him again and returning him to his former place, because of his abuse of power. In a Sufi parable, a master hypnotizes a self-styled godly man, places him on a throne, reveals that he is really greedy, and restores him to his pauperhood, saying to the King and disciples (for whom the demonstration is performed): "This is not our man." The phrase has accordingly become a proverb in the Middle East.

The Desolate Island

There was once a very wealthy man, who was of a kind and generous disposition, and who wanted to make his slave happy. He therefore gave him his freedom, and also presented him with a shipload of merchandise.

"Go," he said, "and sail to various countries. Dispose of these goods, and whatever you may get for them shall be your own."

The freed slave sailed away, across the wide ocean.

He had not been long on his voyage before a storm blew up. His ship was driven on to the rocks and went to pieces, and all on board were lost except the former slave himself. He managed to swim to a nearby island and drag himself ashore.

Sad, despondent, and lonely, naked and with nothing to his name, he walked across the land until he came to a large and beautiful city.

Many people came out to meet him, crying, "Welcome! Welcome! Long live our King!"

They brought a rich carriage and, placing him in it, escorted him to a magnificent palace, where many servants gathered around him. He was dressed in royal garments and they addressed him as their sovereign: they expressed their complete obedience to his will.

The ex-slave was, naturally enough, amazed and confused, wondering whether he was dreaming; and all that he saw, heard or experienced was merely passing fantasy.

Eventually he became convinced that what was happening was in fact real; and he asked some people around him, whom he liked, how he could have arrived in this state.

"I am, after all," he said, "a man of whom you know nothing, a poor, naked wanderer, whom you have never seen before. How can you make me your ruler? This causes me more amazement than I can possibly say."

"Sire," they answered, "this island is inhabited by spirits. Long ago they prayed that they might be sent a son of man to rule over them, and their prayers have been answered. Every year they are sent a son of man. They receive him with great dignity and place him on the throne. But his status and his power end when the year is over. Then they take the royal robes from him and put him on board a ship, which carries him to a vast and desolate island. Here, unless he has previously been wise and prepared for that day, he finds neither subject nor friend: and he is obliged to pass a weary, lonely and miserable life. Then a new King is selected, and so year follows year. The Kings who came before you were careless and did not think. They enjoyed their power to the full, forgetting the day when it would end."

These people counselled the former slave to be wise, and to allow their words to stay within his heart.

The new King listened carefully to all this: and he felt grieved that he should have wasted even the little time which had passed since he came to the island.

He asked a man of knowledge who had already spoken:

"Advise me, O Spirit of Wisdom, how I may prepare

for the days which will come upon me in the future."

"Naked you came among us", said the man, "and naked you shall be sent to the desolate island of which I have told you. At present you are King, and may do whatever you please. Therefore, send workmen to the island, and let them build houses and prepare the land, and make the surroundings beautiful. The barren soil will be turned into fruitful fields, people will go there to live, and you will have established a new kingdom for yourself. Your own subjects will be waiting to welcome you when you arrive. The year is short, the work is long: therefore be earnest and energetic."

The King followed this advice. He sent workmen and materials to the desolate island and, before the end of his term of power, it had become a fertile, pleasant, and attractive place. The rulers who had come before him had anticipated the end of their time with fear, or smothered the thought of it by amusing themselves. But he looked forward to it with joy, for then he could start upon a career of permanent peace and happiness.

And the day came. The freed slave who had been made a king was stripped of his authority. With his royal robes he lost his powers. He was placed naked on a ship, and its sails were set for the island. When he approached its shore, however, the people whom he had sent ahead came forward to welcome him with music, song, and great joy. They made him ruler, and he lived ever after in peace. ∎

Gazelle Horn

*The Hindu and Buddhist scriptures and tale collections contain many stories which are substantially similar to variants known all over the world. Among these ancient writings are the Hindu **Mahabharata** and **Ramayana** and the Tibetan Buddhist **Kahgyur** and **Tangyur,** which have influenced peoples of the Far East with tales which have not diffused westwards: 'Gazelle Horn' is one of the best-known examples of this.*

Some idea of the importance of these books is seen in the fact that one collection of the Kanjur was bartered by a Buriat community for 7,000 oxen: even though, as the Russian authority Vasilev notes, people listen to the recitations and "are edified, even though they do not comprehend" — since they do not understand Tibetan.

*The **Kahgyur** is a translation from Sanskrit sources, made in Tibet between the 7th and 13th centuries, but mostly in the 9th. Its contents were analysed by the Hungarian pioneering scholar Csoma Korosi in Calcutta from a hundred-volume edition. This version is, however, taken from the 108-volume edition printed in Pekin in the 18th century by command of the Emperor, and translated by Professor Anton von Schifner, the specialist in Buddhist legends.*

In very remote times, in a forest region free from villages and richly provided with flowers, fruits, water and roots, there lived a penance-performing holy man, a Rishi. He fed on roots, fruit and water, and clothed himself with leaves and skins.

As he had attained the Five Kinds of Insight, wild gazelles were in the habit of living in his hermitage, keeping him company. One day a gazelle doe came to the spot where he had lately been. And, as the results of human actions are beyond mental comprehension, it happened that she became pregnant. When the time came for her to bring forth, she went back to the same place and there gave birth to a boy.

When she had smelt him and realized that this was a creature that did not resemble herself, she was terrified, and abandoned him. Now the Rishi came to the place and saw the child. He began to consider whose it might be; and he perceived that it was his own child. So he took the baby with him into his hermitage and brought it up there. When the boy had grown, gazelle horns appeared on his head, and because of this the Rishi named him Gazelle Horn.

The Rishi fell ill, and although treated with the right medicines, his sickness did not become less. Seeing that he must die soon, he spoke to the boy thus:

"O son, from time to time many Rishis come to this hermitage from all manner of regions. You must, from love of me, receive them in a friendly manner, invite them to repose on the couch, and set before them roots and fruits according to your means."

It is said that the end of collection is diffusion; the end of the high is to fall; the end of coming together is separation: and the end of life is death. So the holy man discharged his obligations to this law. The youth burnt the Rishi's body in the usual manner and then, as he mourned, being depressed by grief at the loss of his father, he found himself possessed of the Five Kinds of Insight.

One day, when he had gone to fetch water in a pitcher, the deity began to let rain fall. As he walked along with the container, which was quite full, he let it fall, so that it broke. Rishis are very quickly angered; so, spilling the little water that was left, he reproached the deity, saying: "As my full pitcher has been broken because of your bad behaviour, you shall not let rain fall for twelve years from this day!"

Because of this curse, the deity let no rain fall. In consequence, a great famine arose in Varanasi and its people consequently emigrated in all directions.

The King sent for the seers and said to them: "Honoured Sirs, to whose power is it due that the deity sends no rain?"

They replied, "To a Rishi's anger. If he can be disturbed in his penances, the deity will again send rain. Otherwise it is not possible."

The King sat, absorbed in thought. His wives, the Princes, and the Ministers, asked him, "Why, O King, are you displeased?"

He replied: "On account of a Rishi's anger the deity sends no rain. The seers have declared that if the Rishi can be disturbed in his penances the deity will send rain again, but that otherwise it is impossible."

One of the King's daughters, whose name was Shanta, said, "O King, if that is the case, do not be distressed. I will contrive that the Rishi shall be completely distracted from this penance."

The King said, "By what means?"

She replied, "Let me and other women be taught mystic lore by the Brahmins, members of the priestly caste. And let a hermitage, provided with flowers, fruit and water, be prepared on a ferry boat." The King agreed.

Then the Princess gave orders for the preparation of tempting objects, and fruits filled with wine, and other very bright fruits of various kinds. She made herself look like a Rishi, dressed herself in bark and grass, and went to the Gazelle Horn Rishi's hermitage, attended by the women to whom the Brahmins had taught mystic lore.

When they arrived, the pupils of the Gazelle Horn Rishi said to him, "O Teacher! Many Rishis have come to the Hermitage."

He replied: "It is well that Rishis have come. Bring them in."

When they had entered and he had looked at them, he said in verse:

"Alas! A Rishi's appearance was never like this of old:

"A loosely flowing step, a face free from beard, a rising and falling breast."

His mind was a prey to doubt, but he offered his visitors roots and fruit. They ate, and then said to the Rishi, "Your fruits are harsh and acid. The fruits which are to be found at our hermitage on the water are like the drink of the gods. Therefore we invite you there."

He went with them to the pleasure-ground on board the boat. There they spread before him stupefying substances, coconuts filled with wine, and other fruits. When he was drunk with wine and seduced by the alluring things, he gave himself up to pleasure with the women, and his magical power vanished.

The deity, rejoicing in rain, called the clouds together from every side and got the better of the Rishi.

Shanta said, "Now, do you know what the power is?"

Having fettered the Rishi with amorous bonds, she took him to the King and said, "O King! This is the man."

As the deity now sent rain, a good harvest followed. The King gave Shanta to the Rishi as his wife, together with her attendants. But the Rishi, ignoring her, began to indulge in love with other women. She also started to treat him with small respect, as her good nature was destroyed by jealousy.

One day, when she hit him on the head with a shoe during an argument, he said to himself:

"I, who used not to allow power to the thunder of the cloud, must now, being fettered by love bonds, allow myself to be set at naught by a woman!"

Thereupon he again devoted himself to ascetic exertions, and once more became possessed of the Five Kinds of Insight. ■

Tom Tit Tot

The power resident in a person's name is a feature of folklore in widely dispersed cultures. It is very likely that this native English version of the imp and his secret name was current in the British Isles for many centuries before it was driven out by the Grimm Brothers' exportation of the German form—now better known in Anglo-Saxon countries—Rumpelstiltskin. The secret name, and the forfeit which has to be given if it cannot be discovered, is widely reflected in folktales. There is a cognate of Tom Tit Tot in southern Nigeria "The Hippopotamus called Isantim". The tale is found in places as far apart as Iceland and Italy, Mongolia and Sweden. In Cornwall the secret name is Terrytop; in Scotland, Whuppity Stoorie, in France, Ricdin-Ricdon, and in Magyar, Dancing Vargaluska. This English version, taken down from the words of an East Anglian woman a century ago, is beautifully told—the folklorist Joseph Jacobs thought it "far superior to any of the Continental variants".

Once upon a time there was a woman who had baked five pies. When they came from the oven, they had been so over-baked that their crusts were too hard to eat.

So the lady said to her daughter:

"Maiden, you just put those pies on the shelf and leave them there, and the pastry will get soft."

But she didn't say, 'They'll get soft', really; she said, in the way they have in East Anglia, 'They'll come again', meaning the same thing.

But the girl, hearing these words, said to herself:

"Well, if they'll come again, I'll eat them now." And she sat down and, there and then, ate them all up.

When it was time for supper, the woman said to the girl:

"Go and get one of those pies. I expect they've come again now."

The girl went and she looked, and there was nothing there but the pie-dishes. So she went back to her mother, and she said:

"No, they haven't come again."

"Not one of them?" asked the mother.

"Not one of them", she said.

"Well, whether they've come again or not come again," said the mother, "I'll have one for my supper."

"But you can't, if they haven't come", said the girl.

"But I can," said she, "go and bring the best of them."

"Best or worst," said the girl, "I've eaten them all, and you can't have one until it *has* come again."

Well, the woman was really angry, and she took her spinning to the door to spin, and as she spun she sang:

"My daughter has eaten five, five pies today—

My daughter has eaten five, five pies today." The King was coming down the street, and he heard her singing, but he could not make out the words. So he stopped, and he said:

"What was that you were singing about, Mother?"

The woman was ashamed to let him know what her daughter had done, so she sang, instead of that:

"My daughter has spun five, five skeins today—
My daughter has spun five, five skeins today."

"Well!" said the King, "I never heard of anyone who could do that."

Then he said: "Look here, I want a wife, and I'll marry your daughter. But take note: eleven months of the year she shall have all the food she likes to eat, and all the gowns she wants to wear, and all the company she cares to have. But, the last month of the year, she'll have to spin five skeins every day—and if she does not, I'll kill her!"

"All right," said the woman, for she was thinking what a fine marriage that would be. And as for those five skeins, well, there would be plenty of ways of getting out of that—most likely he'd forget about it.

And so they were married. And for eleven months the girl had all the food she wished, and all the dresses she desired, and all the company she wanted. But, when the time was ending, she began to think about those skeins, and she wondered whether the King still had them in mind. But not one word did he say about them: and she thought that he must have forgotten the whole matter.

However, on the last day of the last month of the eleven, he took her into a room which she had never seen before. There was nothing in it but a spinning wheel and a stool.

"Now," he said, "now my dear, you will be shut in here tomorrow with some food and some flax. And, if you haven't spun five skeins by nightfall, your head will come off!"

And away he went, about his business.

Well, she was very frightened indeed. She had always been a useless girl, so much so that she did not even know how to spin. What was she to do tomorrow, with nobody to help her? She sat down on a stool in the kitchen, and how she cried!

Then she suddenly heard a hard kind of knocking on the door. She jumped up and opened it; and what did she see but a small black thing with a long tail, who looked at her strangely, and said:

"What are you a-crying for?"

"What's that to you?" she asked.

"Never you mind" he said, "but tell me what you're crying for."

"It won't do me any good if I do" said she.

"You don't know that" said the visitor, and its tail twirled around.

"Well," she said, "It won't do any harm, even if it does no good," and she told him all about the pies and the skeins and everything.

"This is what I'll do," said the little black thing: "I'll come to your window in the morning and take the flax—and bring it spun at night."

"What would you charge?" she asked.

It looked out of the corner of its eye and said:

"I'll give you three chances every night to guess my name. And, if you haven't guessed it before the month is up, you shall be mine!"

Well, she thought, she'd be sure to guess the name before the month was up.

"All right," said she, and how the thing twisted its tail with delight!

Well, the next day, her husband took her into the room, and there was the flax and the day's food.

"Now, there's the flax," said he, "and if you haven't spun it by night, off goes your head!"

And then he went out and locked the door.

He had hardly gone when there was a knocking on the window. She leapt up and opened it, and there—sure enough—was the little old thing sitting on the ledge.

"Where's the flax?" he said.

"Here it is" she said.

And she handed it over.

Well, when evening came, there was a rapping on the window again. She got up and opened it, and there was the little old thing, with five skeins of flax on his arm.

"Here it is," he said, and he gave it to her.

"Now, what's my name?"

"Is it Bill?" she asked.

"No, it is not" he said.

And he twirled his tail.

"Is it Ned?"

"No it is not."

And he twirled his tail.

"Well, is it Mark?"

"No, it is not." And he twirled his tail harder.

And away he flew.

Well, when her husband came in, there were the five skeins, ready for him.

"I see I shan't have to kill you tonight, my dear" said he. "You'll have your food and flax in the morning"—and away he went.

After that, the flax and food were brought, and every day the little black imp came, morning and evening. And all day the maiden was sitting thinking of names to say when he came at night.

But she never lit on the right one. And, as the days approached the end of the month, the imp began to look really malicious, and twirled his tail faster every time she made a guess.

At last it came to the last day but one. The imp came that night with the usual five skeins and said:

"What, haven't you got my name yet?"

"Is it Nicodemus?" she asked.

"No, it is not" he said.

"Is it Samuel?" she wanted to know.

"No, it is not" said he.

"Well, then is it Methuselah?"

"No, it is not that, either," he said; and he looked at her like a fiery coal, and said:

"Woman, there's only tomorrow night—then you'll be mine!" And away he flew.

Well, she really did feel horrid. But then she heard the King coming along the corridor. In he came, and when he saw the five Skeins, he said:

"Well, my dear, I can see that you'll have your skeins tomorrow night as well and—as I reckon I shan't have to kill you, I'll have supper in here tonight."

So supper was brought, and another stool for him, and down the two sat to eat.

Well, the King had not had more than about a mouthful, when he stopped and began to laugh.

"What is it?" she asked.

"Because," he said, "I was out hunting today, and I got to a place in the wood which I hadn't seen before. And there was an old chalk pit, and a sort of humming sound. So I got off my horse and went very quietly to the pit, and I looked down.

"Well, what should be there, but the funniest little black thing you should ever see. And what was it doing, but spinning wonderfully fast with a little spinning-wheel and twirling its tail. And as it spun, it sang:

'Nimmy nimmy not,
My name's Tom Tit Tot'."

Well, when the maiden heard this, she felt as if she could have jumped out of her skin for joy—but she didn't say a word.

Next day, the little thing looked really nasty when he came for the flax. And, when night fell, the girl heard that tapping again on the window-pane. She opened the window, and the imp came right in on the ledge. It was grinning from ear to ear, and how its tail was twirling!

"What's my name?" it asked, as it gave her the skeins.

"Is it Solomon?" she said, pretending to be afraid.

"No, it is not!" As he said that he came further into the room.

"Well, is it Zebedee?" she said.

"No, it is not!" And then it laughed and twirled its tail until you could hardly see it.

"Take time, woman!" it said, "for there is one more guess and you're mine!" And it stretched out its black hands at her.

She backed away a step or two, and she looked at it, and then she laughed out loud, and she said, pointing a finger at it:

"Nimmy nimmy not,
Your name's Tom Tit Tot."

When he heard that, he gave an awful shriek, and flew into the dark, and she never saw him, ever again.

∎

A famous Scottish ballad, "The Barring of the Door" is essentially the same tale as that of the Silent Couple, which is one of the world's most widely distributed folktales. It is found in Turkey and Sri Lanka, in Venice and Kashmir, in Arabia and Sicily, and quite possibly in many other places as well. If it came from the East, its route to Scotland is mysterious. If it originates in the West, how it found itself in several distinct Asian cultures is no less intriguing. This is the Arabian version.

The Silent Couple

Once upon a time there was a newly-married couple; still dressed in their wedding finery, they relaxed in their new home when the last of the guests at their feast had left.

"Dear husband", said the young lady, "do go and close the door to the street, which has been left open."

"*Me* shut it?" said the groom, "a bridegroom in this splendid costume, with a priceless robe and a dagger studded with jewels? How could I be expected to do such a thing? You must be out of your mind. Go and shut it yourself."

"So!" shouted the bride, "you expect me to be your slave: a gentle, beautiful creature like me, wearing a dress of finest silk—that I should get up on my wedding day and close a door which looks onto the public street? Impossible."

They were both silent for a moment or two, and the lady suggested that they should make the problem the subject of a forfeit. Whoever spoke first, they agreed, should be the one to shut the door.

There were two sofas in the room, and the pair settled themselves, face to face, one on each, sitting mutely looking at one another.

They had been in this posture for two or three hours when a party of thieves came by and noticed that the door was open. The robbers crept into the silent house, which seemed so deserted, and began to load themselves with every portable object of any value which they could find.

The bridal couple heard them come in, but each thought that the other should attend to the matter. Neither of them spoke or moved as the burglars went from room to room, until at length they entered the sitting room and at first failed to notice the utterly motionless couple.

Still the pair sat there, while the thieves collected all the valuables, and even rolled up the carpets under them. Mistaking the idiot and his stubborn wife for wax dummies, they stripped them of their personal jewels—and still the couple said nothing at all.

The thieves made off, and the bride and her groom sat on their sofas throughout the night. Neither would give up.

When daylight came, a policeman on his beat saw the open street door and walked into the house. Going from room to room he finally came upon the pair and asked them what was happening. Neither man nor wife deigned to reply.

The policeman called massive reinforcements and the swarming custodians of the law became more and more enraged at the total silence, which to them seemed obviously a calculated affront.

The officer in charge at last lost his temper and called out to one of his men: "Give that man a blow or two, and get some sense out of him!"

At this the wife could not restrain herself: "Please, kind officers" she cried, "do not strike him—he is my husband!"

"I won!" shouted the fool immediately, "so *you* have to shut the door!" ∎

Childe Rowland

*How can an ancient Inca story have been current in Shakespeare's time as an English folk tale, mentioned in **King Lear**? A Guatemalan Indian provided the traditional materials for the **Popul Vuh**, for the Spanish conquerors, containing this story. It was described by Lewis Spence as 'the only native American work that has come down to us from pre-Columbian times'. It features a game with a ball and the penetration of the underground headquarters of magically-endowed people who capture mortals by two young heirs to a gracious lady, for the purpose of a battle. An adviser warns of the essential taboos to be respected, and the evil ones are vanquished. Each one of these ingredients and incidents, in the same order and down to the detail of the ball-game being the cause of the trouble, is preserved in the Scottish version of **Childe Rowland,** recited by a tailor in 1770 and preserved in the version given here by the folklorist Joseph Jacobs. As if this were not enough, Childe Rowland also has illustrious literary relationships. In addition to Shakespeare's reference, Browning wrote a poem with this title; and the plot of the story is almost identical with that of Milton's **Comus.** Jacobs noted the affinity with **Comus** in 1899, and averred that the resemblance could hardly be a coincidence. He would perhaps have been equally surprised if he had noted the South American version. It was published by Spence in 1913, and although Jacobs died in 1916, apparently he did not see it. When I mentioned the resemblance to Lewis Spence in the nineteen-forties, he had not seen Jacobs' version either.*

Childe Rowland and his brothers twain
　　Were playing at the ball,
And there was their sister Burd Ellen
　　In the midst, among them all.

Childe Rowland kicked it with his foot
　　And caught it with his knee;
At last he plunged among them all
　　O'er the church he made it flee.

Burd Ellen round about the aisle
　　To seek the ball is gone
But long they waited, and longer still,
　　And she came not back again.

They sought her east, they sought her west,
　　They sought her up and down,
And woe were the hearts of those brethren,
　　For she was not to be found.

So at last her elder brother went to the Warlock Merlin, the magician, told him all, and asked him if he knew where Burd Ellen was. "The fair Burd Ellen," said the Warlock Merlin, "must have been carried off by the fairies, because she went round the church 'widershins'—the opposite way to the sun. She is now in the Dark Tower of the King of Elfland; it would take the boldest knight in Christendom to bring her back."

"If it is possible to bring her back," said her brother, "I'll do it, or perish in the attempt."

"Possible it is," said the Warlock Merlin,"but woe to the man, or mother's son that attempts it, if he is not well taught beforehand what he is to do."

The eldest brother of Burd Ellen was not to be put off by any fear of danger, from attempting to get her back, so he begged the Warlock Merlin to tell him what he should do, and what he should not do, in going to seek his sister. And after he had been taught, and had repeated his lesson, he set out for Elfland.

But long they waited, and longer still,
    With doubt and muckle pain,
But woe were the hearts of his brethren,
    For he came not back again.

Then the second brother got tired of waiting, and he went to the Warlock Merlin and asked him the same as his brother. So he set out to find Burd Ellen.

But long they waited, and longer still,
    With muckle doubt and pain,
And woe were his mother's and brother's heart,
    For he came not back again.

And when they had waited and waited a good long time, Childe Rowland, the youngest of Burd Ellen's brothers, wished to go, and went to his mother, the good Queen, to ask her to let him go. But she would not at first, for he was the last and dearest of her children; and if he were lost, all would be lost. But he begged, and he begged, till at last the good Queen let him go; and gave him his father's good brand [sword] that never struck in vain, and as she girt it round his waist, she said the spell that would give it victory.

So Childe Rowland said good-bye to the good Queen, his mother, and went to the cave of the Warlock Merlin. "Once more, and but once more," he said to the Warlock, "tell how man or mother's son may rescue Burd Ellen and her brothers twain."

"Well, my son," said the Warlock Merlin, "there are but two things, simple they may seem, but hard they are to do. One thing to do, and one thing not to do. And the thing you do is this: after you have entered the land of Fairy, whoever speaks to you, till you meet the Burd Ellen, you must out with your father's brand and off with their head. And what you've not to do is this: bite no bit, and drink no drop, however hungry or thirsty you be; drink a drop, or bite a bit, while in Elfland you be, and never will you see Middle Earth again."

So Childe Rowland said the two things over and over again, till he knew them by heart, and he thanked the Warlock Merlin and went on his way. And he went along, and along, and still further along, till he came to the horse-herd of the King of Elfland feeding his horses. These he knew by their fiery eyes, and knew that he was at last in the land of the Fairy. "Can'st thou tell me," said Childe Rowland to the horse-herd, "where the King of Elfland's Dark Tower is?" "I cannot tell thee," said the horse-herd, "but go on a little further and thou wilt come to the cow-herd, and he, maybe, can tell thee."

Then, without a word more, Childe Rowland drew the good brand that never struck in vain, and off went the horse-herd's head, and Childe Rowland went on further, till he came to the cow-herd, and asked him the same question. "I can't tell thee," said he, "but go on a little further, and thou wilt come to the hen-wife, and she is sure to know." Then Childe Rowland out with his good brand, that never struck in vain, and off went the cow-herd's head. And he went on a little further, till he came to an old woman in a grey cloak, and he asked her if she knew where the Dark Tower of the King of Elfland was. "Go on a little further," said the hen-wife, "till you come to a round green hill, surrounded with terrace-rings, from the bottom to the top—go round it three times 'widershins', and each time say:

    'Open, door! open, door!
    And let me come in.'

and the third time the door will open, and you may go in." And Childe Rowland was just going on, when he remembered what he had to do; so he out with the good brand, that never struck in vain, and off went the hen-wife's head.

Then he went on, and on, till he came to the round green hill with the terrace-rings from top to bottom, and he went round it three times, 'widershins', saying each time:

    "Open, door, open!
    And let me come in."

And the third time the door did open, and he went in, and it closed with a click, and Childe Rowland was left in the gloom.

It was not exactly dark, but a kind of twilight or gloaming. There were neither windows nor candles and he could not make out where the twilight came from, if not through the walls and roof. These were rough arches made of a transparent rock, incrusted with sheepsilver and rockspar, and other bright stones. But though it was rock, the air was quite warm, as it always is in Elfland. So he went through this passage till at last he came to two wide and high folding doors which stood ajar. And when he opened them, there he saw a most wonderful and gracious sight. A large and spacious hall, so large it seemed to be as long, and as broad, as the green hill itself. The roof was supported by fine pillars, so large and lofty that the pillars of a cathedral were as nothing to them. They were all of gold and silver, with fretted work, and between them and around them wreaths of flowers, composed of diamonds and emeralds, and all manner of precious stones. And the very key-stones of the arches had for ornaments clusters of diamonds and rubies, and pearls, and other precious stones. And all these arches met in the middle of the roof, and just there, hung by a golden chain, an immense lamp made out of one big pearl hollowed out and quite transparent. And in the middle of this was a big, huge carbuncle gem, which kept spinning round and round, and this was what gave light by its rays to the whole hall, which seemed as if the setting sun was shining on it.

The hall was furnished in a manner equally grand, and at one end of it was a glorious couch of velvet, silk and gold, and there sat Burd Ellen, combing her golden hair with a silver comb. And when she saw Childe Rowland, she stood up and said:

> "God pity ye, poor luckless fool,
>   What have ye here to do?
>
> Hear ye this, my youngest brother,
>   Why didn't ye bide at home?
> Had you a hundred thousand lives
>   Ye couldn't spare any a one.
>
> But sit ye down; but woe, O, woe,
>   That ever ye were born,
> For come the King of Elfland in,
>   Your fortune is forlorn."

Then they sat down together, and Childe Rowland told her all that he had done, and she told him how their two brothers had reached the Dark Tower, but had been enchanted by the King of Elfland; and lay there entombed as if dead. And then after they had talked a little longer Childe Rowland began to feel hungry from his long travels, and told his sister Burd Ellen how hungry he was and asked for some food, forgetting all about the Warlock Merlin's warning.

Burd Ellen looked at Childe Rowland sadly, and shook her head, but she was under a spell, and could not warn him. So she rose up, and went out, and soon brought back a golden basin full of bread and milk. Childe Rowland was just going to raise it to his lips, when he looked at his sister and remembered why he had come all that way. So he dashed the bowl to the ground, and said: "Not a sup will I swallow, nor a bit will I bite, till Burd Ellen is set free."

Just at that moment they heard the noise of someone approaching, and a loud voice was heard saying:

> "Fee, fi, fo, fum,
> I smell the blood of a Christian man,
> Be he dead, be he living, with my brand,
> I'll dash his brains from his brain-pan."

And then the folding doors of the hall were burst open, and the King of Elfland rushed in.

"Strike then, Bogie [goblin], if you darest," shouted out Childe Rowland, and rushed to meet him with his good brand that never yet did fail. They fought, and they fought, and they fought, till Childe Rowland beat the King of Elfland down on his knees, and caused him to yield and beg for mercy. "I grant thee mercy", said Childe Rowland; "release my sister from thy spells and raise my brothers to life, and let us all go free, and thou shalt be spared." "I agree" said the Elfin King, and rising up he went to a chest from which he took a phial filled with a blood-red liquor. With this he anointed the ears, eyelids, nostrils, lips, and finger-tips of the two brothers, and they sprang at once into life, and declared that their souls had been away, but had now returned. The Elfin King then said some words to Burd Ellen, and she was disenchanted, and they all four passed out of the hall, through the long passage, and turned their back on the Dark Tower, never to return again. So they reached home and the good Queen their mother, and Burd Ellen never went round a church "widershins" again. ∎

The Tale of Mushkil Gusha

Traditional tales were felt, in the 18th century, to be "an affront to the rational mind" as the illustrious Iona and Peter Opie remind us in **The Classic Fairy Tales,** *(London: Oxford University Press, 1974). Nowadays, of course, the work of psychologists makes people more open-minded, sometimes even to the point of agreeing with the famous folklorist Joseph Campbell that the folk-tale is "the primer of the picture-language of the soul."*

Never having been through a phase of believing in the complete sovereignty of the intellect at the expense of other sides of humanity, people in the Middle East have for long regarded certain traditional stories as having a real function, and effect on the mind and on the community.

Such a tale is that which is sometimes called The Tale of Mushkil Gusha—the Remover of All Difficulties. It is known in both major and minor communities in India and Pakistan, in Central Asia and Iran, in the Near East and even in Africa and the Yemens. It is believed that if this story is recited on Thursday nights, it will in some inexplicable way help the work of the mysterious Mushkil Gusha, Friend of Man.

Once upon a time, not a thousand miles from here, there lived a poor old wood-cutter, who was a widower, and his little daughter. Every day he used to go into the mountains to cut firewood, which he brought home and tied into bundles. Then he used to have breakfast and walk into the nearest town, where he would sell his wood and rest for a time before returning home.

One day, when he reached home very late, the girl said to him, "Father, I sometimes wish that we could have some nicer food, and more and different kinds of things to eat."

"Very well, my child," said the old man; "tomorrow I shall get up much earlier than I usually do. I shall go further into the mountains where there is more wood, and I shall bring back a much larger quantity than usual. I will get home earlier and I will be able to bundle the wood sooner, and I will go into town and sell it so that we can have more money and I shall bring you back all kinds of nice things to eat."

The next morning the wood-cutter rose before dawn and went into the mountains. He worked very hard cutting wood and trimming it and made it into a huge bundle which he carried on his back to his little house.

When he got home, it was still very early. He put his load of wood down, and knocked on the door, saying, "Daughter, Daughter, open the door, for I am hungry and thirsty and I need a meal before I go to market."

But the door was locked. The wood-cutter was so tired that he lay down and was soon fast asleep beside his bundle. The little girl, having forgotten all about their conversation the night before, was fast asleep in bed. When he woke up a few hours later, the sun was

high. The wood-cutter knocked on the door again and said, "Daughter, Daughter, come quickly; I must have a little food and go to market to sell the wood; for it is already much later than my usual time of starting."

But, having forgotten all about the conversation, the little girl had meanwhile got up, tidied the house, and gone out for a walk. She had locked the door assuming in her forgetfulness that her father was still in the town.

So the wood-cutter thought to himself, "It is now rather late to go into the town, I will therefore return to the mountains and cut another bundle of wood, which I will bring home, and tomorrow I will take a double load to market."

All that day the old man toiled in the mountains cutting wood and shaping the branches. When he got home with the wood on his shoulders, it was evening.

He put down his burden behind the house, knocked on the door and said, "Daughter, Daughter, open the door for I am tired and I have eaten nothing all day. I have a double bundle of wood which I hope to take to market tomorrow. Tonight I must sleep well so that I will be strong."

But there was no answer, for the little girl when she came home had felt very sleepy, and had made a meal for herself and gone to bed. She had been rather worried at first that her father was not home, but she decided that he must have arranged to stay in town overnight.

Once again the wood-cutter, finding that he could not get into the house, tired, hungry, and thirsty, lay down by his bundles of wood and fell fast asleep. He could not keep awake, although he was fearful for what might have happened to the little girl.

Now the wood-cutter, because he was so cold and hungry and tired, woke very, very early the next morning: before it was even light.

He sat up, and looked around, but he could not see anything. And then a strange thing happened. The wood-cutter thought he heard a voice saying: "Hurry, hurry! Leave your wood and come this way. If you need enough, and you *want* little enough, you shall have delicious food."

The wood-cutter stood up and walked in the direction of the voice. And he walked and he walked; but he found nothing.

By now he was colder and hungrier and more tired than ever, and he was lost. He had been full of hope, but that did not seem to have helped him. Now he felt sad, and he wanted to cry. But he realised that crying would not help him either, so he lay down and fell asleep.

Quite soon he woke up again. It was too cold, and he was too hungry, to sleep. So he decided to tell himself, as if in a story, everything that had happened to him since his little daughter had first said that she wanted a different kind of food.

As soon as he had finished his story, he thought he heard another voice, saying, somewhere above him, out of the dawn, "Old man, what are you doing sitting there?"

"I am telling myself my own story," said the wood-cutter.

"And what is that?" said the voice.

The old man repeated his tale. "Very well," said the voice. And then it told the old wood-cutter to close his eyes and to mount as it were, a step. "But I do not see any step," said the old man. "Never mind, but do as I say," said the voice.

The old man did as he was told. As soon as he had closed his eyes, he found that he was standing up and as he raised his right foot he felt that there was something like a step under it. He started to ascend what seemed to be a staircase. Suddenly the whole flight of steps started to move, very fast, and the voice said, "Do not open your eyes until I tell you to do so."

In a very short time, the voice told the old man to open his eyes. When he did he found that he was in a place which looked rather like a desert, with the sun beating down on him. He was surrounded by masses and masses of pebbles; pebbles of all colours: red, green, blue, and white. But he seemed to be alone. He looked all around him, and could not see anyone, but the voice started to speak again.

"Take up as many of these stones as you can," said the voice, "Then close your eyes, and walk down the steps once more."

The wood-cutter did as he was told, and he found himself, when he opened his eyes again at the voice's bidding, standing before the door of his own house.

He knocked at the door and his little daughter answered it. She asked him where he had been, and he told her, although she could hardly understand what he was saying, it all sounded so confusing.

They went into the house, and the little girl and her father shared the last food which they had, which was a handful of dried dates.

When they had finished, the old man thought that he heard a voice speaking to him again, a voice just like the other one which had told him to climb the stairs.

132

The voice said, "Although you may not know it yet, you have been saved by Mushkil Gusha. Remember that Mushkil Gusha is always here. Make sure that every Thursday night you eat some dates and give some to any needy person, and tell the story of Mushkil Gusha. Or give a gift in the name of Mushkil Gusha to someone who will help the needy. Make sure that the story of Mushkil Gusha is never, never forgotten. If you do this, and if this is done by those to whom you tell the story, the people who are in real need will always find their way."

The wood-cutter put all the stones which he had brought back from the desert in a corner of his little house. They looked very much like ordinary stones, and he did not know what to do with them.

The next day he took his two enormous bundles of wood to market, and sold them easily for a high price. When he got home he took his daughter all sorts of delicious kinds of food, which she had never tasted before. And when they had eaten it, the old wood-cutter said: "Now I am going to tell you the whole story of Mushkil Gusha. Mushkil Gusha is 'the remover of all difficulties'. Our difficulties have been removed through Mushkil Gusha and we must always remember it."

For nearly a week after that the old man carried on as usual. He went into the mountains, brought back wood, had a meal, took the wood to market and sold it. He always found a buyer without difficulty.

Now the next Thursday came, and, as is the way of men, the wood-cutter forgot to repeat the tale of Mushkil Gusha.

Late that evening, in the house of the wood-cutter's neighbours, the fire had gone out. The neighbours had nothing with which to re-light the fire, and they went to the house of the wood-cutter. They said, "Neighbour, neighbour, please give us a light from those wonderful lamps of yours which we see shining through the window."

"What lamps?" said the wood-cutter.

"Come outside," said the neighbours, "and see what we mean."

So the wood-cutter went outside and then he saw, sure enough, all kinds of brilliant lights shining through the window from the inside.

He went back to the house, and saw that the light was streaming from the pile of pebbles which he had put in the corner. But the rays of light were cold, and it was not possible to use them to light a fire. So he went out to the neighbours and said, "Neighbours, I am

133

sorry, I have no fire." And he banged the door in their faces. They were annoyed and confused, and went back to their house, muttering. They leave our story here.

The wood-cutter and his daughter quickly covered up the brilliant lights with every piece of cloth they could find, for fear that anyone would see what a treasure they had. The next morning, when they uncovered the stones, they discovered that they were precious, luminous gems.

They took the jewels, one by one, to neighbouring towns, where they sold them for a huge price. Now the wood-cutter decided to build for himself and for his daughter a wonderful palace. They chose a site just opposite the castle of the King of their country. In a very short time a marvellous building had come into being.

Now that particular King had a beautiful daughter, and one day when she got up in the morning, she saw a sort of fairy-tale castle just opposite her father's and she was amazed. She asked her servants, "Who has built this castle? What right have these people to do such a thing so near to our home?"

The servants went away and made enquiries and they came back and told the story, as far as they could collect it, to the Princess.

The Princess called for the little daughter of the wood-cutter, for she was very angry with her, but when the two girls met and talked they soon became fast friends. They started to meet every day and went to swim and play in the stream which had been made for the Princess by her father. A few days after they first met, the Princess took off a beautiful and valuable necklace and hung it up on a tree just beside the stream. She forgot to take it down when they came out of the water, and when she got home she thought it must have been lost.

The Princess thought a little and then decided that the daughter of the wood-cutter had stolen her necklace. So she told her father, and he had the wood-cutter arrested; he confiscated the castle and declared forfeit everything that the wood-cutter had. The old man was thrown into prison, and the daughter was put into an orphanage.

As was the custom in that country, after a period of time the wood-cutter was taken from the dungeon and put in the public square, chained to a post, with a sign around his neck. On the sign was written: "This is what happens to those who steal from Kings".

At first people gathered around him, and jeered

and threw things at him. He was most unhappy.

But quite soon, as is the way of men, everyone became used to the sight of the old man sitting there by his post, and took very little notice of him. Sometimes people threw him scraps of food, sometimes they did not.

One day he overheard somebody saying that it was Thursday afternoon. Suddenly, the thought came into his mind that it would soon be the evening of Mushkil Gusha, the remover of all difficulties, and that he had forgotten to commemorate him for so many days. No sooner had this thought come into his head, than a charitable man, passing by, threw him a tiny coin. The wood-cutter called out: "Generous friend, you have given me money, which is of no use to me. If, however, your kindness could extend to buying one or two dates and coming and sitting and eating them with me, I would be eternally grateful to you."

The other man went and bought a few dates. And they sat and ate them together. When they had finished, the wood-cutter told the other man the story of Mushkil Gusha. "I think you must be mad," said the generous man. But he was a kindly person who himself had many difficulties. When he arrived home after this incident, he found that all his problems had disappeared. And that made him start to think a great deal about Mushkil Gusha. But he leaves our story here.

The very next morning the Princess went back to her bathing-place. As she was about to go into the water, she saw what looked like her necklace down at the bottom of the stream. As she was going to dive in to try to get it back, she happened to sneeze. Her head went up, and she saw that what she had thought was the necklace was only its reflection in the water. It was hanging on the bough of the tree where she had left it such a long time before. Taking the necklace down, the Princess ran excitedly to her father and told him what had happened. The King gave orders for the wood-cutter to be released and given a public apology. The little girl was brought back from the orphanage, and everyone lived happily ever after.

These are some of the incidents in the story of Mushkil Gusha. It is a very long tale and it is never ended. It has many forms. Some of them are even not called the story of Mushkil Gusha at all, so people do not recognise it. But it is because of Mushkil Gusha that his story, in whatever form, is remembered by somebody, somewhere in the world, day and night, wherever there are people. As his story had always been recited, so it will always continue to be told. ∎

'A Band of Pilgrims on the way to Mecca', Persian, dated 1502 A.D.

The Food of Paradise

What does a folk-tale really mean? Scholars and others take them to pieces; ideologues look for those which will support their beliefs about tales; literary people often use them as the basis for their own works. Folk-tales are recited, in many cultures, by professional or at any rate highly expert specialists: and these are sometimes only superannuated and toothless grandmothers. In spite of the enormous amount of work done on the collection, analysis and study of tales, how many collectors have troubled themselves to ask the reciters themselves, the experts, what the tale is supposed to mean, or what effect it is intended to have? I asked a Central Asian bard this question, for he had contributed several hundred tales to an 'ethnographic mission'. He said: "This is one thing I was never asked by the learned men and women."

His explanation of the function of this tale, 'The Food of Paradise' is that it will confirm the bias of those who, for example, believe that humility is really living off the by-products of a total system. It will also, he continued, encourage those who think that even those things which seem wonderful (the sweetmeat) are as nothing, seen from a wider perspective. "But," he continued, "for those who are ready to understand the truth: they will find this tale valuable to take them beyond such simple confirmations."

On the close of my visit to the Holy City Mecca, I joined the caravan of Sheikh Amru, who apart from being a great theological teacher, was a famous narrator of ancient tales. The occasion was when he asked me as to what calling I was going to choose after my wanderings. Somewhat humorously I said that I was going to do nothing for my living since Allah has promised to feed the Faithful.

"Listen my son," said the Sheikh, as he reclined against his camel's saddle; and then I knew that an ancient tale was to be retailed out to us. This is what he said:

In the school founded by the Caliph for the study of divine things sat the devout Mullah Ibrahim, his hands folded in his lap, in an attitude of meditation. Ibrahim taught students from all the countries of Islam, but the work was thankless and ill-paid. And as he sat there he thought on his state for the first time in many years.

"Why is it," he said to himself, "that a man so holy as I am must toil so hard to instruct a pack of blockheads, when others who have merited nothing through piety or attention to the Commands of Allah fare sumptuously every day and neither toil nor spin? O, Compassionate One, is not this thing unjust? Whereof should Thy servant be burdened, like an ass in the market-place, which carries two panniers, both filled to the top, and stumbles at every blow of the driver's stick?"

And as he considered, Ibrahim the Wise, as men called him, brought to mind that verse in the Holy Literature in which it says: "Allah will not let any one

135

starve." And taking deeper counsel with himself, he said: "May it not be that those whom I have blamed for their sloth and inactivity are, after all, the better Moslems, that they have greater faith than I? For, perusing this passage, they may have said to themselves: "I will cast myself upon the mercy of Allah, which in this text is surely extended to all men. Allah in his bounty will surely feed and maintain me." Why then toil and strive as the faithless do? It is those who have faith that are the elect."

At that moment a great pasha halted before the gates of the seminary, in his piety alighting from his palanquin to give alms to a beggar, as all good Moslems do. And as Ibrahim watched him through the lattice, he thought: "Does not the condition of the beggar as well as that of this pasha prove the justice of the text upon which I have been meditating? Neither starves, but the wealthier man is assuredly the more devout, for he is the giver and not the receiver, and for this very purpose has been blest with the goods of this world. Why do I hesitate, wretched man that I am? Shall I not, as the Book ordains, cast myself on the bounty of Allah and free myself forever from the intolerable burden of instructing fools in a wisdom they can never understand?"

So saying, Ibrahim the Sage arose from his place in the College of the Caliph, and walked out of the City of Baghdad where he had dwelt for many years. It was evening, and betaking himself to the banks of the river, he selected a dry and shady spot beneath a spreading cypress tree, and awaiting the bounty of Allah, fell fast asleep in the certainty that the Lord of all Compassion would not fail him.

When he awoke, it was early morning, and a divine hush lay upon everything. Ibrahim lazily speculated as to the manner in which he would be sustained. Would the birds of the air bring him sustenance, would the fishes from the stream leap ashore, offering themselves for the assuagement of his growing hunger? In what way did those who merited the help of Allah first receive it, if not in some miraculous manner? True, the wealthy were bequeathed riches by their parents. But there must be a beginning. A pasha might sail down the river in his barge and supply his wants out of golden dishes and silver cups.

But morning blossomed into day, and day into night, and still the miracle remained unaccomplished. More than one pasha glided past him in his gilded barge, but these made only the customary salutations and gave no other sign. On the road above, pilgrims and travellers passed, but without taking the least notice of him. Hunger gnawed at his vitals, and he thought with envy of the millet porridge with goats' milk which the mullahs would now be enjoying at the seminary. Still was he trustful, and, as he made the customary ablutions in the river, his faith had abated not one jot.

Again he slept, and once more day dawned in scarlet and silver beauty. By this time he felt so faint as scarcely to be able to stand. The hours crept slowly onward, yet no sign came that his hunger was to be satisfied.

At last, as midday approached with its stifling heat, something floating on the surface of the water caught his eye. It seemed like a mass of leaves wrapped up with fibre; and, wading into the river, he succeeded in catching it. Back he splashed with his prize to the bank, and sitting down on the sward, he opened the packet. It contained a quantity of the most delicious-looking halwa, that famous marzipan, of whose making only Baghdad knows the secret, a sweetmeat composed of sugar mingled with paste of almonds and attar of roses and other delicate and savoury essences.

After gorging himself with the delightful fare, Ibrahim the Wise drank deeply from the river, and lolled on the grass, sure that his prayer had been answered, and that he would never have to toil more. There was sufficient of the ambrosial food to serve for three meals a day; and on each day, after the hour of midday prayer, a similar packet of halwa came floating down the stream as though placed there by the hands of angels.

"Surely," said the Mullah, "the promises of Allah are true, and the man who trusts in Him will not be deceived. Truly I did well to leave the seminary, where, day-in, day-out, I had perforce to cram divine knowledge into the heads of idiots incapable of repeating a verse correctly even at the fifteenth attempt."

Months passed, and Ibrahim continued to receive the food that Allah had promised with unfailing regularity. Then, quite naturally, he began to speculate whence it came. If he could find the spot where it was deposited on the surface of the stream, surely he must witness a miracle, and as he had never done so, he felt greatly desirous of attaining the merit such a consummation would undoubtedly add to his repute as a holy man.

So one morning, after eating the last of the halwa he had received the preceding day, he girded up his loins, and taking his staff, began slowly to walk

upstream.

"Now," said he, "if what I suppose be true, I will today receive my luscious food at an earlier hour than usual, as I shall be nearer the place where it is placed on the water and indeed on each day I shall receive at an even earlier hour, until at last I come to the spot where some divine seraph, sent by Allah from Paradise, drops the savoury food of heaven upon the stream in justification of my trust in the most Merciful."

For some days Ibrahim walked up-stream, keeping carefully to the bank of the river and fixing his eyes on its surface in case he should fail to discern the packet of halwa. Every day, at an even earlier hour, it floated regularly past him, carried by the current so near to the shore that he could easily wade out and secure it. At nights he slept beneath a convenient tree, and as men perceived him to be a Mullah and a holy man, no one thought of molesting him.

It was on the fourth day of his journey that he observed the river had widened. In a large island in the midst of the stream rose a fair castle. The island comprised a princely domain of noble meadow-land and rich gardens, crossed and interlaced by the silver of narrow streams, and was backed by the blue and jagged peaks of great mountains. The castle itself was built of marble white as sculptured ice, and its green and shady lawns sloped down to a silent and extensive shore of golden sand.

And when night descended, this wondrous region was illuminated by the romance of moonlight into an almost unearthly radiance; so that Ibrahim, in all his piety, was forced to compare it with Paradise itself. The white castle on its dark rocks seemed like day pedestalled upon night, and from the sea-green of the shadow of myrtles rose the peaks of pavilions, whence came the sound of guitars and lutes and voices more ravishingly sweet than Ibrahim, the son of the seminary, had ever believed earth could hold.

And as Ibrahim gazed spellbound at the wondrous spectacle and drank in the sounds of ecstasy which arose from the garden, wondering whether he were not already dead and in the purlieus of Heaven, a harsh voice hailed him at his very elbow, asking him what he was doing there. He turned swiftly to see standing beside him an ancient man in the garb of a hermit, with long matted hair and tangled beard.

"Salaam, good father," he said, much relieved, for like all men of peace, he feared violence. "The peace of Allah, the Merciful, the Compassionate, be upon you."

"And upon you, my son," replied the anchorite. "But what do you do here at this hour of the night, when all such as you should be asleep?"

"Like yourself, I am a holy man," replied Ibrahim, with unction, "but I travel on a quest the nature of which I may not divulge to any. Passing this spot, I was attracted by the unusual appearance of yonder castle and its surroundings, and would learn its history, if that is known to you."

"It is, though in part only," rejoined the hermit, "for I have dwelt many years in this neighbourhood, but have little converse with men. Know, then, that the place you behold is called the Silver Castle. It was built by a Pasha now dead, who was greatly enamoured of a certain Princess, whose father refused him her hand in marriage. But, not to be gainsaid, so fierce and unruly a thing is love in some men, he built this strength in the midst of the river as you see, and placed upon it so many dark and terrible spells of magic that none could cross to or from it without his sanction. Then, abducting the Princess, he espoused her and placed her in yonder tower. The King, her father, came with an army to besiege the place, but so potent were the necromancies the Pasha had surrounded it with that he was compelled to raise the siege and leave his daughter in the hands of his enemy."

"You amaze me," cried Ibrahim. "And does this Princess remain here still?"

"No, brother," replied the Hermit, "like her lord she has passed away, but they have left behind them a daughter who governs the castle, a lady of surpassing beauty, who spends her days in pleasure and in spending the wealth her father bequeathed her. But she has but one sorrow, and that is that none can dissolve the spells woven by her father the Pasha, so that no one may either gain admittance to the castle or leave it. Her companions are therefore either the very aged or those born on the island and no other, which, for a young and beautiful woman, must be wearisome. But you will pardon me, brother, I am going on a pilgrimage to a certain shrine in Baghdad, where I betake myself once a year to acquire merit. Meanwhile if you choose to rest, you may dwell in my humble cell yonder until I return in seven days' time."

Ibrahim gladly accepted the Hermit's offer, and when he had gone, sat down to ponder over the tale he had told him. Now, among other wisdoms, he had acquired during his years of study a deep knowledge of the magical art, and he bethought him that it might be given to him to rid the castle and the inhabitants of the spells which held them prisoner on the island.

But in the midst of his thoughts he fell asleep, and did not waken until the sun was high in the heavens. Then he made his ablutions, and betook himself to the bank of the river, where he sat and watched the surface of the water for a sign of the appearance of the delicious food he received daily.

And as he watched, he beheld a curious thing. Some three hours before midday, a very beautiful woman appeared on the marble battlements which overhung the river. So fair was she that the Mullah gasped with surprise at the radiance of her beauty, which was that of the houris of Paradise. For her hair was as golden wire which is drawn thin by the cunning of the goldsmith, her eyes were yellow, and bright as topazes found on Mount Ararat, and the colour of her cheeks was as that of the roses of Isfahan. And as for the flesh of her body, it shone with the lustre of silver, so brightly polished it was.

"Can this be the Princess?" thought Ibrahim, or an angel from heaven? Nay, surely it is she, for this woman, though surpassingly beautiful, is still a mortal."

And as Ibrahim stood beholding her, she raised her arm and cast something into the river. And when she had done so, she withdrew from the battlements and disappeared like a star behind clouds.

The Mullah kept his eyes fixed on what she had cast into the stream, and in a little perceived that it was the very packet of leaves which he was wont to receive daily. Wading into the stream, he secured it, unwrapped it, and found it full of the delicious halwa, as usual.

"Ha," said he, as he devoured the savoury sweetmeat. "So now I know at last that radiant being by whose hands Allah, the Just, the Merciful, has ordained I shall be fed daily. Truly, the Compassionate must have put it into the heart of this divine princess to cast this luscious food on the breast of the stream at the self-same hour each day. And shall I not seek to repay her the distinguished kindness she has done me by freeing her from the spells by which she is encompassed, and which keep her a prisoner, she who should be wed to a Sultan at least and should reign in Baghdad itself?"

And with these grateful thoughts, he sat down to consider by what means the spells which surrounded the castle might be broken. Casting himself into a deep trance, he walked in spirit in the Land of the Jinn, where as a holy man, he could come to no harm. And coming to the house of one of the Jinn, whom he knew and whose name was Adhem, he summoned him and had speech with him.

"Hail, holy man," said Adhem, making low obeisance. "I am your servant. In what way can I serve you?"

Ibrahim acquainted him with the reason for his presence there, at which the Jinn assumed an air of the greatest concern.

"What you ask is indeed hard, most wise Ibrahim," he said doubtfully. "But I will take counsel of my brethren on the matter without delay, and shall let you know the result of our deliberations by a speedy and trusty messenger. No more can I say or do at present."

With this Ibrahim departed and soon after awoke from his trance. He seemed only to have been an hour in the Land of the Jinn, but it must have been five hours or more, for the sun was high in the heavens when he fell asleep, and now the moonlight was sparkling on the waters of the river. And the same exquisite music he had heard before arose from the gardens of the castle, as though from the lips of peris.

And as Ibrahim listened, entranced, a shape scarcely more solid than the moonlight rose slowly out of the river and stood before him in the shadowy likeness of a Jinn. Three times it made obeisance before him, then it spoke.

"Most wise and holy Ibrahim" it said, "my master Adhem, a prince among the people of the Jinn, has sent me to acquaint you with the decision of his counsellors. They proffer you this ring set with the diamond which men call adamant, and in whose shining surface if you will gaze, you shall behold the nature of those spells which keep the Princess and her people prisoners in yonder castle. And, having discovered the nature of those spells, if you summon our people to your aid in such shapes as will dissolve or break them, they will come in such guise as will set the Princess free."

With those words the Jinn vanished into the river whence he had come. And, without delay, Ibrahim took the ring which the spirit had cast on the grass at his feet, and peered into the shining stone it held.

And straightaway he beheld the first spell. Close to the shore of the river arose a mighty bastion as of stone, invisible to mortal eyes, which surrounded the castle from shore to shore. And Ibrahim summoned to him the hosts of the Jinns in the guise of sappers, with picks and hammers, and on this wall they fell mightily in their myriads, so that without sound or clamour of any sort, they reduced it to dust ere a man could count a hundred.

Then Ibrahim looked once more in the surface of the diamond and saw a great web like that of a spider hanging in the air round the castle. And he summoned the hosts of the Jinn in the shape of eagles, which so rent the invisible web with their strong beaks that in almost less time than it takes to tell of it, it fell in fragments into the stream.

Once more Ibrahim gazed into the stone, and this time he saw an army of sightless giants, with spear and scimitar in hand, drawn up in array of war on the shores of the island. And he called the Jinn people to him in the likeness of greater and more powerful giants, who did battle with those on the island. Terrible was the strife, and Ibrahim trembled mightily as he watched it. But soon the Jinn prevailed over the giants of the island, and put them to flight.

The spells which had surrounded the castle were now removed, and as day had dawned, Ibrahim cast about for some means of reaching the castle. No sooner had he wished this than by the power of the Jinn a bridge rose out of the stream by which he was enabled to cross to the island. And when he had done so, he was accosted by an old man who held a bared scimitar in his hand, and who asked him by what means he had been enabled to reach the island, which had so long been under enchantment.

"That I may tell only to your lady, the Princess," said Ibrahim. "Admit me to her presence without delay."

The guard, marvelling, ushered him through the great gate of the castle, and across a spacious court where fountains sang mellifluously. Entering a magnificent hall, whose floor was inlaid with squares of blue and white marble and the walls with lapis lazuli and other rare stones, he gave the Mullah into the keeping of a black eunuch, who requested the holy man to follow him.

Upon a dais sat the incomparable Princess whom Ibrahim had beheld on the battlements, and who daily cast the packet of halwa on the waters of the river. To her the Mullah made obeisance, and, kneeling before her, told his tale.

"And what most wise Ibrahim, do you ask in recompense of your so notable offices on my behalf?" asked the Princess. "Speak, and it shall be granted to you, even to the half of my inheritance."

"Nay, noble lady," exclaimed Ibrahim. "For have I not reason enough to be grateful to your Highness for the delicious food with which you have fed me daily? That halwa which you cast every morning from the battlements, and which has floated down stream, I have eaten with thankfulness. Surely only an angel from Paradise could have put it into your heart to despatch it."

The Princess blushed so deeply that her heightened colour could be seen even beneath her veil.

"Alas, good Mullah!" she cried, wringing her hands. "What is this you tell me? Curses on the day on which I first cast that halwa as you call it, on the waters of the river. Know, that each morning it is my custom to take a bath of milk, after which I anoint and rub my limbs with essence of almonds, sugar and sweet-scented cosmetics. These, then, I remove from my nakedness and, wrapping them in leaves, cast them into the stream."

"Ah, now Princess, I see who has been blind," cried Ibrahim, with a wry countenance. "Allah surely gives food to everyone; but its quality and kind are dictated by what man deserves!" ∎

*Although the first recorded literary appearance of the 'stick-fast' tale is in the Indian **Jataka** tales, traditionally dating from over two thousand years ago, it has only been traced in Western writings to a 15th Century English poem, "The Tale of the Basin."*

To the American Blacks goes the credit of carrying the oral version from Africa to the United States, where it may have arrived centuries before Joel Chandler Harris made it famous in 'The Wonderful Tar-Baby Story' in 1881. The tale is, in one form or another, known all over Europe and the Middle East. It was taken to Canada through French influence, and from there, probably, to three or four eastern American-Indian tribes. These Indians have supplied at least twenty-three variants of the tale.

A. M. Espinosa, reviewing over 150 versions, has plotted the three main routes westwards, affording valuable information about the way in which stories are diffused. By the study of the content of the versions, he found that one route was India-Africa-America; a second was India-Europe-Iberia-America and the third was India-Europe-American colonies.

Although some scholars have believed that many tales are found so widely apart because of polygenesis — the 'stick-fast' concept seems so very odd that it could be used as an argument against the polygenetic hypothesis.

The Lamb with the Golden Fleece

There was once a poor man who had a son, and as the son grew up his father sent him out to look for work. The son travelled about looking for a place, and at last met with a man who arranged to take him as a shepherd.

Next day his master gave him a flute, and sent him out with the sheep to see whether he was fit for his work. The lad never lay down all day, very unlike many lazy fellows. He drove his sheep from place to place and played his flute all day long.

There was among the sheep a lamb with golden fleece, which, whenever it heard the flute, began to dance. The lad became very fond of this lamb, and made up his mind not to ask any wages of his master but only this little lamb.

In the evening he returned home; his master waited at the gate; and, when he saw the sheep all there and all well-fed, he was very pleased, and began to bargain with the lad, who said he wished for nothing but the lamb with the golden fleece.

The farmer was very fond of the lamb himself, and it was with great unwillingness he promised it; but he gave in afterwards when he saw what a good servant the lad made.

The year passed away; the lad received the lamb for his wages, and set off home with it. As they journeyed night set in just as he reached a village, so he went to a farmhouse to ask for a night's lodging.

There was a daughter in the house, who, when she saw the lamb with the golden fleece, determined to steal it. About midnight she arose, and lo! the minute she touched the lamb she stuck hard-and-fast to its

fleece, so that when the lad got up he found her stuck to the lamb. He could not separate them, and as he could not leave his lamb, he took them both.

As he passed the third door from the house where he had spent the night, he took out his flute and began to play. Then the lamb began to dance; and, on its wool, the girl.

Round a corner a woman was putting bread into the oven; looking up she saw the lamb dancing; and, on its wool, the girl. Seizing the baker's shovel in order to frighten the girl, she rushed out and shouted, "Get away home with you, don't make such a fool of yourself."

As the girl continued dancing, the woman called out, "What, won't you obey?" and gave her a blow on her back with the shovel, which at once stuck to the girl, and the woman to the shovel, and the lamb carried them all off.

As they went on they came to the church. Here the lad began to play again, the lamb began to dance, and on the lamb's fleece the girl, and on the girl's back the shovel, and at the end of the shovel the woman.

Just then the priest was coming out from matins, and seeing what was going on began to scold them, and bid them not to be so foolish and to go home. As words were of no avail, he hit the woman a sound whack on her back with his cane, when—to his surprise—the cane stuck to the woman, and he to the end of his cane.

With this nice company, the lad went on; and towards dark reached the royal borough and took lodgings at the end of the town with an old woman.

"What news is there?" said he.

The old woman told him they were in very great sorrow: for the King's daughter was very ill, and no physician could heal her, but if she could but be made to laugh she would be better at once. No one had as yet been able to make her smile; and moreover the King had issued that very day a proclamation stating that whoever made her laugh should have her for his wife, and share the royal power.

The lad with the lamb could scarcely wait till daylight, so anxious was he to try his fortune.

In the morning he presented himself to the King and stated his business and was very graciously received.

The daughter stood in the hall at the front of the house; the lad then began to play the flute, the lamb to dance, on the lamb's fleece the girl, on the girl's back the shovel, at the end of the shovel the woman, on the woman's back the cane, and at the end of the cane the priest.

When the princess saw this sight she burst out laughing, which made the lamb so glad that it shook everything off its back, and the lamb, the girl, the woman, and the priest each danced by themselves for joy.

The King married his daughter to the shepherd, the priest was made court-chaplain; the woman, court bakeress, and the girl, lady-in-waiting to the Princess.

The wedding lasted from one Monday to the other Tuesday, and the whole land was in great joy, and if the strings of the fiddle hadn't broken they would have been dancing yet! ■

In Europe, this tale is known as 'The Presents of the Little Folk', as collected by the Brothers Grimm in Germany; and it most usually features two hunchbacks. It is quite widely distributed in France and Italy, and Turkish and other versions are also known. The following presentation is interesting because it is found in a collection of tales of Japan dated 1664, and believed to date from a much earlier time there. The behaviour of the goblins, with their piping and dancing and tricks, seems very close to that of the Irish little folk. Indeed, a similar fiction is found in Ireland, where it is known as the Legend of Knockgrafton. Supporters of the migration theory have suggested that it dates from times when a Turanian tribe occupied Ireland, even before the Celts; though such a supposition is not essential to explain its diffusion.

The Man with the Wen

Once long ago, in old Japan, there was a man who spent his days trudging up and down the mountains collecting wood. This he used to burn, and to make charcoal, for he was unable to make a living in any other way. This unfortunate fellow thought that the gods were in some way displeased with him, for he had on his left cheek a large and disfiguring swelling: what people call a wen.

He had gone to many doctors, but whatever treatment they had prescribed had never been of any use. In fact, whatever medicine he tried, the wen grew larger and larger day by day. He was so distressed at his appearance, that he shunned other people, and gradually became more and more miserable. His wife tried to be cheerful about the matter and pretended to be unaware of it—the wen and the depression into which her husband was falling—however, in the end it made her hate him.

Their life as charcoal burners was not one of much happiness; and for all the wood he could gather, there seemed to be very little financial gain. The poor woman was seriously thinking of running away, back to her own village, and leaving him and his monstrous wen forever.

One day, with an uncomfortable bundle of wood on his back in an osier basket, the charcoal burner went slowly up the mountain track, fingering his wen with

exploring fingers, positive that it was larger than the day before.

Suddenly, the thunder rolled, the lightning flashed, and heavy slanting rain began to fall.

"O Merciful Heaven," he cried, "so far from home and so little wood, and now this downpour. Where can I shelter?"

Stumbling and falling, half blinded, he was at the end of his strength, when his hands touched the bark of a hollow tree. Gratefully, he eased the basket off his thin shoulders, and covered the top with his wide hat. He saw that there was enough space for him to creep into the hollow of the ancient tree-trunk. There was scarcely a drop of rain on his head and shoulders as he crouched there, and he pulled his thin coat around him, removing his sandals to rest his aching feet. The thunder rolled and it seemed as if the world was about to crack into millions of pieces. But, as quickly as it had begun, the storm ceased. The charcoal burner fingered his wen, and was just about to creep out of the tree when he heard the tramp of feet. The rays of the setting sun played on a group of people who came marching along the mountain path, lighting them with a crimson glow.

"Whoever can they be?" wondered the man, quickly retrieving his sandals and slipping his feet into them. He still remained inside the tree hollow, for the sound

of wild piping came to his ears. With staring eyes he gazed at a multitude of creatures; they were the strangest he had ever seen in his life. There must have been about a hundred of them, a troop of what he now realised were some sort of enchanted beings.

They were all of strange shapes; some were tall, covered with creepers, hung with curious beads. Others were small and shrunken like skeletons with phosphorus eyes, dancing disjointedly, yet with a gay abandon. Some had the mouths of crocodiles, snapping like castenets, keeping in time to the sound of drums almost martial in their rhythms. There were elves with one eye in the middle of their foreheads, dwarves with tremendous feet, all stamping and leaping along the mountain path in perfect time with the shrill piping and drumming. There were pale witches with long black hair, and huge dark giants, dressed in bear-skins. Those who did not have musical instruments had magic wands in their hands, or claws, or paws; but each was leaping and pirouetting in joy and excitement. Some had two horns, some had only one, but each contributed noisily to the general merriment and air of carnival.

Not daring to show himself, the frightened charcoal burner peeped through a knothole, and held his breath. They came to a stop just near his hiding place, and the stamping and music grew louder.

They made a large circle, ambling or hopping, round and round, with one of their number in the middle, (the head demon evidently), jumping as high as the others' heads in a series of extraordinary leaps. They lit a huge bonfire, and holding up torches which they ignited there, shouted and sang at the top of their voices.

The firelight gleamed on furry legs, shining tusks, or flashing eyes. As he watched, and heard the music, the charcoal burner became as gay as they. Forgotten was his wen, and his predicament; he leaped into the firelight and his feet carried him round in a most lively dance. His wen bobbed about, but he did not even try to cover it as usual with one hand. His arms were flung into the air, and he danced crazily, willing and fey, with all the others enjoying themselves round the fire.

"Well done! Excellent timing!" shouted the head demon, "Keep it up, human being, we are much entertained!" Each demon roared or screeched encouragement.

The man danced like one whose very life depended on his feet not touching the ground for more than a split second.

The lesser demons piled more wood on the flames, others carried torches round and round. The laughter and screeching grew in intensity, and so did the intricate dancing of all present. The charcoal burner managed to hold his own in that mighty throng. He laughed as he had not done since the night of his wedding so many years ago, when he felt himself to be the happiest and most favoured man of the village where he was born.

At last, completely worn-out, he came to a sudden stop, and felt terribly thirsty. As if he had read the charcoal-burner's mind, the head demon handed him a bowl of wine. The flavour was amazingly good, and it slipped down his throat like a priceless elixir. He felt as good as ever within a few seconds of having drunk, and felt the gleaming eyes of the head demon upon him. "You have danced well," said the demon with sincerity. "We have been immensely privileged to have you in our little company. Never have we seen a human who could keep up with our ideas of revelry, let alone surpass us!"

"No, no," said the charcoal burner politely, "It was most remarkably good of you to allow my faltering steps to . . ."

"Faltering steps! You are a master of the dance!" roared the demon, pressing the wine bowl upon the man once more. "I speak for all of my people when I say we have tonight, in fact, learned much in the way of steps from you! You must come tomorrow night and teach us more."

Very flattered by the important demon's attentions, the human being could scarcely believe his ears. "Tomorrow night? Oh, Noble Entity. I would like nothing better in this world. Just let me recover my strength and I will with all my heart attend your revels here, for I am most amazed by your frivolity," he answered gallantly.

"Just a moment though," said the head demon, as his minions refilled his wine bowl, and lavished every attention on him, "Human beings sometimes find life so demanding that they forget our invitations . . . Let us see what sort of a pledge you can leave with us so that we can be sure that you will come back."

A few of the demons held a consultation, and when they had made a decision, they came to the head demon and said, "Lord Demon, we have democratically decided that, as some humans consider a wen to be a very fortunate thing to have, we will ask the man to leave that as a sign of his good faith."

"Done," said the head demon, "with your permission,

good sir, of course, just a small prick!"

The charcoal burner's finger went up to his cheek in his usual gesture of dismay. He felt a minute twinge, as if a gnat had stung him, and at that moment the entire devilish company vanished. And, with them, his wen had also disappeared.

He could not believe his good fortune. The moon was now up, all signs of the fire the demons had lit and danced around had gone. He slipped his osier-basket onto his back, loaded with the wood he had collected, and made his way home with his mind in a turmoil.

His wife was delighted to see him, without the monstrous wen. Her heart was uplifted, and she decided not to run away after all. Life would now be much better, with the hideous lump removed from her husband's face. He told her everything, from start to finish, and her eyes were like a faun's in the lamplight. All the love she had had for him on their wedding day returned. But more was to come. In the bottom of his osier-basket, when the wood was all taken out and stacked in the hut, were a hundred pieces of finest silver money.

"Husband! Husband! You will never have to work again collecting wood, we can enter some other, nice clean business. Let us give thanks to the gods for what they have caused to happen tonight!" cried the woman in the height of excitement.

Now, next morning, the tale was told all round the charcoal-burner's circle of friends. One neighbour, a baker said:

"O, dear brother, let me go in your place, please, so that I could have this wen removed from my cheek, for it has plagued me greatly since it appeared a few months ago.

"If only I could go and meet those demons, the dancing would be quite easy to do, I'm sure, and I certainly could do with a hundred pieces of finest silver to get myself a new oven!" His wife added her screams and tears to his request.

So the kindly charcoal-burner told the baker where to go, and the neighbour set off gaily up the mountain track. He reached the hollow tree, and settled down for a long wait, eating some salted fish and bread while he looked forward to the devilish train's arrival. He had a large osier-basket with him, in which he hoped to take his silver home. No sooner had the sun disappeared than he heard the tramp of the approaching throng. Pipes, flutes and drums grew louder and louder. Singing and shouting, the demons came, as before, into the clearing. Their heads tossed, their eyes and teeth gleamed in the starlight. The festivities began, the fire was lit, and the demons started dancing. Soon the whole mountainside was reverberating with sound.

"Has the man not come, as he promised he would?" some of the demons began to ask each other. "Here I am, just as I agreed!" shouted the baker, running towards them. He took out his fan, and covering his wen, began to dance and sing as hard as he possibly could. But, his feet were not as nimble as that of the charcoal-burner, and he had no natural rhythm at all. He just seemed to shuffle and hop, with no more grace than a goat. The demons looked on with distaste, and several gave him the thumbs-down sign. The head demon snarled with rage as the man cavorted clumsily round the fire. "Your feet are like lead, nothing like last night's performance!" he roared, and the others screeched insults, spitting at the baker like wildcats. "This won't do, we are not at all amused by this behaviour. Where is your heart tonight? Here take your pledge and go, leave us this instant!" Thunder rolled, lightning flashed, rain fell. The roaring and offensive remarks hurled at him so terrified the baker that he ran for his life, a wen on either cheek. ∎

This story has wandered across the world, perhaps from the Kalmucks to Norway; and it is as well known in Japan as it was to the Brothers Grimm. The details vary from place to place, for the chivalric chase is variously aided by magical horses, telescopes, medical skill, military prowess, knowledge of everything in the world, or the power to run faster than thought. In Iceland, the girl is sick; in Arabia a magic carpet is called into play; in Grimm, a tailor is one of the heroes— his skill is such that he can even sew eggs together. In the version of the **Tales of a Parrot,** *set in Afghanistan, a dispute about the girl arises between the heroes which may continue to this day; and in the Mongolian version the youths kill one another when they realise how beautiful the Princess is.*

In the Arabian telling, the lady's problem is that she is ill with a mysterious disease; in Germany and Japan, her captor is a dragon, in India, a demon, in the Mongolian, a wicked Khan has stolen her.

In the ancient Indian version, there is only one hero; in one Persian variety and the Arabic, three; Grimm and another Persian recension have four brothers; the Kalmucks prefer six— and the Albanians opt for seven. The 47th tale of the Italian Basile's **Pentamerone** *is very close to the Arabic; yet the Italian version was known in Europe long before the modern translations of the* **Arabian Nights** *were published. This is the Albanian telling.*

The Skilful Brothers

Once upon a time there was a King who had a beautiful daughter. They lived happily until, one day, the Devil took it into his head to carry her away. This he did, conveying her to his dwelling-place, deep in the earth, where human beings cannot normally reach.

The King was distraught beyond measure; and he announced that whoever should save the girl could have her hand in marriage, provided that she agreed to accept him.

Seven intelligent, noble, and skilful youths each volunteered to rescue the Princess, and they set out together to seek the hiding-place.

Now these brothers were well equipped for their task. The first had such acute hearing that he could hear any sound, even from the most remote distances. The second had the power of making the very earth open to any depth. The third could steal anything from anyone without their knowing it. The fourth could hurl any object to the very confines of the world. The fifth was able to build a lofty and impregnable castle in an instant. The sixth was such a marksman that he could hit anything, no matter how high in the air it was, or how distant. The seventh could catch, and safely hold, anything which fell from the sky, whatever the altitude.

The seven had not gone very far when the youth with the acute hearing put his ear to the ground and heard that under that very spot was the Devil's hideout. He said to the second young man:

"Cause the earth to open at this point!"

Instantly, by the second youth's magical power, the earth opened; and the party descended into the ground to where they saw the Devil, deeply asleep and snoring, clutching the maiden to him.

The third youth stole the Princess from the diabolical grasp by his power to abstract anything from anywhere without it being known. In her place he put a toad.

The fourth companion took off one of the Devil's unique shoes, and hurled it so far that it descended at the other end of the earth.

Carrying the Princess, the brothers started their journey back to her father's palace.

Very soon, however, the Devil awoke. He roared and screamed with fury when he found the toad, the Princess gone, and his irreplaceable shoe missing. He threw himself into the air and sped to the end of the world to recover the footgear, and then started off in hot pursuit of the travellers.

As soon as they saw him coming in the distance, the fifth young man caused by his art a mighty and almost inaccessible tower to be built. The eight fugitives went inside, and the door closed, just at the moment when the Devil arrived.

Try as he might, the fiend could not get into the tower. Resorting to guile, he said:

"I will go away in peace, if you will only just let me have one final look at the Princess."

Foolishly, as it turned out, they made a very small

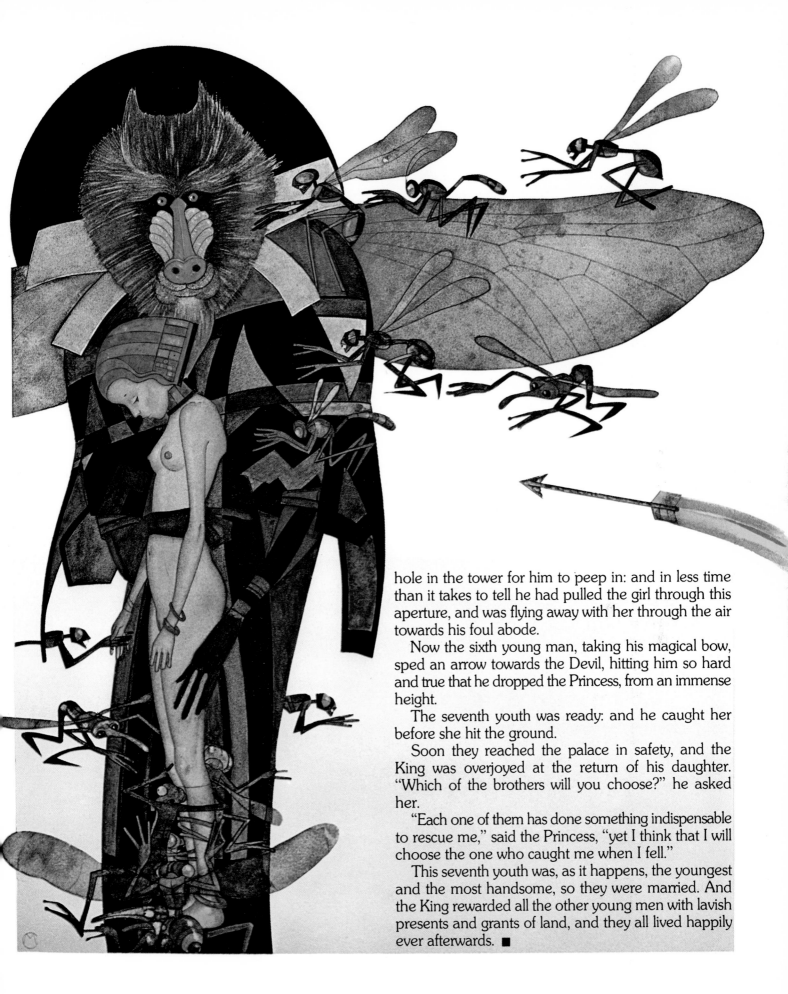

hole in the tower for him to peep in: and in less time than it takes to tell he had pulled the girl through this aperture, and was flying away with her through the air towards his foul abode.

Now the sixth young man, taking his magical bow, sped an arrow towards the Devil, hitting him so hard and true that he dropped the Princess, from an immense height.

The seventh youth was ready: and he caught her before she hit the ground.

Soon they reached the palace in safety, and the King was overjoyed at the return of his daughter. "Which of the brothers will you choose?" he asked her.

"Each one of them has done something indispensable to rescue me," said the Princess, "yet I think that I will choose the one who caught me when I fell."

This seventh youth was, as it happens, the youngest and the most handsome, so they were married. And the King rewarded all the other young men with lavish presents and grants of land, and they all lived happily ever afterwards. ■

At the end of the last century, Mrs. M. R. Cox collected three hundred years of Cinderella-type stories. They totalled 345 versions: and she added that they could be multiplied. This may be one of the most enduring of all tales—a variety has been noted (by Arthur Waley) in a Chinese book of the ninth century A.D. My father published a Vietnamese variant, claimed to be thousands of years old, in 1960. It has also been observed that the story of Aslaug, daughter of Siegfried and Brunhild in the Volsung Saga, is a striking parallel. Apart from the now-popular version of Perrault, published in the 18th century, there are other intriguing and excellent tales featuring the pathetic Cinders. Of these, the Scottish variant is 'Rashin Coatie'—Coat of Rushes— and there is an English one: 'Cap o' Rushes'. People have argued about the slipper—should it have been glass or fur. Children love the details of the ball, the magic pumpkin, the wicked stepmother, and why should they not? But for sheer beauty and delight, this American version, found among the Algonquin Indians, seems hard to beat.

The Algonquin Cinderella

There was once a large village of the MicMac Indians of the Eastern Algonquins, built beside a lake. At the far end of the settlement stood a lodge, and in it lived a being who was always invisible. He had a sister who looked after him, and everyone knew that any girl who could see him might marry him. For that reason there were very few girls who did not try, but it was very long before anyone succeeded.

This is the way in which the test of sight was carried out: at evening-time, when the Invisible One was due to be returning home, his sister would walk with any girl who might come down to the lakeshore. She, of course, could see her brother, since he was always visible to her. As soon as she saw him, she would say to the girls:

"Do you see my brother?"

"Yes," they would generally reply—though some of them did say "No."

To those who said that they could indeed see him, the sister would say:

"Of what is his shoulder strap made?" Some people say that she would enquire:

"What is his moose-runner's haul?" or "With what does he draw his sled?"

And they would answer:

"A strip of rawhide" or "a green flexible branch", or something of that kind.

Then she, knowing that they had not told the truth, would say:

"Very well, let us return to the wigwam!"

When they had gone in, she would tell them not to sit in a certain place, because it belonged to the Invisible One. Then, after they had helped to cook the supper, they would wait with great curiosity, to see him eat. They could be sure that he was a real person, for when he took off his moccasins they became visible, and his sister hung them up. But beyond this they saw nothing of him, not even when they stayed in the place all the night, as many of them did.

Now there lived in the village an old man who was a widower, and his three daughters. The youngest girl was very small, weak and often ill: and yet her sisters, especially the elder, treated her cruelly. The second daughter was kinder, and sometimes took her side: but the wicked sister would burn her hands and feet with hot cinders, and she was covered with scars from this treatment. She was so marked that people called her *Oochigeaskw*, the Rough-Faced-Girl.

When her father came home and asked why she had such burns, the bad sister would at once say that it was her own fault, for she had disobeyed orders and gone near the fire and fallen into it.

These two elder sisters decided one day to try their luck at seeing the Invisible One. So they dressed themselves in their finest clothes, and tried to look their prettiest. They found the Invisible One's sister and took the usual walk by the water.

When he came, and when they were asked if they could see him, they answered: "Of course." And when asked about the shoulder strap or sled cord, they answered: "A piece of rawhide."

But of course they were lying like the others, and they got nothing for their pains.

The next afternoon, when the father returned home, he brought with him many of the pretty little shells from which wampum was made, and they set to work to string them.

That day, poor little Oochigeaskw, who had always gone barefoot, got a pair of her father's moccasins, old ones, and put them into water to soften them so that she could wear them. Then she begged her sisters for

a few wampum shells. The elder called her a 'little pest', but the younger one gave her some. Now, with no other clothes than her usual rags, the poor little thing went into the woods and got herself some sheets of birch bark, from which she made a dress, and put marks on it for decoration, in the style of long ago. She made a petticoat and a loose gown, a cap, leggings and a handkerchief. She put on her father's large old moccasins, which were far too big for her, and went forth to try her luck. She would try, she thought, to discover whether she could see the Invisible One.

She did not begin very well. As she set off, her sisters shouted and hooted, hissed and yelled, and tried to make her stay. And the loafers around the village, seeing the strange little creature, called out "Shame!"

The poor little girl in her strange clothes, with her face all scarred, was an awful sight, but she was kindly received by the sister of the Invisible One. And this was, of course, because this noble lady understood far more about things than simply the mere outside which all the rest of the world knows. As the brown of the evening sky turned to black, the lady took her down to the lake.

"Do you see him?" the Invisible One's sister asked.

"I do, indeed — and he is wonderful!" said Oochigeaskw.

The sister asked:

"And what is his sled-string?"

The little girl said:

"It is the Rainbow."

"And, my sister, what is his bow-string?"

"It is The Spirit's Road—the Milky Way."

"So you *have* seen him," said his sister. She took the girl home with her and bathed her. As she did so, all the scars disappeared from her body. Her hair grew again, as it was combed, long, like a blackbird's wing. Her eyes were now like stars: in all the world there was no other such beauty. Then, from her treasures, the lady gave her a wedding garment, and adorned her.

Then she told Oochigeaskw to take the *wife's* seat in the wigwam: the one next to where the Invisible One sat, beside the entrance. And when he came in, terrible and beautiful, he smiled and said:

"So we are found out!"

"Yes," said his sister. And so Oochigeaskw became his wife. ■

The Kindly Ghost

The Biblical story of "Joseph and His Brothers" appearing as an African folk-tale, surprised some collectors. But the Sudan, where this example was collected by Amina Shah, is geographically and historically linked with Egypt, and the diffusion problem is not great, though it is not known how long this tale has been extant in oral form.

Much more puzzling is the appearance of this story in Hawaii (as "Aükele and the Water of Life" and in at least one other version as well.) This tale was recited to amazed missionaries by Polynesians before they had been told the Biblical versions. This narrative, and other recognizably related tales from the world stock of stories, are found among the Maoris of New Zealand, and in Tonga, the Marquesas, and Samoa. They are, in fact, pan-Polynesian, and the themes involved are encountered too, in cultures ranging from Zulu to Eskimo to Semitic.

Once there were three brothers, who were wandering about looking for water.

After a lot of walking, they got to where one tree was standing alone, far away from any other. They were very thirsty and tired, so they sat down under the tree. Presently, when they felt better, the two elder brothers said to each other "Let us go on further, and leave Ahmad here, as he will only be troublesome to us, for he cannot walk as fast as we can. And, if we do find water, why should we have to have one third each instead of half?"

So, when the younger brother slept, they both ran off and left him.

At last it was evening, the sun had gone down, and Ahmad woke with a start. "Where are you, brothers?" he cried in fear, in the darkness. But there was no reply. He was terrified, and called again.

Suddenly a ripe fruit fell out of the tree and hit him on the shoulder. He ate it greedily, as it tasted delicious, and he thought he would not save any for his brothers. Wild animals began to call in the surrounding desert land, so Ahmad quickly got into the hollow of the tree. It was comfortable and safe from the prowling creatures that hunted at night. When his eyes were accustomed to the dark, he saw that he was in a little room inside the tree, and there was a fine bow lying at his feet with a set of hunting arrows beside it. There was also an axe, made of sharpest steel. In the morning, after he had had a good sleep, he went out with the axe, cut bark and creepers from the tree, and made a snare for

animals. Hunting far and wide, he shot game. When he was thirsty the tree seemed to know, and dropped a sweet juicy fruit from its topmost branches.

Time went by—he did not know how long—but day after day he managed to feed himself, and to quench his thirst from the fruit of the tree. In all that time there was no rain.

He was happy, though he kept wondering when his brothers would be returning. He never gave up hope that they would come back to find him when they discovered where there was water.

One day, he found there was a small rat in his snare. He bent over it and heard it squeak: "Let me out, let me out, and when you need me, I will repay your kindness."

He was very surprised to hear the rat speak with a human voice. He released it, and it darted away.

The next day, when he came back from hunting, he found he had trapped a falcon. "If you will let me free, I shall repay your kindness just when you need it," said the bird, in a human voice.

Ahmad released it, and it flew away high into the sky, without saying any more.

When night came, he squeezed himself into the hollow of the tree, and inside he saw the vision of a small grey man. "How are you, my son? Have you got everything you need?" he asked, kindly.

"Not everything, father," said Ahmad, "but sufficient for each day and night, I thank you."

The old man said "Once upon a time, in the distant past, I, too, lived in this tree, and I was so skilled in magical things that I only wished for a thing for it to immediately appear before me. But of what use is anyone's poor magical power in the World of Worlds?"

Ahmad looked on in amazement, hearing the old man talk, and seeing how radiant he appeared in the darkness of the tree's hollow. He could not speak for wonder. "This will be of use to you," went on the old man, "It is a magical pouch, and if you wish for something, it will make that thing happen. But wish for no evil thing, or evil will come upon *you*. Take your rest now, and when you need something, wish upon my magic pouch." The vision vanished, and Ahmad scarcely knew whether he had imagined him or not, except that the magic pouch was in his own hand.

When morning came he rose, and went out into the dawn and looked around. All was desolate as before. With the magic pouch clasped in his fingers, he wished with all his heart for a village to spring up there, and

trees, water, and friendly people. No sooner had he wished than there was a great rushing sound in his ears. He closed his eyes, and when he opened them, there was so much activity around him he was nearly pushed over. There were people buying and selling under his tree, there were goats bleating, small boys running and shouting, women carrying huge bundles hither and thither on their heads. There were several huts nearby, and old men were sitting outside them, smoking. Best of all, there flowed nearby a fine, sparkling river.

Ahmad ran to the water and, throwing himself down, splashed cold water on his face. He was in Paradise, he thought. Now, walking around, with the magic pouch tied to his belt, he found it was a real village, though it also appeared to be the village of his dreams.

A respectable-looking elder beckoned him over to his doorway. "Ahmad, welcome to your very own village," said he, "Go, take those cattle over there; they are yours." And he pointed to a large herd of the finest animals Ahmad had ever seen. The days passed with many delights, and soon he was married to a pretty wife.

One night, the little old ghost appeared to him and Ahmad said to him, "Thank you so much for all the wonderful things I have got through the miraculous pouch."

"Do not thank me," said the old man, "I am not the One who has wrought these things."

"Well, take the pouch back, then, and give it to whomsoever it belongs," said Ahmad.

"No, my son, you will still have need of it, it is yours for life," said the ghostly visitor, and vanished.

One evening, just as the sun had set, Ahmad and his wife were looking out towards the river, when they saw two dusty, dirty, dishevelled men staggering towards the village. They were none other than Ahmad's two brothers.

"Brother, brother!" cried the elder, throwing himself at Ahmad's feet, "let us stay here and rest, we have searched so long for water, and now we have been told that you own this village and this river, and all these cattle. Please forgive us for leaving you, take us in and let us stay for a little while!"

Ahmad raised them up, and gave them clean clothes, food and shelter. He asked them to stay in his village, and be with him and his wife for as long as they wished.

But instead of being really grateful, the two brothers

began to be jealous of all that Ahmad now owned, and the respect which he was given by the villagers. One night they came to him and said, "O brother, we are nothing here compared to you; we are going away."

And Ahmad clenched his hands over the magic pouch and said, "Let my brothers have each as fine a house as I have, and pretty wives, and cattle, and let them be content." New houses sprang up, more cattle appeared, and two pretty wives came to the two men.

The brothers were amazed at the magical properties of the pouch which was hanging from Ahmad's belt, and asked, "Is that the source of all your wealth?" and Ahmad told them, "Yes, it was given to me in a dream by a little old man, and it is by holding it and wishing, that I have got everything I have today."

Then the brothers said, "Let us have a look at that fabulous pouch, then, so that we can see for ourselves," and Ahmad handed it over.

No sooner had the elder brother got the pouch in his grasp than he cried, "Let this village and all that is in it be swept away to a faraway place, and this part become desert again, with our dear brother Ahmad wandering about in it!" No sooner were the words out of his mouth than the village, the river, the cattle and the people completely disappeared. Ahmad once more found himself alone, without anything to his name but a ragged shirt and broken sandals.

He could not understand what had happened. Surely it could not be due to his two brothers' greed and jealousy?

"Please, old grey father, tell me what to do!" he cried in vain. No voice answered him, no kindly old man appeared.

Far away, far from where Ahmad was lamenting, the happy people of his village laughed and played no more. They went about the day's work sadly, and with averted faces. The wicked brothers lived like despotic monarchs, forcing everyone to bow down to them.

Ahmad's pretty young wife sat alone in her house, eating nothing, grieving for her husband. What had happened, she did not know, except that without him she wanted to die, as Ahmad seemed to have deserted her.

But, now something else happened. Each night, the two brothers got no peace at all, for the ghost of the old grey man went from one to the other, singing and moaning, and wailing, giving out strange sounds all night long. They got up in the morning weary and fretful, and dared not go to bed for fear of the old

ghost. No matter where they slept, they could not escape him.

All this time Ahmad was wandering and looking for his village and his wife, when one day a rat jumped out of a hole in the ground at his feet. "Ahmad, good Ahmad, listen to me . . . You allowed me to escape when I was caught in your snare, I will help you now. You are apparently in trouble, with no bow or arrows, no food in your belly, so far from water. What is the matter?"

Ahmad told the rat the whole story from beginning to end.

"Good deeds are not often repaid by kindness," said the rat, "bitter indeed is ingratitude. But wait, I will get the magic pouch back for you." And he darted away.

Ahmad sat down beside the rat's hole and waited. After all, he had nothing to lose by waiting, the sun was not yet overhead, and he needed to rest, anyway.

The two brothers were fighting at that moment as to who was the true owner of the pouch. As it went from one to the other, it fell on the ground. In came the rat and snatched it between his teeth. "Stop that rat, it's taking away the magic bag!" cried the elder brother. The second brother picked it up, with the rat still clinging to it. They beat the rat with sticks, but still it held on. Then, from the sky swooped a falcon, the one which Ahmad had released, and took the pouch in its beak. The rat escaped and ran away.

Soon the pouch was laid at Ahmad's feet by the falcon. As soon as the pouch was in his fingers Ahmad wished that his village could be returned to him with all it contained. No sooner were the words out of his mouth than he heard the lowing of his cattle, and his pretty wife came towards him, with laughing eyes. But the two false brothers came to Ahmad with false smiles on their faces, and pretended that they knew nothing about the matter of the village being spirited away.

Ahmad looked at them, and saw them for what they were. He knew that if they remained there, trouble would always be in the air.

"Their ways are not my ways," said Ahmad to the magic pouch, "please let them be taken away to a village of their own where I will never go, and may I never set eyes upon them again!" The two brothers vanished before his very eyes.

So, ever afterwards, the rat played in Ahmad's hut, and the falcon flew over the roof, and the magic pouch hung in readiness at his waist. ∎

While such fables as the Fox and the Grapes and the Wolf in Sheep's Clothing have become proverbial in many countries, this one is important in the literary history of 'Aesopian' teachings. It originates with the **Panchatantra** *('The Five Books'), dating at the latest from 500 A.D., and perhaps as old as 100 B.C. It was compiled for the instruction in government of princes in India. It is one of the most widely translated books in the world; there are over two hundred versions in more than fifty languages.*

This particular fable is of interest because it is one of the only two stories from the **Panchatantra** *which are attributed to Aesop (the other is the 'Ass without Heart and Ears'), and also because it is found in the works of Lucian and the Fables attributed to Babrius (third century A.D. and also in the Fables of Avian.*

Professor Franklin Edgerton of Yale University (The **Panchatantra;** *London: Allen & Unwin, 1965) has pointed out that part of the original zest of the story is the fact that, in India, the ass is considered the epitome of lecherousness.*

The 'Five Books' is a very worldly primer, preaching mainly that one should look out for oneself. This may not have been so true of the original work which seems to have foreshadowed it. The translations, starting from the 6th century A.D. Pahlavi Iranian version, are from a lost Sanskrit original. There is a persistent belief in the Middle East and West Asia that the versions which we have are superficial in having been adapted from spiritual into political teaching. One interpretation of the following tale, for instance, along these lines, states that the skin covering the ass stands for hypocrisy or the assumption of mystical knowledge, which are thrown off when the real nature of the human being (the braying) breaks through under stress.

Illustration from an early printed edition of Aesop's Fables

The Ass in Pantherskin

There was once a donkey belonging to a washerman, which was exhausted through carrying heavy loads of laundry. His owner, to help him recover, put a panther's skin over him for warmth and turned him into someone else's field to graze.

The ass could eat as much as it liked, for people thought that he was a panther and did not drive him off, and so he revived somewhat.

A certain farmer, glimpsing the wild animal's skin, was greatly afraid and stole away as cautiously as he might, wrapped in his grey cloak.

But the donkey, seeing what he took for a female ass in the distance, started to run after it. The man put on speed. The ass thought that he would give a mating-call, in case his quarry had mistaken him for a panther.

As soon as the man heard the donkey braying, he knew what he was, and, drawing his bow, killed him on the spot. ■

The Water of Life

*The idea of the Water of Life is very widespread in European traditional lore and in the East. This tale from the Grimm collection resembles one from the **Thousand and One Nights.** This version of the story was shown, over a hundred and fifty years after being published in Germany from a narrative of the countryfolk of Hesse, to a Yemenite bard. This interesting experiment showed that the illiterate reciter of tales claimed instantly to recognize it as a metaphor of the spiritual search and its perils. He interpreted the 'water' as mystical understanding, the 'father' as the community, the 'bad brothers' as spurious religionists, and much more. Story-tellers like this Taimur Rasuli draw great crowds in the Middle East, and have repertoires of some hundreds of tales and variants.*

Once upon a time, many many years ago, in a far distant land, there was a King who had three sons. One day, this King became ill and nobody knew how to cure him.

His sons were very sad about this, and one day, as they were walking in the gardens of the palace, wondering what to do, they suddenly saw an old man who came up to them and asked them what the matter was. When they told him, the old man said: "There is something that will cure your father. It is the Water of Life. All he needs is one drink of it, but it is very difficult to find."

Now the eldest son said to himself: "If I manage to find the Water of Life for my father, he is sure to appoint me as the next King." In that country the King always appointed his own successor.

At first the King said: "No, I have heard that the search for the Water of Life is dangerous, and I would not have you do such a thing." But the young man insisted, and finally the father gave him permission to go.

So the Prince set out on horseback. After journeying for some time, he came to a very deep valley with rocks all around him, and he saw a little man with a strange hat and cloak. And the little man said:

"Where are you going, Prince?" The Prince said: "That's nothing to you, you insolent fellow," and he rode his horse impatiently past the little man.

Now the little man thought that this Prince was being discourteous and through his special powers he made it impossible for the Prince to move any further. The Prince found that he couldn't go forward, he couldn't go back, he couldn't get off the horse. In fact, he couldn't do anything, and all he heard was laughter all round him.

Now, in the meantime, the old King was waiting and waiting, and so were the brothers, for the return of the eldest Prince. And when they got no news, the

second son said: "Father, I shall now go and bring back the Water of Life."

At first the King did not want to let him go, but in the end he gave his permission, and the second son set out. As he went on his way this Prince said to himself: "I shall bring back the Water of Life to cure my father and he will surely make me his heir."

Now, the Prince, as he went along the road, met the same little man who stopped his brother. And the little man said: "Prince, where are you off to?" The Prince, who was very rude, said: "Be off with you! I have no time for you." And he rode scornfully past. The little man put the same spell on this Prince as he had put on his eldest brother; and he, too, found himself paralysed and unable to move.

Now, when the second Prince didn't come back when the old King and the youngest son had waited and waited for news, the youngest Prince went to his father and said: "Father, *I* will now go and bring the Water of Life for you." At first the father did not want him to go, but finally he reluctantly agreed.

So the young man set off, and when he got to the same spot where his brother had met the little man, he saw him sitting there, with his funny hat and cloak. The little man said to him: "Where are you going, Prince?" And the Prince said: "I am going to find the Water of Life to cure my father. Can you help me?"

And the little old man said: "Do you know anything about how or where to find the Water of Life?"

"No," said the Prince.

"Well," said the little man, "since you have been courteous to me and you are intelligent enough to know that you need advice, I will tell you. The Water of Life is found in a well, in a magic castle. Now I will give you a wand of iron and two loaves of bread. When you get to the castle, strike its door of iron three times with the rod, and it will open. Inside you will find two hungry lions. Throw down the loaves, and you will be able to pass them safely. Then, hurry on to the well inside and take some of the Water of Life before the bell strikes. But if you stay there too long, the door of iron will close—and you will never be able to escape."

The Prince thanked the little man and took the rod and the bread and went on, and on, over sea and over land, until he came to the end of his journey. And he found everything as the little man had said. When the door had flown open, and when the lions were eating the bread, he saw he had come into a huge, enormous hall. In the hall there were a number of people sitting around, as if in a trance. And he took rings off their hands and put them on his fingers; and in another room there was a table with a sword and a loaf of bread on it, which he also collected.

Then he came to a room where there was a beautiful maiden sitting on a couch, and she welcomed him and said: "Set me free, and you may have my kingdom. If you come back in a year and a day the magic spell will have worn out, and we shall be able to get married." He said: "I must go and get the Water of Life for my father who is ailing, but I shall return in a year and a day." And the Princess said: "Very well, go through that door and you will find the Water of Life."

He went through the door, and saw a well in the inner gardens of the castle, and he took some water and put it into a bottle.

Now the youngest Prince felt that his mission was all but accomplished; and when he saw a beautiful couch with silken draperies on it, he thought he would just sit down and rest.

He sat down, but he soon fell asleep. Then, suddenly he woke, hearing a sort of rattle, which was the bell starting to strike. So he jumped up from the couch and, taking up the bottle of water, the loaf, and the sword, he managed to get out of the iron door just before it closed.

Then the young Prince started to journey homeward, and his way led through a country where everybody was starving. He gave them some of the bread which he had taken from the table in the magic castle, and they found that there was magic bread enough for everybody in the whole country. But the Prince did not have time to receive their thanks. He spurred his horse on; and then he came to a country which was dreadfully threatened by a terrible enemy. So he handed the sword from the castle to the King of that country, because it was a magic sword which would defeat any enemy. Then the young man urged his horse on, and finally he came to the little man who had told him where to look for the Water of Life. He said to the little man: "I am in a great hurry to get back to my father, but I wonder what happened to my two brothers who set off in front of me to find the Water of Life?"

The little man said: "They were so insolent, they were so arrogant, and they valued advice and knowledge so little, that I have paralysed them with a spell." The young Prince asked that they should be released, and the little man said: "Very well then, I shall release them for your sake, but I warn you, they are very bad people and no good will come of this."

"They are my brothers, however," said the youngest Prince. And so, eventually, the little man let them go.

The three princes now set off for their father's bedside. And, as they went, the youngest Prince told his brothers the whole story of his adventures.

But when the young man was asleep one night on the homeward journey, the two brothers plotted his downfall. They stole the Water of Life and put some ordinary water instead into the bottle in which he carried it. And so, when all three arrived back at their father's Court, the elder brothers had the real Water of Life.

The young Prince went forward and gave his water to his father, and since it was only ordinary water the old King was not made any better at all. Then the two other Princes produced their water, saying: "Here, father, is the *real* Water of Life. Our brother is not telling the truth. He never found the real Water of Life. *We* had the adventures which he claims to have been his."

The old King sipped the water; and as he did, he was completely and at once restored to health. He became so angry at what he thought was the deceitfulness of his youngest son that he sent him away with a soldier to be killed, and then he rewarded his two other sons with costly gifts.

Now the young Prince was led into the forest by the soldier, and the soldier seemed rather sad. So the young Prince said to him: "My friend, I have been unjustly accused. I am quite innocent of the charges laid against me."

The soldier said: "I am afraid it is my duty to kill you."

But the young Prince said: "Give me your cloak and I will give you mine. You can take my cloak back to the King and say that you have killed me. And I promise to disappear forever."

The soldier agreed, and the young man plunged into the forest. Now, it was not long afterwards that a resplendent embassy arrived from the country which had been saved from famine by the young Prince, with the full story of how it had been he, and no one else, who had saved their country. And then, not long afterwards, rich gifts were sent from the second kingdom, which had been saved by the young man through the magic sword.

Now, the old King realized that his two elder sons had not been telling the truth. And he said "It is very sad that I had him put to death without giving adequate thought to the matter."

And the soldier, as it happened, was present in Court when the King said this aloud. And he stepped forward and said: "Your Majesty, he is still alive. I took pity on him, although I did disobey your orders." And he explained what had happened.

The King was overjoyed and sent messages to all the Kings and Princes of the world, explaining that he had unjustly accused his son and that he wanted him to come home again.

Meanwhile the Princess in the enchanted castle was eagerly awaiting the return of the youngest Prince. She had a road of gold made leading from the palace some distance to the main highway. And she gave orders that whoever came straight up the golden road and did not follow it to the right or left, would be her lover. And anybody else would not be the true youngest Prince and should be taken into custody.

The young Prince, meanwhile, was making his way as well as he could, to try to fulfil his promise to rescue the Princess in a year and a day.

Now the two other brothers, knowing the story of the Princess in the magic castle, and fearing the wrath of their father, decided to go and try to capture her for themselves. They got on their horses, and they rode far and they rode fast.

When they got to the golden road, one said: "This road is too beautiful to ride on," and he turned his horse and rode on the right-hand side of it. The guards, when they saw him do this, took him immediately in charge.

And the second Prince, when he saw the golden road thought: "This road is too beautiful, I must not tread on it," and he, too, turned; and he rode on its left side. And the guards, when they saw this, imprisoned him.

Eventually, travelling slowly, the young Prince arrived at the golden road. And when he got to its edge he just glimpsed the castle and he thought only of the Princess and could see no other form of beauty. The road was completely invisible to him, because he thought only of being reunited with his beloved. He went straight down the middle of the road, up to the iron gates. And the guards let him in.

The Princess was overjoyed at his arrival and after they had embraced one another, she told him that she had received a message from his father the King, saying that all was now well. The young Prince told her the whole story of the treachery of his brothers, and the Princess said: "They are here, my guards are holding them in the dungeons."

So the young Prince said: "Let them go."

And as soon as they were released, they fled by ship to some very remote place, and have never been seen since.

So the young man and the Princess went to celebrate their wedding at the court of the old King. And they invited everybody, including the first old man and the little old man who had advised them so well.

And everyone lived happily ever after. ∎

The animal fable has long been one of the most favoured formats for preaching and the inculcation of morals in both East and West. In the East, notably India, while animals are generally shown to be good rather than bad, fables are often employed to warn against giving trust or making assumptions where certain kinds of people—symbolized by animals—are concerned.

The fable of the serpent was for centuries one of the most popular and most widely used. In the Middle Ages, it did service to Christianity, through the **Clerical Discipline** *of the baptized Jew Petrus Alfonsus of 800 years ago, in the monkish*

Gesta Romanorum *of the 13th century, and John of Capua's* **Directorium Humanae Vitae.** *Before that, it served Islam in the Persian* **Fables of Bidpai;** *and even earlier it is found counselling Hindus in the pages of an anecdote of King Vikramaditya of Ujjain and elsewhere. The story has been found extant and still flourishing in popular narrative in both Italy and the Himalayan region of Asia. Choosing a version which is geographically in between, we can look at the Balkan one, collected in Albania.*

The Serpent

There was once a hunter who, while passing by a quarry, noticed that a serpent was trapped by a large stone or rock.

The snake called out when it saw him: "Please help me, lift the stone."

The hunter answered: "I cannot help you, because you are likely to devour me."

The reptile asked again for aid, promising that he would not eat the man.

And so the man released the the snake. It immediately made a movement towards him, as if to attack.

"Did you not promise not to eat me, if I let you go?" the man asked.

The snake said: "Hunger is hunger."

"But," said the hunter, "if you are doing something wrong, what has hunger to do with it?"

The man then suggested that they should put the matter to the adjudication of others.

They went into some woods, where they found a hound. They asked him whether he thought that the snake should eat the man, and he replied:

"I was once owned by a man. I caught hares, and he would provide me with the very best meat to eat. But now I am old, and I cannot even catch a tortoise, so he wants to kill me. Since I have only been given evil in return for good, this is what the snake should give to you. I claim that he should eat you."

"You have heard" said the snake to the man, "That is the judgement."

But they decided to take three pieces of advice, not one, and continued on their way. Presently they met a horse and asked him to judge between them.

"I think that the serpent should be allowed to eat the man" said the horse. It continued:

"I once had a master. He fed me for so long as I could travel. Now that I am feeble and cannot continue my duties, he desires to kill me."

The serpent said to the man: "We now have the unanimity of two judgements."

Further along, they came across a fox. The hunter said:

"Dear friend, come to my help! I was passing a quarry and I found this huge serpent under a stone and almost dead. He asked me to release him. I got him out, and yet he now wishes to eat me."

The fox answered:

"If I have to give a decision, let us return to the place where you met. I have to see the actual situation."

They went back to the quarry, and the fox asked for the rock to be placed over the serpent, to reconstruct the situation. This was done. He asked: "Is this how it was?"

"Yes," said the serpent.

"Very well," the fox told him, "You shall now stay there until the end of your days." ∎

An early European, hand coloured, book illustration of Alladin.

Ordinary readers have always associated the tale of Aladdin and the Wonderful Lamp with the **Arabian Nights.** *Scholars, who could not find it in any version known to them, accused the French translator Galland of making it up himself and passing it off as an Eastern story. They were far too hasty. It has, since the 18th century, been found in Oriental manuscripts of South India and Burma and in Albania. It exists in the oral literature of the Mongolians, in Greek and in Czech. Ms. M. H. Burke took the following oral version from the lips of an almost illiterate woman in Rome, where it may have been current for centuries.*

The Wonderful Lamp

One day a kindly-looking old man knocked at the door of a poor tailor's house. His small son opened the door, and the visitor said that he was his uncle, and gave the lad a coin to buy himself a meal. Now the tailor, who was out of work, was away at the time, but later he came home, and was rather surprised to find his guest calling him his brother. Still, as he seemed to be rich, he did not feel inclined to object too strongly.

The newcomer spent some time with the family, spending liberally on their upkeep; but finally said that he had to leave, and wanted to take the boy, Cajusse, with him, so that he might learn something and so become a businessman. Of course the tailor agreed.

As soon as they had left the town, however, the man said, "I am not really your uncle at all. I need a strong lad to perform a task which I am too old to complete. I am a magician. Now, don't try to get away—you cannot."

Cajusse was not particularly alarmed, and asked the wizard what he had to do. The man took up a stone

slab from the ground and told the boy that he had to go down into the earth. "When you get to the bottom of the cave, continue along until you come to a beautiful garden, where you will find a fierce dog, keeping guard. Give him this bread. Do not, on any account, look back if you hear any noise behind you. You will see an ancient lamp on a shelf. Take it down and bring it back to me."

Then the wizard gave Cajusse a ring. "If anything happens," he said, "rub the ring and wish to be saved from it."

Cajusse duly made his way underground, where he found all kinds of amazing things. Precious jewels hung like fruit from trees, and he picked many and filled his pockets with them. When he got back to the entrance of the cave, the old man asked him to hand up the lamp.

"Not until you have pulled me up" said Cajusse, fearful that he might be left behind on his own.

The magician, to frighten Cajusse, dropped the stone slab back into the cave's entrance. But Cajusse simply rubbed his ring, and an apparition manifested itself. "Bring food for supper!" cried Cajusse. He also ordered his parents to be brought to him, so they all had a wonderful meal.

Cajusse returned to his home. Some time later, he heard that the town was to be illuminated to celebrate the wedding of the Sultan's daughter to the son of the Chief Minister. He had an idea. "Mother," he said, "I want to marry the Princess. Take this basket of priceless jewels to the Sultan, and say that we ask for his daughter in marriage."

The old woman did as she was bid, and the Sultan was truly astonished when he saw that the jewels were more precious than anything which he had in his own treasury. He promised to give his answer at the end of a month.

It was so arranged, however, that the Princess and the Minister's son were married within the week. Cajusse rubbed the magic lamp and said, "Tonight go and take away the daughter of the Sultan, and place her on a mattress of straw in our outhouse."

When the Princess appeared on the paliasse, Cajusse placed a naked sword between them in token of the purity of his intentions, and laid beside her, wanting to talk. But the Princess—not unnaturally—was far too afraid of him to reply.

Cajusse had the Princess carried three times, one night after another, to his home; and the girl told her mother about it, unable to understand what was happening.

The Queen told the Sultan, and he was just as puzzled. And the Minister's son complained to his father that his bride kept disappearing when night fell, and returned in some inexplicable way, at dawn.

Cajusse sent his mother to the Sultan again, this time with three baskets of priceless gems, asking if he could be allowed to see the Princess. "Very well," said the Sultan, "he may come to the Palace."

As soon as he heard that he was to be received by the royal family, Cajusse rubbed his magical ring and caused magnificent robes of gold and silver to be brought, together with a beautiful horse and attendants, who walked ahead of him strewing money and crying: "Make way for Signor Cajusse!"

The Princess obtained her liberty from the Minister's son, and she and Cajusse were married.

But the wizard, of course, heard about Cajusse's successes, and he decided to get hold of the magical lamp. Dressing himself as a pedlar, he stood outside Cajusse's house, calling out: "Old lamps taken and new ones given for them!" Cajusse was not at home, and the Princess sent out the ancient lamp in the hands of a servant, which the magician exchanged for a new one. Then he rubbed the lamp and caused the palace to be borne away by magic to an island somewhere in the remote seas.

When Cajusse arrived home, he realized what had happened and rubbed his magical ring, which never left his finger, asking to be carried by the slave of the ring to where the palace was now located.

When he got there, Cajusse blew his horn outside the window of his wife, and she rushed to it, to assure him that she would refuse the magician's attempts to make her his wife. Cajusse advised her: "Arrange a feast tonight. Tell the magician that you will marry him only if he will tell you what thing would be deadly for him, so that you can protect him against it."

Sure enough, there was such a secret, and during the feast the wizard confided it to the lady. "In a far-away forest" he said, "there is a beast called a hydra, which has seven heads. Someone desiring my death would have to go there, find the animal and cut off his seven heads. When the middle head is split open, a young hare will leap forth and run away. If the hare's head is split open, a bird will fly out. If the bird is caught and split open, a precious stone will be found in his body. If that stone is placed under my pillow, I shall die."

Now, of course, Cajusse knew what to do. He travelled to the forest, and found the hydra, which he killed. When he split its middle head, the hare jumped out. Cajusse caught the hare and cut its head open. out flew the bird. He managed to catch the bird and open it up. Inside was the stone, which Cajusse hastened to take to the Princess, together with a bottle of opium.

In the evening, the girl slipped some of the drug into the magician's wine, and he fell into a deep sleep. As soon as the stone was placed under his pillow, he uttered three terrible cries, turned around three times, and died.

Now that the awful sorcerer was dead, Cajusse and his wife, by means of their magical things, had the palace returned to where it had been before, and lived happily ever afterwards. ■

The kind of tale which was enjoyed in Europe about six hundred years ago is that of the freeholder (The Franklin) in Chaucer's **The Canterbury Tales.** Like the Italian Boccaccio, whose hundred tales were published when Chaucer was a child, Chaucer incorporated this tale of effort and generosity plus romance into his stories. These were supposedly told by a group of people to each other to pass the time.

The theme of the lady who is reluctant to yield to a suitor and who therefore sets him tests—which may or may not be successfully carried out—seems to have been of abiding interest to all kinds of writers and readers in the past. On this theme, numerous ancient Hindu story-tellers contrive to make the would-be lover ashamed; so do the Arabians. The Persians have the husband test his wife, and she turns the tables on him. In an English story of 1430—'The Lady Prioress and her Three Wooers'—the devout lady punishes a knight, a priest, and a merchant, who all have designs on her chastity. An unexpected twist occurs in the story of the 'Lady of Antwerp'; she sets tests for three lovers and herself dies in the end.

Chaucer's 'Franklin's Tale' covers much of the same ground, but it introduces the question of chivalry, and gives an insight into what must have been the way of thinking of those remote times, from the pen of the first writer of relatively modern English. It certainly is unusual to find the husband, the wife, and the lover and his accomplice all tied for the accolade of generosity—and the moral left open for the reader.

Who Was the Most Generous?

Once there was a noble cavalier who loved a beautiful Lady. After he married her, another cavalier courted her secretly, which she abominated, but she dared not tell her husband of the intrigue, lest there be bloodshed.

Tarolfo, the second nobleman, troubled her so much by letters, flowers, and small gifts of love, that the Lady told him she must see him. He arrived at a hidden bower, feeling that he must surely have won her.

But he was in for a surprise.

"My good sir," said she, "there is only one situation in which we can be lovers. When my garden shall bloom in cold January with the flowers of mild June."

"I swear that I shall not rest until I have learned how this can be done, dear Lady," said he, leaving with his head high.

"That shall never be," said she, and went to her boudoir, secure in the belief that she would not see him again.

But Tarolfo went to Thessaly, where he chanced upon an ancient man, gathering herbs in a dark wood. "What do you do, Sir?" he asked the old man, and the answer was "I am collecting for physic. Who are you and what do you here?" "I am from the farthest West, I grieve over a most hopeless position, yet I have still hope, for the prize is very great," said Tarolfo.

The old man, who was called Tebano, said, "I will help you if you tell me what it is that you have to do."

The cavalier told him, "I must make a garden blossom in January with all the flowers of summer." "It can be done," said the old man. "Do you not know this is an uncanny place you have come to?" "God will protect me" said the nobleman.

"Do not judge me by my outside appearance. I can do anything that is required, if the payment is right. What will you give me if I perform this service for you?"

"You shall have half of whatever I own, half of my horses, half of my sheep, treasure, and houses," promised Tarolfo, so eager was he to gain the love of the Lady.

The magician agreed, and they went to the garden, in January, on the night of a full moon. With mystic movements and strange utterances, the old man cavorted around the garden. By dawn everything was in flower as if it were midsummer. Roses and fair blossoms were everywhere. "By my faith," cried the Lady, upon rising, "the garden is blooming with every flower of summer. I am undone!"

Soon a message came from her would-be lover, requesting that she give him a time when they could be together, as he had fulfilled her condition.

Nearly out of her mind with distress, she sent him a letter to say that she must wait until her husband was away from home.

Now, her husband, loving her much, noticed that she neither smiled nor ate for the space of a week, and questioned her. "Is it your health, my love, or your mind?" he asked anxiously. Unable to bear the shame, she told him everything, and waited for his condemnation. It did not come. Instead he said gravely, "You made a promise, even though it was a rash one, but as you are bound by your word, you must keep it. You should go to him, but, my dear, do not in future make any promise such as this—even though it does seem impossible."

"You mean I should let him enjoy me as he wishes?" she cried. "Yes," said he, "Tarolfo has earned his reward. He has kept his word, now you must do so."

With her maidens around her, she sadly went to meet the cavalier at the appointed place. All adorned she went, yet her heart was heavy and she dreaded his approach. "Does your husband know?" was his first question. "Yes, he sent me to you so that I should keep my word," she replied.

Tarolfo thought for a moment, then he said:

"Please return to your husband. He is so generous a man that I cannot take what is rightfully his." A look of shame came to his face. "Beg him to forgive me, I will never do anything so ignoble as this again."

She thanked him and returned to her husband, full of joy. Her lesson had been hard, but she had learned it.

Now, the magician, when Tarolfo went to him and said "Come, take your half of my possessions" was not pleased. "I cannot take payment for what has not been a successful enterprise," he said, shaking his head. "I have a pride in my work. After all, am I not a craftsman just as any carpenter or builder is? The gods forbid that I should be less generous than the husband has been." And he disappeared before Tarolfo's very eyes.

Now, which of the three was the most generous? ∎

Cupid and Psyche

The strange fascination of legends in which people turn into animals — or the other way about — have given us both Beauty and the Beast and the Frog Prince. The forbidden, the taboo of looking or of knowing something before due time, is usually integral with the legend, found all over Europe and in Asia. Thomas H. Moore has collected a version from Chile. Sometimes, as in the Indian tales, the lady is an enchanted snake; in Norway the girl is married to a white bear; elsewhere, she may have a magical bird-costume which effects the transformation. Some scholars think that the whole idea is derived from ancient Egypt, and alludes to the metamorphosis of the Butterfly, Aurelia, and hence is a parable of the ascent of the human soul. One of the most distinguished versions of the legend is this one, from Apuleius' **The Golden Ass,** *of the 2nd Century A.D.*

'Cupid & Psyche' by Francois Gerard, 1778

Once upon a time there was a great King, who had three fair daughters. And they were so beautiful that from many lands suitors came to seek their hands in marriage.

The youngest was the loveliest of all, so that people said that she was like the goddess Aphrodite, and they bowed low as she passed through the streets of the city.

Now it was not long since Paris had given the goddess Aphrodite the apple for being the fairest of all the goddesses, and she was jealous. She summoned her son, Cupid, and said to him, "Come, let us fly together to see this mortal maiden whom men say is the image of me." They reached the palace where Psyche was sleeping, and when his mother showed the girl to him, she said to him: "Prick her with one of the arrows of love so that she will feel the deepest affection for one of the basest of mortal men. Avenge me, my son." Then she departed.

Cupid, however, gazing upon the girl, was stricken with pity and said "I will never do you so much wrong as to mate you with some wretch not good enough for you. You are safe from my darts." And he flew away.

Now, though all men bowed down before Psyche, none dared marry her, for she seemed too good and pure. So while her sisters married, and had husbands whom they loved, Psyche remained untouched and unsought. When she had reached the age when Greek maidens should be wed, the King grew anxious, and went to consult the oracle. When he returned, with ashen face, his Queen asked him what had been the oracle's answer. "Psyche must be left on a desolate mountainside until some monster comes to devour her," said the King. "Men have paid her honours only reserved for the gods, and the gods require vengeance."

The Queen and her maidens wept and wailed, but Psyche remained calm. At last a white-clad priest came to tell the King he must tarry no longer. Soon a procession, each person clad in black, left the city, Psyche led by her father and mother, and singers sang

a mournful dirge. The sun was rising when they reached a bare rock; and here it was that the oracle had directed Psyche should be left to perish.

When for the last time her parents took her in their arms, Psyche never shed a tear in farewell. After all, what good was it to mourn, when it was surely all the will of the gods?

Not daring to look back, in case they should see the dreadful monster actually devouring their daughter, the King and Queen went away with their retainers. Psyche was very tired, for she had walked a long way, so she leaned wearily against the rock. Soon a deep sleep came over her, and her sorrows were forgotten.

While she slept, Cupid was looking down at her, and at his bidding Zephyr lifted her up gently and carried her away to lay her down upon a bed of lilies in the valley.

While she slept, beautiful dreams wafted through her mind. She woke feeling happy, she did not know why, and, getting to her feet, began to walk towards a beautiful palace made of ivory and gold. A little timidly, she stepped into the palace, and passed from room to room without coming to the end of the wonders there. Out of the silence a voice said in her ear: "Everything you see is yours, so enjoy the palace and its contents as if it were your own home." There was a table set with every delicacy, forks and spoons of gold, and unseen fingers played music upon the harp.

When evening came, a great calm came upon Psyche, and she heard someone say "Place this veil upon your head, for you are to be a bride," and a golden veil descended upon her, covering her face. Then a cake was put into her hand, and the same voice said "Eat half of this cake and I will eat the other half." She did so with trembling fingers, and she saw that the rest of the cake had vanished. "Now listen to what I say," she heard the voice again, "You are now my wife, and you will live in this palace with me as long as you live. But, one word of warning: your sisters may find you here, and if they come, do not tell them anything about this ceremony, for their love can turn to hate very quickly, out of jealousy."

Psyche nodded, and promised that she would do as her unseen husband decreed. But after a few weeks of bliss she began to feel unhappy at being without friends of her own age, and sometimes cried beside the fountain. One evening she felt her husband's fingers stroking her hair, asking, "What makes you so unhappy, my dear?" "It is because I miss my sisters and my friends," she answered, and continued, "Could I not see my sisters even for a little while? After all, I have not been devoured by any monster, they might like to know what has happened to me." There was silence for a few moments; then the voice said "I am afraid that ill may come of your wish, but if you remember what I told you and do not tell them everything, I am happy for you to invite your sisters here." Psyche was overjoyed, and promised to tell them nothing.

"Then, tomorrow," said he, "I shall tell my servant, Zephyr, to carry them here". And next morning Zephyr found her sisters seated on the rock, beating their breasts and crying. Suddenly, they found themselves wafted gently to the palace where Psyche was sitting. Soon they were laughing together, and the great table was groaning with food and silver, and they ate till they could eat no more.

"Now, tell us what happened to you after you were left on that dreadful rock" asked the eldest sister; and the other inquired "Where is your husband? and *who* is he?" Their growing suspicion boded no good for Psyche, and she began to be afraid for her secret. "Oh, he goes out hunting a lot," she said, "I would like you to come into the treasure-room with me and choose some presents." The sight of so much gold and so many jewels and precious objects turned their heads completely. The gifts they were given were of immense value, and when Zephyr bore the girls away, unknown to them, Psyche felt that she did not want to see her sisters again for quite some time.

"You told them nothing, I hope?" asked her husband that night, "For they could be plotting your downfall, you know . . ."

"No, I remembered what you said, husband, and indeed I was glad to see them go, for they have become very jealous of me," said Psyche.

"Good," said he, sighing, "for the present moment all seems well, but be careful that you do not let them know the true state of affairs, or much ill fortune will come to us."

"I promise you," said Psyche, "I will never tell them. Let them come again, and I will show you how I can be silent!"

So the sisters came again, Psyche wanting to show her husband that he could trust her completely.

At first the other two girls behaved as if they were glad of their sister's good fortune, then one said "Oh, dearest sister, I've been so worried about you and the dreadful thing which had happened to you that I can scarcely speak."

"Why, what do you mean?" asked Psyche, trembling.

Her blood ran cold when she saw the look on their faces. "Tell me, and do not beat about the bush. What is it?"

"Your husband, dear sister, who is he? Where is he from? From where does he get all this treasure? My dear, believe us, we are only thinking of your own good . . ." and the two sisters began to wring their hands.

Psyche shook her elder sister's arm and said: "Tell me, what have you heard about my husband?"

"We have it on the very best authority," said her sister, "that your husband is not as you think, but a huge and poisonous snake which is full of venom. People working in the fields have seen it swimming across the river. Believe us, we would not like to tell you this, but . . ."

Psyche recoiled with horror. "It is true I have never yet seen my husband's face," she cried, "He warned me that if ever I were to look upon him he would be forced to abandon me forever. And yet, and yet, he is always so gentle to me."

"We have something here to help you see his true form," the sisters chorused, placing a small oil-lamp into Psyche's hand, "Tonight, when he is asleep, light this and look upon that dreadful face. Then you can happily return with us and be free of him!"

They both embraced her, and were wafted home on the wings of Zephyr.

Left alone, Psyche wept, and for hours tried to subdue her misery. When at last her husband came in, she managed to hide her deceit. So well did she feign happiness that he did not suspect anything was wrong as she welcomed him. Soon he was asleep by her side. For a few moments Psyche wondered whether she dare light the lamp or not, then she felt she had to know. She leaned over the bed and held the flame close to him. Instead of the dreadful monster she had expected there was the most beautiful of all the gods, Cupid himself.

At this sight Psyche started and a drop of burning oil fell on Cupid's shoulder. He woke, and looked at her reproachfully. He turned, and would have flown away, but Psyche grasped his leg, and was borne up with him into the air, till she fell to the ground and fainted away.

Then, after she had regained consciousness, she spent a long time searching and calling for her husband, weeping and begging him to return. Wandering through the country, one day she came to a temple, where she saw sheaves of oats, ears of corn, and scythes all scattered in wild confusion. Attempting to bring some order to the chaos, she began to tidy the place; and then she heard a loud voice from afar: "Unhappy girl! You have brought down the wrath of the goddess Aphrodite on your head. Go, leave this temple in case you also draw down on me the fury of the goddess."

Not knowing where her feet would lead her, Psyche wandered on, still searching and crying. At last she was tracked down by one of Aphrodite's servants, who took her to the sacred presence of the goddess herself. Here she was whipped and beaten, and was made to separate a large heap of seeds of all kinds — wheat, millet, barley. The task seemed to be hopeless, but Aphrodite left her to do it, under strict instructions from the goddess to put each of them in an individual pile. As she sat and wept, a tiny ant came, and seeing her plight, brought all his brothers, and by nightfall every grain was sorted and in its own bag. Psyche waited, trembling with fear, for Aphrodite to enter the room.

When she did enter, Aphrodite was seized with anger and cried: "Wretched girl! It is not through your own labour that this has been done! Now, in yonder glade, there are some sheep whose coats are as bright as gold and as soft as silk. Tomorrow morning at dawn I want you to go out there, shear them, and bring in enough wool to make me a robe. And this time I do not think you will have any help!" So saying, she disappeared.

Next day, very early, Psyche went out to the glade, and looked into the clear waters of the river. A reed sang to her: "O Psyche, fear nothing. The sheep must be shorn at evening, for during the day you will not be able to catch them. When they lie exhausted, you can gather all the wool you need from the branches of the shrubs and the hedges through which they have been rushing wildly all day."

So Psyche did as the reed told her, and waited till the cool of the evening, and gathered enough wool for the goddess. But when she gave it to Aphrodite, she was greeted with scowls of rage and ordered to go to the top of a lofty mountain to fill an urn from a fountain of black water. The urn was of the finest crystal, and Psyche carried it up most carefully in case she should drop it. But when she got there she found the fountain was guarded by two terrible dragons. She would have started back without the water, had not a giant eagle taken the vessel from her hand and filled it, telling the dragons that Aphrodite needed the precious water to add fresh lustre to her beauty.

Joyfully the eagle brought Psyche the precious urn filled with the black water, and she gave it to the goddess. But still Aphrodite was not satisfied. Each time she was given new tasks and errands, birds and beasts helped her, and the goddess was quite frustrated in her desire to destroy Psyche.

If Cupid had only known that Psyche was suffering so many privations, he would have somehow contrived to save her, but the wound where the boiling oil had fallen took a long time to heal. At last, when it was completely healed, he visited Psyche, and she was overjoyed at the sound of his voice. She poured out all the story of her sufferings, and Cupid was grieved for her. He said "Your punishment has been more than a mortal ought to be asked to endure, and though I am not able to save you from my mother's wrath, I will fly to Mount Olympus, and beseech the gods to grant you forgiveness."

And so he did. In the fullness of time Psyche was rescued from her trials on Earth, and left the world of humans, to sit among the immortals on Mount Olympus, forever immortal herself. ∎

The historian Herodotus, in the fourth century B.C., recorded this tale from, as he says, ancient Egyptian priests: a narrative which has been called the first detective story. Yet it is one of the world's most widely distributed folktales, and is known to the people of Scotland and Mongolia, Norway and Tibet, Cyprus and Russia, as well as in France, Germany, Greece, Armenia, Wales and North Africa. It is very widely dispersed among the world's gypsies, in the Master-Thief versions. One scholar believes that the Gypsy telling is the original one, even more complete than the ancient Egyptian. It is believed to have entered European literature in the 12th century, in the Latin 'Seven Wise Masters'. Many versions claim or imply that they are historical fact, and supply names and places where the events are said to have happened. Six hundred years ago the place given is the palace of the Doge of Venice and the thief is named Bindo; in Denmark, the robber is Klaus and the treasury that of Count Geert of Jutland. For the French, the crime took place at Morlaix, the Russian name of the robber is Chibarca, and in Holland he is from Bruges.

The Royal Detectives

The Egyptian king Rhampsinitus had a great abundance of silver, at that time rarer and more valuable than gold. He ordered a certain builder to make a treasure-house abutting upon the wall of the palace.

Now this builder, when he was about to die, called his two sons to him and told them that he had placed one of the stone blocks on pivots so that even one man could move it, and thus enter the chamber from outside. In this way the sons would be able to steal as much of the King's wealth as they wished.

As soon as their father was dead, these two young men went to the palace wall at night, found the stone and entered the treasure-room. They took away a considerable quantity of the treasure.

The King could not understand what had happened to his silver, when he entered the room whose seals were unbroken and saw how much was missing. So he set a trap after the third opening of the room.

One of the lads was caught in this trap, and could not move. He at once asked his brother to cut off his head and carry it away, so that he could not be recognised and bring trouble upon the whole family.

This the brother did, leaving the treasury by the same secret way in which he had entered it.

The King was astonished to see the headless body, and wondered how he could track down the thieves. He decided to have the trunk hung on the palace's outside wall under guard. The guards were to arrest and bring to the King anyone seen weeping or making a commotion before the body.

The dead thief's mother, when she came to know that the body of her son was suspended in this way, was greatly disturbed. She asked the surviving son to do anything he could to get the body back. If he did not obey her, she said, she would go to the King and confess.

So the youth took some donkeys and loaded them with skins full of wine. He drove them past the guards and made sure that some of the skins fell to the ground, while he pretended to be occupied with the donkeys. The guards stole some of the wine-skins, thinking themselves very clever.

Then the thief acted as if he was very angry with the guards, but they spoke kindly to him, and he appeared to be mollified. He got his asses into proper order again, and then became so friendly with the guards that he gave them some more of his wine. They all began to drink, and they consumed one wineskinful after another until the guards were befuddled and lay down to sleep.

In the dead of night the thief stepped over the sleeping guards and took his brother's body away on his donkeys.

The King, when he heard of this exploit, was naturally furious, and was even more determined than ever to locate the thief. He told his daughter to receive and to make friends with anyone from the city who came to her, and to challenge him to tell her the greatest trick and crime he could think of. If anyone told her the story of the headless thief, she should seize hold of his hand and cry out so that he could be arrested.

The thief, however, heard of the plan, and went to the girl with a dead man's arm concealed under his robe. He told her that his greatest crime had been to rob the King's treasure in the way already described, and that his greatest trick had been to fool the palace guards as he had done.

When the Princess seized the arm which he held out, he stole away in the darkness, leaving her with the severed limb.

When the King heard of this, he announced that if the thief would declare himself, he would be rewarded. the thief revealed himself, and the King gave him his daughter as a reward for his cleverness. ∎

184

Conflict of the Magicians

*The 'Magical Conflict' theme is found in the **Arabian Nights** and Germany (in the collection of the Grimms); in Mongolia and Norway: in Gaelic, Danish, Welsh, Italian, and many other languages. People as diverse as the Albanians of East Europe, the Tamils of South India, the Austrians, and the Kalmucks have thrilled to its incidents, which have few variations, for longer than any recorded literature can tell. The story given here is from the great Kalmuck collection, the **Siddhi Kur,** translated by Professor Jülg. The teacher Nagarguna referred to at the end of the story died in 212 B.C. This and other supposedly Buddhist legends are found in the great Welsh traditional collection, **The Mabinogion.** In this version, the story is given as an account of Taliesin, the Welsh bard of the 6th century in the Library of Jesus College, Oxford, in the distinguished translation of Lady Charlotte Guest, believed to be the earliest European version.*

In the Kingdom of Magadha there once lived seven brothers, and the strange thing about them was that they were all magicians: they could do all kinds of amazing things, and nobody knew how they carried out their enchantments.

A mile or so from where they lived was the house of two brothers who were the sons of a Khan, a local ruler. The elder of these two wanted to learn magic; so he went to the seven magicians, and he said:

"Teach me to understand your art," and he stayed with them for seven years, trying to find out their secrets.

But the magicians kept him very busy, doing all kinds of tasks, and they never taught him the key to their mystic knowledge.

One day, however, the younger brother came to visit him and, looking through a crack in the door into the room where the magicians were at work, managed to learn and to understand the whole of their magical science.

And so the two sons of the Khan went home together: the elder because he could never learn anything from the magicians and the younger because he had learnt everything that they knew.

As they went along, the younger brother said:

"Now that I have obtained all their secrets, the seven magicians will probably want to do us some harm. So you go to the stable—which we left empty. There you will now find a wonderful horse. Put a bridle on him, and lead him out to sell. Make sure that you do not go in the direction of the magicians. When you have sold him, bring back the money you have received."

When he had said this, he went away, turned himself into a horse with the spells he had learnt, and entered the stable to wait for his brother to collect him for sale.

But the elder brother, since the magicians had told him nothing, was not afraid of them at all. He said to himself:

"If my brother is so clever that he can conjure a fine horse into the stable, let him produce another one for us to sell: I'll keep this one for myself."

So he saddled and bridled the horse; but he found that he could not control him. Because he was not taking him to sell, and having forgotten to avoid the magicians' house, he soon found that the animal had borne him away and was standing by the door of the house of the warlocks.

The elder brother now decided that the best thing to do would be to sell the horse, and he offered it to the magicians at a high price. They realized that it was magical, and they said to one another:

"We must prevent the spread of magical horses and things of that kind; otherwise they will become too common, and people will not come to us to buy our wonders. Let us get this horse and kill it."

The magicians paid the asking price, took the horse which was really the enchanted younger brother, and shut it up in a dark stall. When they were ready to slaughter it, one of them held it by the tail, another by the head, and the others by its legs, so that it could not break away.

When the young man who had become a horse realized what they were about to do, seeing the knife in the hand of the seventh magician, he thought:

"I wish that any other living being could appear, so that I might put myself into it!"

Hardly was this thought formed in his head than a little fish came swimming down a nearby stream, and the son of the Khan, in some strange way, went into it: he became the fish.

But the seven magician brothers knew what had happened, and they turned themselves into seven large fish, which followed the small one. When they were very close to the little fish, with their mouths wide open to swallow him, the son of the Khan said, within himself:

"I wish that any other living being could appear, so that I might put myself into it!"

All at once there was a dove, flying in the air, and the Khan's son became the dove. The seven magicians, seeing what had happened, transformed themselves into seven hawks, and pursued the dove over hills and dales, and nearly overtook him when it took refuge in Tibet.

There is a shining mountain southwards in Tibet, and the dove managed to enter a cave there, called the Giver of Rest. There the dove went into the presence of the Great Teacher Nagarguna.

The seven magicians, at the entrance to the cave, changed themselves into pious men, dressed in cotton garments.

They entered the presence of the Master, and humbly requested that he give them his rosary: because, by then, the dove had changed itself into a single bead on the string carried by the Great Teacher.

But Nagarguna understood inwardly what was happening. He handed them the chaplet: but not before he had taken off the single bead which was the dwelling of the son of the Khan. He dropped the bead out of his mouth: and it instantly became a man again, with a great and wonderful stick. Now the son of the Khan took the stick and slew the magicians who had been posing as pilgrims. ■

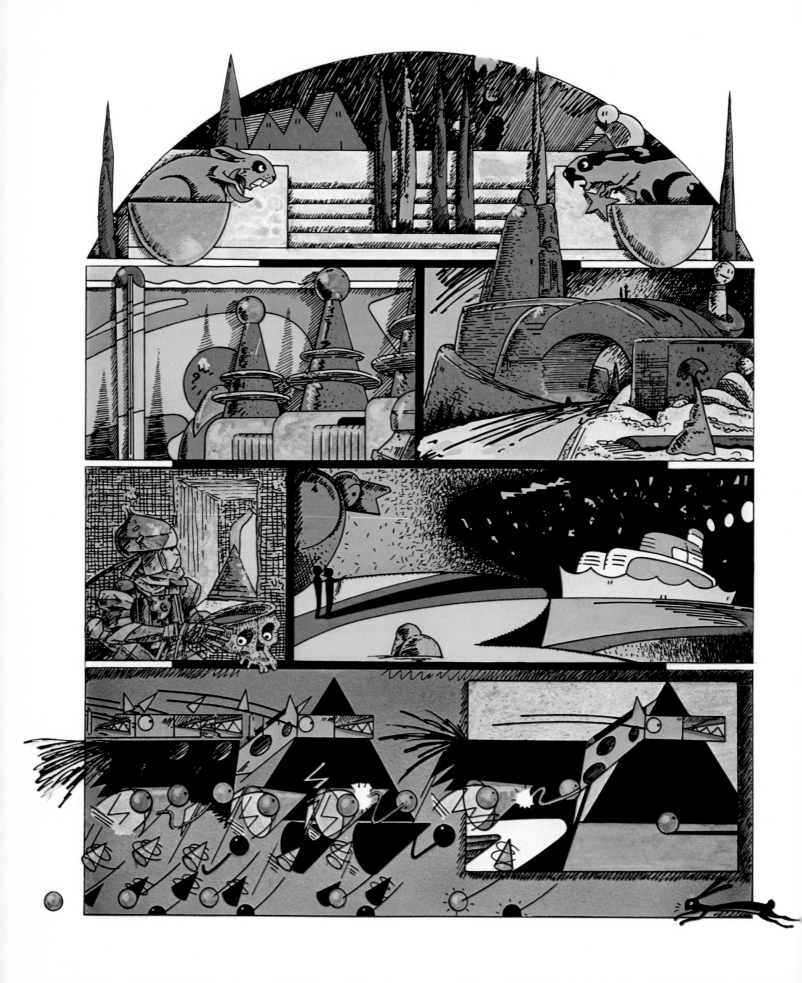

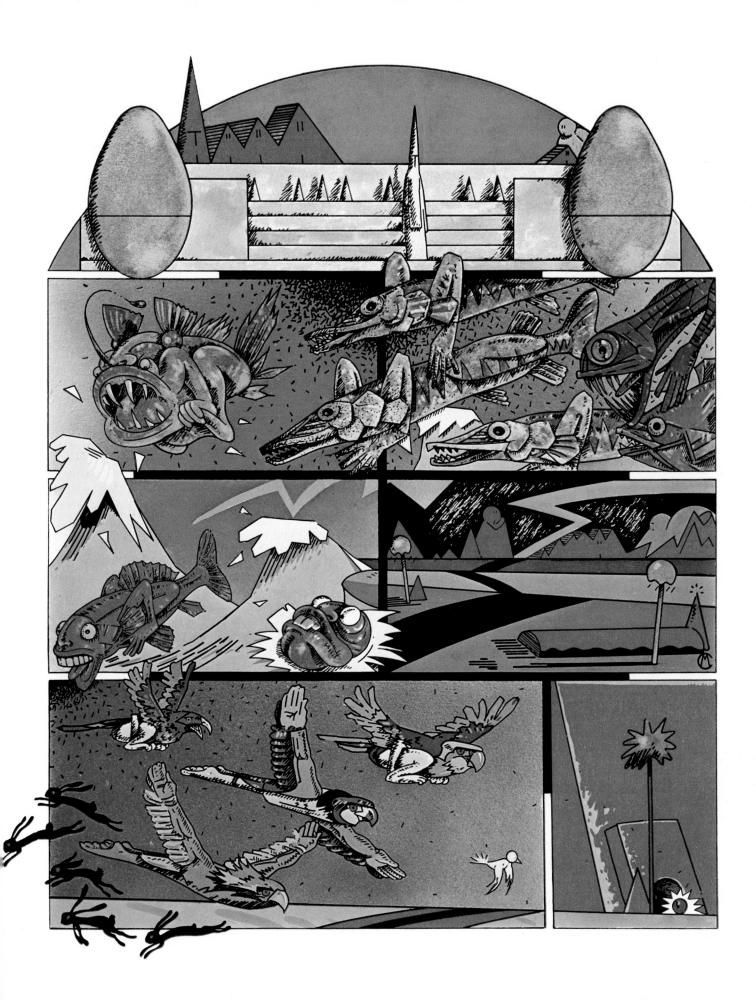

False Witnesses

This tale is thought to have been brought to the West by Jacques, Bishop of Acre, Palestine, who took part in the Crusades and died in Rome in 1240 A.D. Its message — that people will often accept the assertions of the majority however contrary to the evidence of their own senses — has been verified in the 20th-century by psychologists. The earliest English version is that of 1518, and it is found in Hebrew, Persian, German, Spanish, Syriac, and Latin as well. The essential idea, however, has been traced back nearly fifteen centuries, but it may have been first composed more than 2000 years ago. This version is from the 15th-century German adventures of the Saxon rogue, Till Eulenspiegel, called in English "Howelglass" or "Owlglass".

14th Century English Woodcut Adventures of Till Eulenspiegel

The cunning Owlglass went to a fair where all kinds of things were being sold, to see what he could get for nothing. He laid his plans to see whether he could trap a peasant. After looking around for a time, he espied a countryman buying a nice piece of green cloth. "This," he decided, "will do for me, I shall get hold of the cloth . . ."

"Good morning" he said to the farmer, "and where did you buy that fine bolt of blue cloth."

"It isn't blue, it is green."

"What nonsense" said Owlglass, "you must be blind: anyone can see that it is the deepest and surest blue."

The argument went on, with the peasant getting more and more annoyed, until they decided that the first person to come along should be asked to judge the colour. "What is more," said the peasant, "if this cloth is blue, then I'll forfeit it, and you can have it yourself, for nothing!"

Now Owlglass had a friend, a rogue priest, with whom he had already arranged the trick. At a signal, the priest came out of where he was hiding, looking like the first passer-by.

"Hey, there!" shouted the villain, "Sir Priest, will you pronounce upon the colour of this cloth, to settle an argument?"

"Indeed I will my son," said the priest, "it is undoubtedly blue, as anyone can see."

"Now give me the cloth, you ignorant oaf!" cried Owlglass.

"Not likely"—the peasant was cunning—"for how do I know that you have not arranged all this with the priest, to steal my cloth?"

"Very well," said the crook, "let us wait until the next man approaches."

Sure enough, within a minute or two, another figure strode past, and was called in to judge. He, too, was a confederate of the first two confidence men—and he insisted that the cloth was blue.

So Owlglass won his wager, the cloth was handed over, and the three crooks divided the spoils. ∎

The theme of surprise: things turning out well when the opposite is expected, and the other way about, is today as well represented in detective and science fiction as it has been in world tales of the past. Whether it is the nagging wife or some other external cause, the principle in this kind of story is that someone is set on a course not of his — or her — own choosing. Beyond the exciting cause, however, there is the stream of destiny, which has its own plans, which themselves interlock with the fates of the other characters in the narrative. In this case there is an interplay among the lives of the cobbler, the jeweller, the Queen, the thieves, and so on, which seeks to indicate — so say traditional story-tellers — that people and events do not exist in isolation. Furthermore, the results of actions cannot be predicted only from expectation, however well-informed.

It is believed by some Oriental thinkers that tales such as this illustrate the workings of the extra-dimensional world which can sometimes be entered by those who have been prepared to handle its seeming confusion — by means of a tale such as this:

The Cobbler Who Became an Astrologer

There was in the city of Isfahan a poor cobbler called Ahmed, who was possessed of a singularly greedy and envious wife. Every day the woman went to the public baths, the Hammam, and each time saw someone there of whom she became jealous. One day she espied a lady dressed in a magnificent robe, jewels on every finger, pearls in her ears, and attended by many persons. Asking whom this might be, she was told,"The wife of the King's chief astrologer".

"Of course, that is what my wretched Ahmed must become, an astrologer," thought the cobbler's wife, and rushed home as fast as her feet would carry her.

The cobbler, seeing her face, asked, "What in the world is the matter, my dear one?"

"Don't you speak to me or come near me until you become a Court Astrologer!" she snapped, "Give up your vile trade of mending shoes! I shall never be happy until we are rich!"

"Astrologer! Astrologer!" cried Ahmed, "What qualifications have I to read the stars? You must be mad!"

"I neither know nor care how you do it, just become an astrologer by tomorrow or I will go back to my father's house and seek a divorce," she said.

The cobbler was out of his mind with worry. How was he to become an astrologer — that was the question? He could not bear the thought of losing his wife, so he went out and bought a table of the zodiac signs, an astrolabe and an astronomical almanac. To do this he had to sell his cobblers' tools, and so felt he must succeed as an astrologer. He went out into the market-place, crying "O people, come to me for all answers to everything! I can read the stars, I know the sun, the moon and the twelve signs of the zodiac! I can foretell that which is to happen!"

Now, it so happened that the King's jeweller was passing by, in great distress at losing one of the crown jewels which had been entrusted to him for polishing. This was a great ruby, and he had searched for it high and low without success.

The Court Jeweller knew that if he did not find it his head would be forfeit. He came up to the crowd surrounding Ahmed, and asked what was happening.

"Oh, the very latest astrologer, Ahmed the Cobbler, now promises to tell everything there is to know!" laughed one of the bystanders.

The Court Jeweller pressed forward and whispered into Ahmed's ear,"If you understand your art, discover for me the King's ruby, and I will give you two hundred pieces of gold. If you do not succeed, I will be instrumental in bringing about your death!"

Ahmed was thunderstruck. He put a hand to his brow and shaking his head, thinking of his wife said: "O woman, woman, you are more baneful to the happiness of man than the vilest serpent!"

Now, the jewel had been secreted by the jeweller's wife, who, guilty about the theft, had sent a female slave to follow her husband everywhere. This slave, on hearing the new astrologer cry out about a woman who was as poisonous as a serpent, thought that all

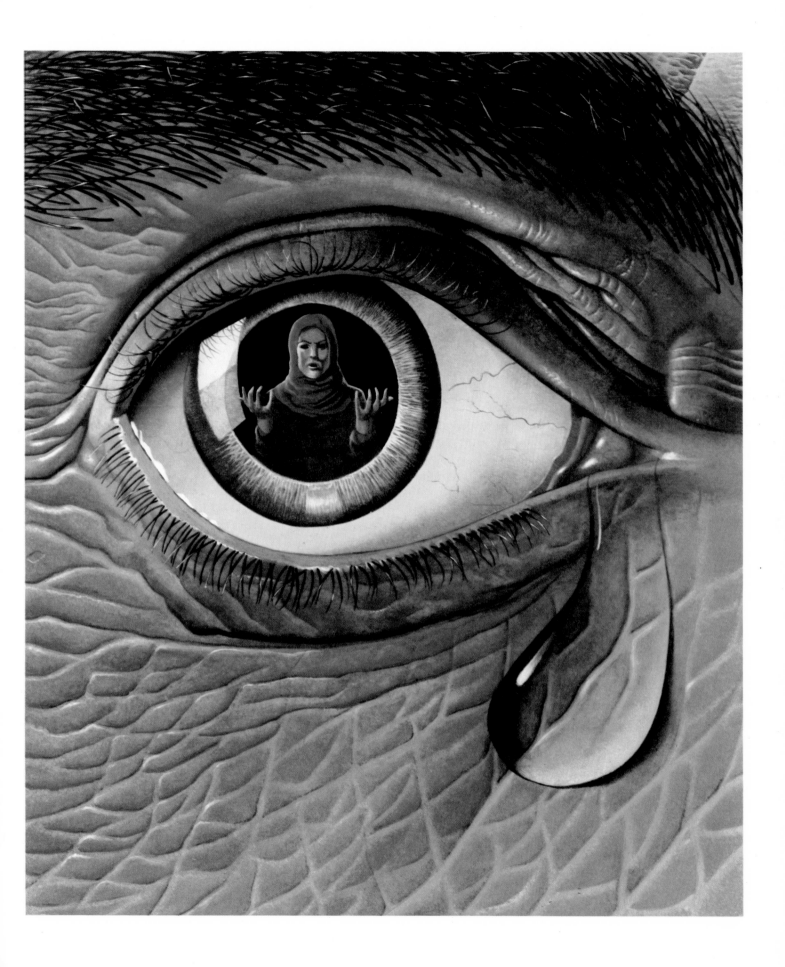

must be discovered, and ran back to the house to tell her mistress. "You are found out, dear mistress", she panted, "You are discovered by a hateful astrologer! Go to him, lady, and plead with the wretch to be merciful, for if he tells your husband you are lost."

The woman then threw on her veil, and went to Ahmed and flung herself at his feet, crying, "Spare my honour and my life and I will tell all!"

"Tell what?" inquired Ahmed.

"Oh, nothing that you do not know already!" she wept, "You know well I stole the ruby. I did so to punish my husband, he uses me so cruelly! But you, O most wonderful man from whom nothing is hidden, command me, and I will do whatever you ask that this secret never sees the light."

Ahmed thought quickly, then said, "I know all you have done, and to save you I ask you to do this: Place the ruby at once under your husband's pillow, and forget all about it."

The jeweller's wife returned home, and did as she was bidden. In an hour Ahmed followed her, and told the jeweller that he had made his calculations, and by the sun, moon and stars the ruby was at that moment lying under his pillow.

The jeweller ran from the room like a hunted stag, and returned a few moments later the happiest of men. He embraced Ahmed like a brother, and placed a bag containing two hundred pieces of gold at his feet.

The praises of the jeweller ringing in his ears, Ahmed returned home grateful that he could now satisfy his wife's lust for money. He thought he would have to work no more, but he was disenchanted to hear her say, "This is only your first adventure in this new way of life! Once your name gets known, you will soon be summoned to court!"

Unhappily, Ahmed remonstrated with her. He had no wish to go further in this career of fortune-telling, it simply was not safe. How could he expect to have further strokes of luck like the last, he asked? But his wife burst into tears, and again threatened him with divorce.

Ahmed agreed to sally forth next day to the market-place, to advertise himself once more.

He exclaimed loudly as before "I am an astrologer! I can see everything which will happen, by the power given to me by the sun, the moon and the stars!"

The crowd gathered again, and a veiled lady was passing, while Ahmed was holding forth. She paused with her maid, and heard of the success he had had

the day before with the finding of the King's ruby, together with a dozen other stories which had never happened. The lady, very tall and dressed in fine silks, pushed her way forward and said, "I ask you this conundrum: where are my necklace and earrings which I mislaid yesterday? I dare not tell my husband about the loss, as he is a very jealous man and may think I have given them to a lover. Do you, astrologer, tell me at once where they are, or I am dishonoured! If you give me the right answer, which should not be difficult for you, I will at once give you fifty pieces of gold."

The unfortunate cobbler was speechless for a moment, on seeing such an important-looking lady before him, plucking at his arm, and he put a hand over his eyes. He looked at her again, wondering what he should say. Then he noticed that part of her face was showing, which was quite unsuitable for one of her social level, and the veil was torn, apparently in her pressing through the crowd. He leaned down and said in a quiet voice: "Madam, look down to the rent, look to the rent!" He meant the rent in her veil, but it immediately touched off a recollection in her mind. "Stay here, O Greatest of Astrologers," she said, and returned home to her house, which was not far away. There, in the rent in her bathroom wall she discovered her necklace and earrings, where she herself had hidden them from prying eyes. Soon she was back, wearing another veil and carrying a bag containing fifty pieces of gold for Ahmed. The crowd pressed around him in wonder at this new example of the brilliance of the cobbler astrologer.

Ahmed's wife, however, could not yet rival the wife of the Chief Court Astrologer, so she still urged her husband to continue seeking fame and fortune.

Now, at this time, the King's treasury was robbed of forty chests of gold and jewels. Officers of state and the chief of police all tried to find the thieves but to no avail. At last, two servants were despatched to Ahmed to ask if he would solve the case of the missing chests.

The King's Astrologer, however, was spreading lies about Ahmed behind his back, and was heard to say that he gave Ahmed forty days to find the thieves, then, he prophesied, Ahmed would be hanged for not being able to do so.

Ahmed was summoned to the presence of the King, and bowed low before the sovereign.

"Who is the thief, then, according to the stars?" asked the King.

"It is very difficult yet to say, my calculations will take some time," stammered Ahmed, "But I will say this so

far, Your Majesty, there was not one thief, but forty who did this dreadful robbery of Your Majesty's treasure."

"Very well," said the King, "Where are they and what have they done with my gold and jewels?"

"I cannot say before forty days," answered Ahmed, "If Your Majesty will grant me that time to consult the stars. Each night, you see, there are different conjunctions to study . . ."

"I grant you forty days, then," said the King, "But, when they are past, if you do not have the answer, your life will be forfeit."

The Court Astrologer looked very pleased, and smirked behind his beard, and that look made poor Ahmed very uncomfortable. Suppose the Court Astrologer was right after all? He returned to his home, and told his wife "My dear, I fear that your great greed has meant that I have now only forty more days to live. Let us cheerfully spend all we have made, for in that time I shall have to be executed."

"But husband," said she "You must find out the thieves in that time by the same method you found the King's ruby and the woman's necklace and earrings!"

"Foolish creature!" said he, "Do you not recall that I found the answers to those two cases simply by the Will of Allah! I can never pull off such a trick again, not if I live to a hundred. No, I think the best thing will be for me each night to put a date in a bowl, and by the time there are forty in it, I shall know that is the night of the fortieth day, and the end of my life. You know I have no skill in reckoning, and shall never know if I do not do it this way."

"Take courage," said she, "Mean, spiritless wretch that you are, and think of something, even while we are putting the dates in the bowl, so that I may ever yet be attired like the wife of the Court Astrologer's wife, and placed in that rank of life to which my beauty has entitled me!" Not a word of kindness did she give him, not a thought for the turmoil that was in his heart, she only thought of herself and her personal victory over the wife of the Court Astrologer.

Meanwhile, the forty thieves, a few miles away from the city, had received accurate information regarding the measures taken to detect them. They were told by spies that the King had sent for Ahmed, and hearing that the cobbler had told of their exact number, feared for their lives. But the captain of the gang said "Let us go tonight, after dark, and listen outside his house, for in fact he might have made an inspired guess, and we

might be worrying over nothing."

Everybody approved of this scheme, so after nightfall one of the thieves listening on the terrace just after the cobbler had offered his evening prayer, heard Ahmed say "Ah, there is the first of the forty!" He had just been handed the first date by his wife. The thief, hearing these words, hurried back in consternation to the gang and told them that somehow, through wall and window, Ahmed had sensed his unseen presence and said "Ah, there is the *first* of the *forty!*"

The tale of the spy was not believed, and the next night two members of the band were sent to listen, completely hidden by darkness, outside the house. To their dismay they both heard Ahmed say quite distinctly: "My dear wife, tonight there are two of them!" Ahmed, of course, having finished his evening prayer, had been given the second date by his wife.

The astonished thieves fled into the night, and told their companions what they had heard.

The next night three men were sent, and the fourth night four, and so for many nights they came just as Ahmed was putting the date into the bowl. On the last night they all went, and Ahmed cried loudly, "Ah, the number is complete! Tonight the whole forty are here!"

All doubts were now removed. It was impossible that they could have been seen, under cover of darkness they had come, mingling with passers-by, and people of the town. Ahmed had never looked out of the window; had he done so, he would not even have been able to see them, so deeply were they hidden in the shadows.

"Let us bribe the cobbler-astrologer!" said the chief of the thieves, "We will offer him as much of the booty as he wants, and then we will prevent him telling the chief of police about us tomorrow," he whispered to the others.

They knocked at Ahmed's door; it was almost dawn.

Supposing it to be the soldiers coming to take him away to be executed, Ahmed came to the door in good spirits. He and his wife had spent half of the money on good living, and he was feeling quite ready to go. He did not even feel sorry that he was to leave his wife behind. She, in fact, was secretly pleased at having quite a lot of money left over to spend solely on herself.

"I know what you have come for!" he shouted out, as the cock crowed and the sun began to rise, "Have patience, I am coming out to you now. But, what a wicked deed you are about to do!" and he stepped forward bravely.

"Most wonderful man," cried the head of the thieves, "We are fully convinced that you know why we have come, but can we not tempt you with two thousand pieces of gold and beg you to say nothing about the matter!"

"Say nothing about it?" said Ahmed, "Do you honestly think it possible that I should suffer such gross wrong and injustice without making it known to all the world?"

"Have mercy upon us," exclaimed the thieves, and most of them threw themselves at his feet, "Only spare our lives and we shall return the treasure we stole!"

The cobbler was not sure if he were indeed awake or perhaps still sleeping, but, realising that these were the forty thieves, he assumed a solemn tone and said "Wretched men! You cannot escape from my penetration, which reaches to the sun and the moon, and knows every star in the sky. Your repentance has saved you. If you will restore every chest of the forty I will do my very best to intercede with the King on your behalf. But go now, get the treasure and place it in a ditch a foot deep which you must dig under the wall of the Old Hammam, the public baths. If you do this before the people of the city of Isfahan are up and about, your lives will be spared. If not, you shall all hang! Go, or destruction will fall upon you and your families!"

Stumbling and falling and picking themselves up, the band of thieves rushed away.

Would it work? Ahmed knew he only had a short time to wait and find out. It was a very long shot, but he knew that he had only one life to lose, and that he was in great danger anyway.

But Allah is just. Rewards suitable to their merits awaited Ahmed and his wife.

At midday Ahmed stood cheerfully before the King, who said "Your looks are promising, have you good news?"

"Your Majesty," said Ahmed, "The stars will only grant one or the other — the forty thieves or the forty chests of treasure. Will Your Majesty choose?"

"I should be sorry not to punish the thieves," said the King, "but if it must be so, I choose the treasure."

"And you give the thieves a full and free pardon, O King?"

"I do," said the monarch. "Provided I find my treasure untouched."

"Then follow me," said Ahmed, and set off to the Old Hammam.

The King and all his courtiers followed Ahmed, who most of the time was casting his eyes to Heaven and murmuring things under his breath, describing circles in the air the while.

When his prayer was finished, he pointed to the southern wall, and requested that His Majesty ask the slaves to dig, saying that the treasure would be found intact. In his heart of hearts he hoped it were true.

Within a short while all the forty chests were discovered, with all the royal seals intact.

The King's joy knew no bounds. He embraced Ahmed like a father, and immediately appointed him Chief Court Astrologer. "I declare that you shall marry my only daughter," he cried delightedly, "as you have restored the fortunes of my kingdom, and to thus promote you is nothing less than my duty!"

The beautiful Princess, who was as lovely as the moon on her fourteenth night, was not dissatisfied with her father's choice, for she had seen Ahmed from afar and secretly loved him from the first glance.

The wheel of fortune had taken a complete turn. At dawn Ahmed was conversing with the band of thieves, bargaining with them; at dusk he was lord of a rich palace and the possessor of a fair, young, high-born wife who adored him. But this did not change his character, and he was as contented as a prince as he had been as a poor cobbler. His former wife, for whom he now had ceased to care, moved out of his life, and got the punishment to which her unreasonableness and unfeeling vanity had condemned her. Thus is the tapestry which is our life completed by the Great Designer. ■

The moral and magical tale of 'The Two Travellers' is found in a twelve-hundred-year-old Chinese book: and also in Norway, Africa, North America, and Siberia. Its incidents are almost always very closely similar.

There are two men, one is treacherously blinded by the other. Deserted, he finds out (usually supernaturally) how to cure both himself and someone else who is in trouble. He does this and is rewarded: and then, in his honesty, tells the villain how he came about his fortune. The evildoer tries to copy his formula, but something dreadful happens to him instead.

In some versions (the African and one Gypsy telling) it is a bird or birds that save him. But, as often happens in traditional tales, the figure intervening changes according to cultural taste. In the Kirghiz form, it is a tiger, a fox, and a wolf. In the Norse—where no tigers are to be found—the animals become a wolf, a fox, and a hare. In the **Thousand and One Nights** *we find demons, as also in Bengal—and a spirit turns up again in Portugal. In south India, the secret knowledge comes from the goddess Kali, ordinarily a tutelary of destruction; but the Persian narrative softens the figure into that of a poor shepherd with special insights.*

In addition to folk versions, the story has a formidable literary pedigree. In Tibet, it is in the **Kanjur,** *in India it figures in the* **Panchatantra;** *in Iran the classical Nizami embodied it into his* **Seven Portraits** *of 1197. The Hebrew* **Midrash Haggadol,** *of about the 14th century, also has the story. Balkan Gypsy versions are known; and it was so popular in Russia that Afanasief's important collection contains no less than seven variants of the plot. This account embodies the usual common features of the tale.*

The Two Travellers

There were once two men, one good and one bad, who went on a journey together. They were in quest of their fortune. The good man shared his food with his companion until it was all finished.

The good man then asked: "May I have some of your food?"

"Certainly not" said the other, and he became so irrationally infuriated that he plucked out the eyes of his unfortunate partner, robbed him of everything he had, and left him alone and helpless in the wilderness.

The blinded good man became aware of some birds singing, and decided to climb, feeling his way, into the tree in whose topmost branches they were, to be safe from any prowling wild beasts, at least until the morning, when he might be able to think of some way of continuing his journey.

Now it so happened that he found that he could understand the language of the birds. As he listened, he learnt from their discussions that any blind person who bathed his eyes in the dew of that place would have his sight restored. Further, the birds said that the daughter of a certain King was ill, but could be healed by the use of a flower which grew nearby. The same flower had the power of locating water and restoring fertility to gardens.

The blind man immediately bathed his eyes in the dew and found that he could see. Then he plucked the plant. He made his way to the place where the Princess was ill and, having gained admittance, cured her. When he made the King's garden flourish again and found water which was badly needed, he was rewarded by being given the hand of the Princess in marriage.

He continued happily in this life, until the villain who had blinded him turned up again, having heard of his inexplicable good fortune. The miscreant asked him how he had arrived at such a happy and prosperous state.

"It was quite simple, in fact" said the honest man, for he was one who bore no ill-will, "All I did was go up a certain tree, and I heard what to do from the birds, whose speech I suddenly understood."

The bad man thereupon hurried to the place where he had blinded his companion, and waited. Presently the birds arrived and perched on the top of the tree. He found that he understood their speech. They said:

"Someone has overheard our conversation, for the King's daughter is now well, the garden is blossoming, and water has been found!"

They looked all around to see whether an eavesdropper was about, saw the bad man, flew down—and pecked out his eyes. ■

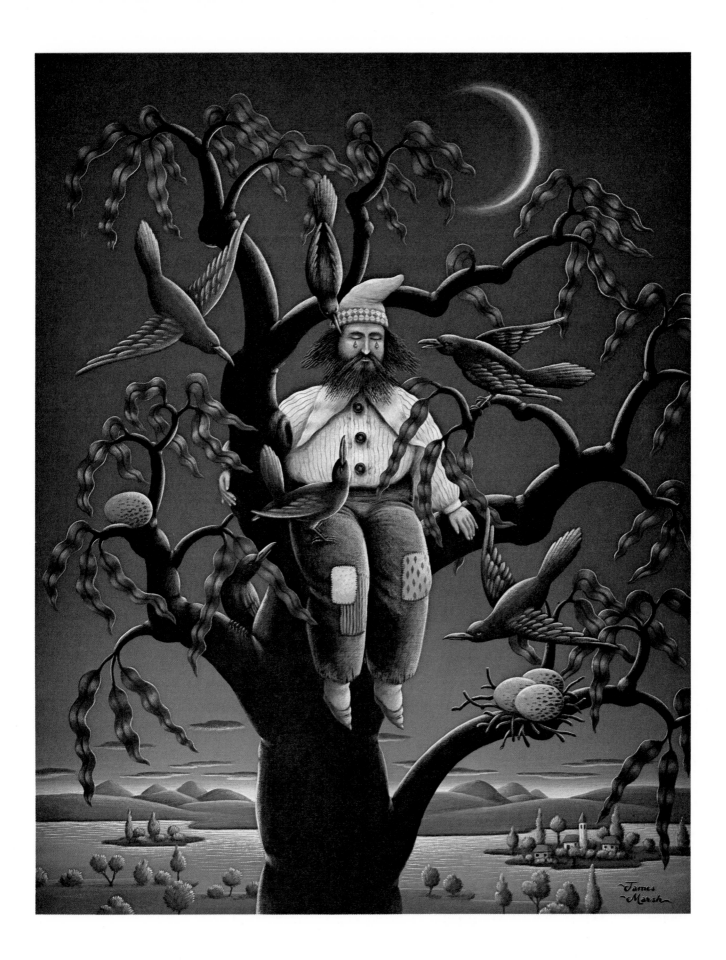

The Fisherman and His Wife

Maxim Gorky, no victim of the sensation that world tales were merely irrationalities produced by disordered primitive brains, freely admitted that such stories "opened up for me a new world where some free and all-fearless power reigned and inspired me to a dream of a better life".

This tale certainly emphasises that there is another 'world' or system which can cause changes in this dimension which are utterly inexplicable. It also claims, implicitly, that there are rules connected with such phenomena which have to be observed.

In the oldest form of this recital, the Tibetan tale of King Mandhatar, the ruler conquers the whole earth and then desires to overwhelm heaven. Soon afterwards, he dies. A Polynesian connection has been noted, and there are many versions in Europe. Although the vanity and ambition of the King changes, in European hands, into that of a covetous woman, it might be noted that a check of folk-tale content has shown that more delinquent men than women appear in them, as a matter of statistics: and the sex of the culprit does not matter when it comes to the moral.

The following version gives a good idea of the climate and projection of the story in Germany of the time of the Grimm collection, with terminology somewhat modernized.

There was once upon a time a fisherman and his wife, Isabel, who lived together in a little hut near the sea.

Every day he went down to fish, and sat with his rod for many an hour at a time, looking out upon the blank water.

One day, the line went right down to the bottom, and when he drew it up a great flounder was on the hook.

The flounder said: "Fisherman, let me go, for I am not a real fish. I am an enchanted fish. What good will it do if you pull me up? I shall not taste good. Throw me back; you will soon catch another fish."

"Ah," said the fisherman, "Don't worry — as you can speak, you are obviously no ordinary fish. I will set you free." So saying, he threw the fish back into the water. It swam away, leaving a streak of blood behind it.

Then the fisherman got up, and went back to his wife to tell her the strange happening.

No sooner did he get inside the hut than she said to him "Have you caught nothing today, husband?"

"Oh," said he, "I caught the most amazing fish. It could speak. It said that it was an enchanted fish, so I threw it back."

"Did you do what you should have done, asked the fish for a wish first?" she asked.

"No." said he, "Why do you say that, wife?"

"Ah" said she, "That is very unlucky. Is one to remain in this hut forever? You might have asked for a better place in which we could live, at least. Go again, and call him, and say we need a better house. I'm sure out of gratitude he'll give it to you."

"But how can that be managed?" he inquired.

"Well, catch him again, and before you release him, ask him quickly."

The man was not very pleased, but his wife insisted, so more to get away from her than to catch the fish he went back to the sea. It looked grey and green, cold and uninviting. He stood by it and said:

"FLOUNDER, FLOUNDER IN THE SEA,
HITHER QUICKLY COME TO ME!
FOR MY WIFE, DEAR ISABEL,
WISHES WHAT I DARE NOT TELL."

No sooner had he said this, than the Flounder came swimming up, and asked; "What do you want with me?"

The man said, shamefacedly, "My wife said I was to catch you again, and when I turned you loose I was to ask you if we could have a nice house instead of the hut."

"Go home," said the Flounder, "You will be pleased."

So the fisherman went home, and found instead of the hut, a clean cottage, with a white-painted gate. His wife was standing in the doorway, and said to him: "Look, this is more like it. See the fine curtains, and the brass bed, the bright shiny copper pots."

In the garden was a large apple tree, hens, chickens, plenty of flowers and vegetables.

"Are you content?" asked the fisherman when they went to bed that night. "I shall have to think about that," said the wife, sleepily.

About fourteen days passed, and the fisherman caught enough for them each day. But his wife began to complain about the cottage, saying "Husband, the bed is too narrow, the parlour is too crowded, the kitchen much too small. The garden is draughty, the gate squeaks. Go, then to the Flounder, and ask him for a castle for us."

"Wife," said he, exceedingly annoyed, "I cannot do that again. Surely, this cottage is good enough for us."

"Good enough for you, but not for me, I can tell you!" she replied angrily, "Have you no ambition? Do you want to be a poor benighted fisherman living in a cottage like this all your life. Go, tell him what I have said."

"It isn't right." said the husband, "I don't suppose I will ever see the Flounder again," but he went down to the sea and looked out. The sea was quite choppy, with great waves topped by white crests. It looked green and grey no longer, but dangerous. "The Flounder may be quite angry," he thought, "but I'd better try, just to tell Isabel that I did so."

"FLOUNDER, FLOUNDER IN THE SEA,
HITHER QUICKLY COME TO ME!
FOR MY WIFE, DEAR ISABEL,
WISHES WHAT I SCARCE CAN TELL."

"What do you want now?" asked the Flounder swimming up with some difficulty.

"Oh," said the man, half-frightened, "she wants to live in a great big castle."

"Go home," said the Fish, "she has it already."

The fisherman went away, and could scarce believe his eyes. Where the cottage had been was a great stone castle, with turrets and battlements, slits for arrows and fifty stone steps. His wife called to him from the top of the stairs, and taking him by the hand, said, "Now, let us walk about in our new home."

So they walked about, in the great panelled hall, with tapestries hanging everywhere, and huge paintings of ancestors. There were gigantic oak tables, and silver, glass, linen; candelabras of Venetian work, rooms of treasure, many servants scurrying hither and thither. There were crystal looking-glasses, priceless carpets from the East, valuable hounds sitting beside the log fire. Outside there were stables, cow-sheds, dove-cots of gigantic size, waggons, flowers and fruit-trees. There were meadows full of deer, and oxen in the pasture, fat sheep in pens.

"Is this not charming?" said the wife.

"I hope you will be satisfied for life, with all this style," said the bewildered fisherman, looking everywhere for his rod. "We shall talk about that some other time," said his wife.

All went well for about two or three weeks, then the wife said to her husband: "Look from this window. Would it not be fine if you and I were King and Queen of all the land?"

"Woman, you must be mad!" said he, "Have you not got enough?"

"Go," she insisted, "Tell the Flounder we wish to be King and Queen."

"I do not want to be King," he shouted, "I am a fisherman!"

"Be what you like," she said, "Just go and tell the Flounder that I want to be Queen. I *must* be Queen!"

He turned away and went down to the sea.

Stupefied, he looked out at the water. It was quite black, and when it splashed up it smelled most disagreeably. But he stood still and repeated as before:

"FLOUNDER, FLOUNDER IN THE SEA,
HITHER QUICKLY COME TO ME,
FOR MY WIFE, DEAR ISABEL,
WISHES WHAT I CANNOT TELL."

"What does she want now?" asked the Flounder, swimming up with some difficulty.

"Ah," said he, "She wants to be Queen now."

"Go home," said the Flounder. "She is Queen already."

The man returned home, and when he came nearer to his castle he saw it had become much larger, and that it had flags flying from the turrets, and soldiers on horseback standing guard everywhere. Before the gate was a herald, with a blaring trumpet, and there were other soldiers with kettledrums and fifes. When he went into the palace he saw there were items made of gold everywhere, plates and bowls set with precious gems. Magnificent curtains fringed with gold hung at all the windows. Tables were made of marble and gold, serious-looking courtiers strolled through the halls, deep in conversation.

He went into the great court apartments, and there sat his wife, with fountains playing jets of wine instead of water, upon a throne of gold and diamonds. She had a crown upon her head glittering with rubies and pearls, her hair in a net of gold. On her neck was a golden chain, in her hands a golden orb and sceptre. At each side stood six young pages, each dressed more gorgeously than the last. The fisherman went up to his wife and said "Ah, Isabel, I see you are the Queen now." "Yes," she said "I am Queen." "Do you like being Queen?" he asked, "Now there is nothing else you can be."

"Oh yes there is," she snapped, "Go to the Flounder right away and tell him that I must be, and shall be Pope."

"Oh wife, wife," said he "you cannot be Pope: the Pope is the head of Christendom and there is only one Pope. The Flounder cannot make you that!"

"I *will* be Pope," said she, and he went off to find the Flounder.

When he came to the shore the sea was running

extremely high, and the sky was so black he was quite terrified. The fisherman could hardly make himself heard above the sound of the mountainous waves which were breaking upon the rocks. He cried:

"FLOUNDER, FLOUNDER IN THE SEA,
QUICKLY, QUICKLY COME TO ME,
MY DEAR WIFE, QUEEN ISABEL,
WISHES WHAT I DARE NOT TELL."

"What now?" asked the Flounder. "She wants to be Pope," said the man. "Go home and find her so," was the reply.

So he went back, and found a huge church, in which his wife was sitting upon a much higher throne than before, with two rows of candles on each side, and before her on footstools were Kings, Queens and Princes kneeling.

"Wife," said he, "Be content. Since you are Pope, you can not be anything higher."

"I will consider that," she said haughtily, and turned her head away.

She rose very early next day, and looked out of the window, watching the sun rising.

"Why should I not make the sun rise and set?" she asked herself. So she roused her poor husband, and said to him:

"I have thought of something. Go, tell the Flounder that I want to make the sun rise and set. Go quickly, I *must* be the Ruler of the Universe."

Stumbling and falling, the fisherman made his way to the sea. There a tremendous storm was raging. Ships and boats of all shapes and sizes were tossing about in all directions. Then he shouted out, though the wind whipped his words away and he could not hear the sound of his own voice:

"FLOUNDER, FLOUNDER, IN THE SEA,
QUICKLY, QUICKLY, COME TO ME,
FOR MY WIFE, POPE ISABEL,
WISHES WHAT I DARE NOT TELL."

"What would she have now?" asked the Fish.

"She wants to be Ruler of the Universe!" shouted the Fisherman.

"Return, and find her back in her hovel of a hut," said the Flounder, and disappeared.

And in that hut the Fisherman and his wife remained for the remainder of their lives. ∎

Impossible Judgement

Nobody can be sure whether any given tale originates with the written form and has from there passed into folklore: or the other way about. Some traditional tales are actually presented as true stories, even in modern biographies. Among these is this one, claimed to be an incident in the life of Lord Chancellor Egerton of England (died 1617) and also attributed to a case of Attorney-General William Noy (died 1634). Yet the same story is found in the writings of Valerius Maximus, nearly two thousand years ago! It is attributed to Demosthenes, who died in 322 B.C., and reappears, according to a cardinal, as having actually happened in the Italian family of Lambertini in the 14th century. Here is a version taken from the novel by Le Sage, **The History of Vanillo Gonzales,** *supposedly from a Spanish original, published in 1734, two thousand years after its first attribution. Presumably the modern writers had not heard of the judgement scene in Shakespeare's* **The Merchant Of Venice.**

'The Merchant of Venice', a Victorian Illustration

Three merchants, named Charles Azarini, Peter Scannati and Jerom Avellino, went to the house of a venerable citizen of Palermo, Sicily, taking with them a notary public and ten thousand gold pieces. The old man agreed, in writing, to look after the money and not to give it up to any one of them unless in the presence of the two others. The agreement was duly notarized.

The money was carefully looked after until, some months later, Avellino knocked on the door during the night, most urgently, saying that the money was needed. Azarini, Scannati, and he, he said, had an opportunity of buying a valuable cargo if they could move quickly.

"But you seem to forget that I cannot give you the money, according to our contract, unless all of you are present," said the old man.

"I do indeed remember it," said Avellino, "but Azarini and Scannati are ill, and cannot come. But they are in agreement that you yield the money to me. Surely you remember that you have known me for a long time, and that I am an honest man?"

The old man was at first uncertain what he should do; but eventually he overcame his fears, and parted with the gold.

Avellino, of course, made off with the money, and thenceforward was nowhere to be found. No sooner did Azarini and Scannati hear what had happened than they brought a suit against the old man for the recovery of their money.

The case was heard by the Duke of Ossuna, Governor of Sicily, who, after the plaintiffs had been heard, asked the ancient, whose name was Giannetino, what answer he had to the charge.

"None whatever, Sir".

Now the Duke said:

"He has no answer to make. He accepts that he owes you ten thousand crowns, and he is ready to do so. By the terms of the agreement, however, he can only pay you if and when all three of you are present together. Therefore bring Avellino into court, and the money shall be paid to you." ∎

Hudden and Dudden and Donald O'Neary

This Irish presentation of a very ancient tale, known for centuries among disparate peoples, was collected by Alfred Nutt in the nineteenth century, and it gives the literal narrative flavour of local phrase and emphasis, with no literary polishing. The theme is that of the trickster—Uncle Capriano in Sicily, Capdarmère in Gascony, Unibos in the eleventh-century Latin, Kibitz (Lapwing) in Germany—who profits from others' weaknesses. Incidents vary, but some are remarkably consistent in the various countries. The hero sells things to people whose avarice makes them believe that these things are, for instance, gold-giving hides. Hypocrites (like the priest who is a woman's illicit lover in certain variants) are trapped; 'magic' is performed by extra information concealed from the audience. The tale is found in the earliest European collection of popular tales, Staparola's published in Venice in 1550, and is reported from Africa, India, and Scandinavia in numerous varieties. An analysis of incidents may show something about the connections of the several versions, but it gives few clues as to how the diffusion may have come about. Some of this information is surprising: the Norse and Italian cognates are unusually close; so are the Icelandic and Indian versions—and the German and some Indian renderings. For some reason, the trickster's career is often initiated by some act of aggression of theft against him: before this event he seems to have been an ordinary, innocent, and law-abiding person. Commentators have been known to state that this fact proves that the story is a prefiguring of the theory that people may be forced into a life of crime or deception by the actions of others. Whether this delinquency, however occasioned, is likely to end, as these tales do, with the complete victory of the trickster, is another matter.

Once upon a time there were two farmers, and their names were Hudden and Dudden. They had poultry in their yards, sheep on the uplands, and scores of cattle in the meadow-land alongside the river. But for all that they were not happy. For just between their two farms there lived a poor man by the name of Donald O'Neary. He had a hovel over his head and a strip of grass that was barely enough to keep his one cow, Daisy, from starving; and, though she did her best, it was but seldom that Donald got a drink of milk or a roll of butter from Daisy. You would think that was little here to make Hudden and Dudden jealous, but so it is, the more one has the more one wants, and Donald's neighbours lay awake of nights scheming how they might get hold of his little strip of grass-land. Daisy, poor thing, they never thought of; she was just a bag of bones.

One day Hudden met Dudden, and they were soon grumbling as usual, and all to the tune of "If only we could get that vagabond Donald O'Neary out of the country."

"Let's kill Daisy," said Hudden at last; "if that doesn't make him clear out, nothing will."

No sooner said than agreed, and it wasn't dark before Hudden and Dudden crept up to the little shed where lay poor Daisy trying her best to chew the cud, though she hadn't had as much grass in the day as would cover your hand. And when Donald came to see if Daisy was all snug for the night, the poor beast had only time to lick his hand once before she died.

Well, Donald was a shrewd fellow, and downhearted though he was, began to think if he could get any good out of Daisy's death. He thought and he thought, and the next day you could have seen him trudging off early to the fair, Daisy's hide over his shoulder, every penny he had jingling in his pockets. Just before he got to the fair, he made several slits in the hide and put a penny in each slit. Then he walked into the best inn of the town as bold as if it belonged to him, and, hanging the hide up on a nail in the wall, sat down.

"Some of your best whiskey," said he to the landlord. But the landlord didn't like his looks. "Is it fearing I won't pay you, you are?" said Donald; "why I have a hide here that gives me all the money I want." And with that he hit it a whack with his stick and out hopped a penny. The landlord opened his eyes, as you may fancy.

"What'll you take for that hide?"

"It's not for sale, my good man."

"Will you take a gold piece?"

"It's not for sale I tell you. Hasn't it kept me and mine for years?" and with that Donald hit the hide another whack and out jumped a second penny.

Well, the long and short of it was that Donald let the hide go for a pile of gold; and, that very evening, who but he should walk up to Hudden's door?

"Good-evening, Hudden. Will you lend me your best pair of scales?"

Hudden stared and Hudden scratched his head, but he lent the scales.

When Donald was safe at home, he pulled out his pocketful of bright gold and began to weigh each piece in the scales. But Hudden had put a lump of butter at the bottom, and so the last piece of gold stuck fast to the scales when he took them back to Hudden.

If Hudden had stared before, he stared ten times more now, and no sooner was Donald's back turned, than he was off as hard as he could pelt to Dudden's.

"Good-evening, Dudden. That vagabond, bad luck to him . . ."

"You mean Donald O'Neary?"

"And who else should I mean? He's back here weighing out sackfuls of gold."

"How do you know that?"

"Here are my scales that he borrowed, and here's a gold piece still sticking to them."

Off they went together, and they came to Donald's door. Donald had finished making the last pile of ten gold pieces. And he couldn't finish because a piece had stuck to the scales.

In they walked without an "If you please" or "By your leave."

"Well, I never!" was all they could say.

"Good-evening, Hudden, good-evening Dudden. Ah! you thought you had played me a fine trick, but you never did me a better turn in all your lives. When I found poor Daisy dead, I thought to myself, 'Well, her hide may fetch something', and it did. Hides are worth their weight in gold in the market just now."

Hudden nudged Dudden, and Dudden winked at Hudden.

"Good-evening, Donald O'Neary."

"Good-evening, kind friends."

The next day there wasn't a cow or a calf that belonged to Hudden or Dudden but her hide was going to the fair in Hudden's biggest cart drawn by Dudden's strongest pair of horses.

When they came to the fair, each one took a hide over his arm, and there they were walking through the fair, bawling out at the top of their voices, "Hides to sell! hides to sell!"

Out came the tanner.

"How much for your hides, my good men?"

"Their weight in gold."

"It's early in the day to come out, of the tavern." That was all the tanner said, and back he went to his yard.

"Hides to sell! Fine fresh hides to sell!"

Out came the cobbler.

"How much for your hides, my men?"

"Their weight in gold."

"Is it making game of me you are! Take that for your pains," and the cobbler dealt Hudden a blow that made him stagger.

Up the people came running from one end of the fair to the other. "What's the matter? What's the matter?" cried they.

"Here are a couple of vagabonds selling hides at their weight in gold," said the cobbler.

"Hold 'em fast, hold 'em fast!" bawled the innkeeper, who was the last to come up, he was so fat. "I'll wager it's one of the rogues who tricked me out of thirty gold pieces yesterday for a wretched hide."

It was more kicks than halfpence that Hudden and Dudden got before they were well on their way home again, and they didn't run the slower because all the dogs of the town were at their heels.

Well, as you may fancy, if they loved Donald little before, they loved him less now.

"What's the matter, friends?" said he as he saw them tearing along, their hats knocked in, and their coats torn off, and their faces black and blue. "Is it fighting you've been? Or mayhap you met the police, ill luck to them?"

"We'll police you, you vagabond. It's mighty smart you thought yourself to be, deluding us with your lying tales."

"Who deluded you? Didn't you see the gold with your own two eyes?"

But it was no use talking. Pay for it he must, and should. There was a meal-sack handy, and into it Hudden and Dudden popped Donald O'Neary, tied him up tight, ran a pole through the knot, and off they started for the Brown Lake of the Bog, each with a pole-end on his shoulder, and Donald O'Neary between.

But the Brown Lake was far, the road was dusty, Hudden and Dudden were sore and weary, and they were parched with thirst. There was an inn by the roadside.

"Let's go in," said Hudden, "I'm dead beat. It's heavy he is for the little he had to eat."

If Hudden was willing, so was Dudden. As for Donald, you may be sure his leave wasn't asked, but he was dumped down at the inn door for all the world as if he had been a sack of potatoes.

"Sit still, you vagabond," said Dudden, "if we don't mind waiting, you needn't."

Donald held his peace, but after a while he heard the glasses clink, and Hudden singing away at the top of his voice.

"I won't have her, I tell you; I won't have her!" said Donald. But nobody heeded what he said.

"I won't have her, I tell you; I won't have her!" said Donald, and this time he said it louder; but nobody heeded what he said.

"I won't have her, I tell you; I won't have her!" said Donald; and this time he said it as loud as he could.

"And who won't you have may I be so bold as to ask?" said a farmer, who had just come up with a drove of cattle and was turning in for a glass.

"It's the King's daughter. They are bothering the life out of me to marry her."

"You're the lucky fellow. I'd give something to be in your shoes."

"Do you see that now! Wouldn't it be a fine thing for a farmer to be marrying a Princess, all dressed in gold and jewels?"

"Jewels, do you say? Ah, now, couldn't you take me with you?"

"Well, you're an honest fellow, and as I don't care for the King's daughter though she's as beautiful as the day, and is covered in jewels from top to toe, you shall have her. Just undo the cord, and let me out, they tied me up tight, as they knew I'd run away from her."

Out crawled Donald, in crept the farmer.

"Now lie still, and don't mind the shaking, it's only rumbling over the palace steps you'll be. And maybe they'll abuse you for a vagabond, who won't have the King's daughter, but you needn't mind that. Ah! it's a deal I'm giving up for you, sure as it is that I don't care for the Princess."

"Take my cattle in exchange," said the farmer; and you may guess it wasn't long before Donald was at their tails driving them homewards.

Out came Hudden and Dudden, and the one took one end of the pole, and the other the other.

"I'm thinking he's heavier," said Hudden.

"Ah, never mind," said Dudden; "it's ony a step now to the Brown Lake."

"I'll have her now! I'll have her now!" bawled the farmer, from inside the sack.

"By my faith, and you shall though," said Hudden, and he laid his stick across the sack.

"I'll have her! I'll have her!" bawled the farmer louder than ever.

"Well, here you are," said Dudden for they were now come to the Brown Lake, and, unslinging the sack, they pitched it plump into the lake.

"You'll not be playing your tricks on us any longer," said Hudden.

"True for you," said Dudden. "Ah, Donald, my boy, it was an ill day for you when you borrowed my scales."

Off they went, with a light step and an easy heart, but when they were near home, who should they see but Donald O'Neary, and all around him the cows were grazing, and the calves were kicking up their heels and butting their heads together.

"Is it you, Donald?" said Dudden. "Faith, you've been quicker than we have."

"True for you, Dudden, and let me thank you kindly; the turn was good, if the will was ill. You'll have heard, like me, that the Brown Lake leads to the Land of Promise. I always put it down as lies, but it is just as true as my word. Look at the cattle."

Hudden stared, and Dudden gaped, but they couldn't get over the cattle, fine fat cattle they were too.

"It's only the worst I could bring up with me," said Donald O'Neary, "the others were so fat, there was no driving them. Faith, too, it's little wonder they didn't care to leave, with grass as far as you could see, and as sweet and juicy as fresh butter."

"Ah, now Donald, we haven't always been friends," said Dudden, "but, as I was just saying, you were ever a decent lad, and you'll show us the way, won't you?"

"I don't see that I'm called upon to do that, there is a power more cattle down there. Why shouldn't I have them all to myself?"

"Faith, they may well say, the richer you get, the harder the heart. You always were neighbourly lad, Donald. You wouldn't wish to keep all the luck to yourself?"

"True for you Hudden, though 'tis a bad example you set me. But I'll not be thinking of old times. There is plenty for all there, so come along with me."

Off they trudged, with a light heart and an eager step. When they came to Brown Lake, the sky was full of little white clouds, and, if the sky was full, the lake was just as full.

"Ah! now, look, there they are," cried Donald, as he pointed to the clouds in the lake.

"Where? Where?" cried Hudden, and "Don't be greedy!" cried Dudden, as he jumped his hardest to be up first with the fat cattle. But if he jumped first, Hudden wasn't long behind.

They never came back. Maybe they got too fat, like the cattle. As for Donald O'Neary, he had cattle and sheep all his days to his heart's content. ■

Riquet with the Tuft

*The earliest collection of popular tales in relatively modern times is the **Piacevoli Notte** of Straparola, published in Venice in 1550—some three thousand years after the Egyptians were recording some of their own legends. The book was banned in 1606 and placed on the Vatican **Index,** as two centuries later the Grimms' work was banned in Vienna for 'encouraging superstition'.*

*Apart from often ignoring the question of a sound moral, the traditional story's 'superstitious' content may have included deeper implications. The **Riquet** tale, transmitted by Charles Perrault in the 18th century, could be taken as suggesting that humanity, within its often somewhat ugly outer husk, has a potential for transformation and inner beauty.*

'Beauty and the Beast' has been characterized, for similar reasons, as a Buddhist-inspired tract, though the transformation or development theme is far from being a Buddhist monopoly.

'Riquet with the Tuft' is one of the first eight tales in the book which includes 'Sleeping Beauty', 'Little Red Riding-Hood', 'Bluebeard', 'Puss-in-Boots' and 'Cinderella'. These 'Mother Goose's Tales', issued in 1697 and translated thirty-two years later into English, are thought to have hit the British Isles with such force as to knock out most of the ancient English stories, which thereafter became difficult to locate.

Written for the French Court and dedicated to the niece of King Louis XIV, the stories are certainly romaticized from what one would expect from the lips of country folk-reciters, but yet they have a far greater flavour of recitation than the stories of other collectors. Altogether, this specimen gives an excellent example of how Perrault handled his themes.

Once upon a time there was a Queen, who brought into the world a son so ugly and so ill-shaped that it was for a long time doubtful if he possessed a human form. A Fairy, who was present at his birth, affirmed that he would not fail to be amiable, as he would have much good sense. She added that he would be able, because of the gift with which she had endowed him, to impart equal intelligence to the person he should love best.

All this consoled the poor Queen a little, who was much distressed at having brought into the world so hideous a little monkey. It is true that the child was no sooner able to speak than he said a thousand pretty things, and that there was in all his actions an indescribable air of intelligence which charmed one.

I had forgotten to say that he was born with a little tuft of hair on his head, which caused him to be named Riquet with the Tuft, for Riquet was the family name.

At the end of seven or eight years, the Queen of a neighbouring kingdom gave birth to two daughters. The first that came into the world was fairer than day. The Queen was so delighted that it was feared her great joy would prove hurtful to her. The same Fairy who had assisted at the birth of little Riquet with the Tuft was present upon this occasion, and to moderate the joy of the Queen, she declared to her that this little Princess would have no mental capacity, and that she would be as stupid as she was beautiful.

This mortified the Queen exceedingly, but a few minutes afterwards she experienced a very much greater annoyance, for the second girl to which she gave birth proved to be extremely ugly. "Do not distress yourself so much, Madam," said the Fairy to her. "Your daughter will find compensation; she will have so much sense that her lack of beauty will scarcely be perceived." "Heaven send it may be so," replied the Queen; "but are there no means of giving a little sense to the elder, who is so lovely?"

"I can do nothing for her, Madam, in the way of wit," said the Fairy, "but everything in that of beauty; and as there is nothing in my power that I would not do to gratify you, I will endow her with the ability to make beautiful the person who shall please her."

As these two Princesses grew up, their endowments increased in the same proportion, and nothing was talked of anywhere but the beauty of the eldest and the intelligence of the youngest.

It is true that their defects also greatly increased with their years. The younger became uglier every instant, and the elder more stupid every day. She either made no answer when spoken to, or she said something foolish. With this she was so awkward, that she could not place four pieces of china on a mantelshelf without breaking one of them, nor drink a glass of water without spilling half of it on her dress.

Notwithstanding the great advantage of beauty to a girl, the younger bore away the palm from her sister nearly always in every society. At first they gathered round the handsomer to gaze at and admire her; but they soon left her for the wittier, to listen to a thousand agreeable things; and people were astonished to find that, in less than a quarter of an hour, the elder had not a soul near her, and that all the company had formed a circle round the younger. The former, though very stupid, noticed this, and would have given without regret, all her beauty for half the sense of her sister.

The Queen, discreet as she was, could not help reproaching her frequently with her folly, which made the poor Princess ready to die of grief.

One day when she had withdrawn into a wood to bewail her misfortune, she saw a little man approach her, of most disagreeable appearance, but dressed very magnificently. It was the young Prince Riquet with the Tuft. He had fallen in love with her from seeing her portraits, which were sent all round the world, and had quitted his father's kingdom to have the pleasure of beholding her and speaking to her. Enchanted to meet her thus alone, he accosted her with all the respect and politeness imaginable.

Having remarked, after paying the usual compliments, that she was very melancholy, he said to her, "I cannot comprehend, Madam, how a person so beautiful as you are can be so sad as you appear; for though I may boast of having seen an infinity of lovely women, I can say that I have never beheld one whose beauty could be compared to yours."

"You are pleased to say so, Sir," replied the Princess; and there she stopped.

"Beauty," continued Riquet, "is so great an advantage that it ought to surpass all others. When one possesses it as you do, I do not see anything that could very much distress you."

"I would rather," said the Princess, "be as ugly as you, and have good sense, than possess the beauty I do, and be as stupid as I am."

"There is no greater proof of good sense, Madam, than the belief that we have it not; it is the nature of that gift, that the more we have, the more we believe we are deficient of it."

"I do not know how that may be," said the Princess, "but I know well enough that I am very stupid, and that is the cause of the grief which is killing me."

"If that is all that afflicts you, Madam, I can easily put an end to your sorrow," said Riquet. "And how would you do that?" said the Princess.

"I have the power, Madam," said Riquet with the Tuft, "to give as much wit as any one can possess to the person I love the most; and as you, Madam, are that person, it will depend entirely upon yourself whether or not you will have so much wit, provided that you are willing to marry me."

The Princess was thunderstruck, and replied not a word.

"I see," said Riquet with the Tuft, "that this proposal pains you; and I am not surprised at it; but I give you a full year to consider it."

The Princess had so little sense, and at the same time was so anxious to have a great deal, that she thought the end of the year would never come; so she accepted at once the offer that was made her.

She had no sooner promised Riquet with the Tuft that she would marry him that day twelve months ahead than she felt herself to be quite another person from what she was previously. She found she possessed an incredible facility of saying anything she wished, and of saying it in a shrewd, yet easy and natural manner.

She commenced on the instant, and kept up a sprightly conversation with Riquet with the Tuft, during which she chatted away at such a rate, that Riquet with the Tuft began to believe he had given her more wit than he had kept for himself.

When she returned to the palace, the whole court was puzzled to account for a change so sudden and extraordinary, for in proportion to the number of foolish things they had heard her say formerly, were the sensible and exceedingly clever observations to which she now gave utterance.

All the court was in a state of joy which is not to be conceived. The younger sister alone was not very much pleased. No longer possessing over her elder sister the advantage of wit, she now only appeared, by her side, as a very disagreeable-looking person. The King was now led by his elder daughter's advice, and sometimes even held his council in her apartment.

The news of this alteration having spread abroad, all the young Princes of the neighbouring kingdoms exerted themselves to obtain her affection, and nearly all of them asked her hand in marriage; but she found none of them sufficiently intelligent, and she listened to all of them without engaging herself to any one.

At length arrived a Prince so rich, so witty, and so handsome that she could not help feeling an inclination for him. Her father, having perceived it, told her that he left her at perfect liberty to choose a husband for herself, and that she had only to make known her decision.

As the more sense we possess, the more difficulty we find in making up the mind positively on such a matter, she requested, after having thanked her father, that he would allow her some time to think of it.

She went, by chance, to walk in the same wood where she had met with Riquet with the Tuft, in order to ponder with greater freedom on what she had to do. While she was walking deep in thought, she heard a dull sound beneath her feet, as of many persons running to and fro, and busily occupied.

Having listened more attentively, she heard one say, "Bring me that saucepan;" another, "Give me that kettle," another, "Put some wood on the fire."

At the same moment the ground opened, and she saw beneath her, what appeared to be a large kitchen, full of cooks, scullions, and all sorts of servants necessary for the preparation of a magnificent banquet. There came forth a band of from twenty to thirty cooks, who went and established themselves in an avenue of the wood at a very long table, and who, each with a larding-pin in hand, set to work, keeping time to a melodious song.

The Princess, astonished at this sight, inquired for whom they were working.

"Madam," replied the most prominent of the troop, "for Prince Riquet with the Tuft, whose marriage will take place tomorrow."

The Princess, still more surprised than she was before, and suddenly recollecting that it was just a twelvemonth from the day on which she had promised to marry Prince Riquet with the Tuft, was lost in amazement. The cause of her not having remembered her promise was, that when she made it she was a fool, and on receiving her new mind, she forgot all her follies.

She had not taken thirty steps in continuation of her walk, when Riquet with the Tuft presented himself before her, gaily and magnificently attired, like a Prince about to be married.

"You see, Madam," said he, "I have kept my word punctually, and I doubt not but that you have come hither to keep yours, and to make me, by the gift of your hand, the happiest of men."

"I confess to you frankly," replied the Princess, "that I have not yet made up my mind on that matter, and that I do not think I shall ever be able to do so to your satisfaction."

"You astonish me, Madam," said Riquet with the Tuft.

"I have no doubt I do," said the Princess; "and assuredly, had I to deal with a stupid person—a man without mind—I should feel greatly embarassed. 'A Princess is bound by her word,' he would say to me, 'and you must marry me, as you have promised to do so.' But as the person to whom I speak is the most sensible man in all the world, I am certain he will listen to reason. You know that, when I was no better than a fool, I nevertheless could not resolve to marry you—how can you expect, now that I have the sense which you have given me, and which renders me much more difficult to please than before, that I should take a decision today which I could not do then. If you seriously thought of marrying me, you did very wrongly to take away my stupidity, and enable me to see more clearly than I saw then."

"If a man without sense," replied Riquet with the Tuft, "should meet with some indulgence, as you have just intimated, were he to reproach you with your breach of promise, why would you expect Madam, that I should not be equally so in a matter which affects the entire happiness of my life? Is it reasonable that persons of intellect should be in a worse condition than those that have none? Can you assert this—you who have so much and have so earnestly desired to possess it? But let us come to the point, if you please. With the exception of my ugliness, is there anything in me that displeases you? Are you dissatisfied with my birth, my understanding, my temper, or my manners?"

"Not in the least," replied the Princess; "I admire in you everything you have mentioned."

"If so," rejoined Riquet with the Tuft, "I shall be

happy, as you have it in your power to make me the most agreeable of men."

"How can that be done?" said the Princess.

"It can be done," said Riquet with the Tuft, "if you love me sufficiently to wish that it should be. And in order, Madam, that you should have no doubt about it, know that the same fairy who, on the day I was born, endowed me with the power to give understanding to the person I chose, gave you also the power to render handsome the man you should love, and on whom you wished to bestow that favour."

"If such be the fact," said the Princess, "I wish, with all my heart, that you should become the handsomest Prince in the world, and I bestow the gift on you to the fullest extent in my power."

The Princess had no sooner pronounced these words than Riquet with the Tuft appeared to her eyes, of all men in the world, the handsomest, the best made, and most amiable she had ever seen.

There are some who assert that it was not the spell of the Fairy, but love alone that caused this metamorphosis. They say that the Princess, having reflected on the perseverance of her lover—on his prudence, and all the good qualities of his heart and mind, no longer saw the deformity of his body nor the ugliness of his features—that his hunch appeared to her nothing more than the effect of a man shrugging his shoulders, and that instead of observing, as she had done, that he limped horribly, she saw in him no more than a certain lounging air, which charmed her.

They say also that his eyes, which squinted, seemed to her only more brilliant from that defect, which passed in her mind from a proof of the intensity of his love, and, in fine that his great red nose had in it something martial. However this may be, the Princess promised on the spot to marry him, provided he obtained the consent of the King, her father.

The King having learned that his daughter entertained a great regard for Riquet with the Tuft, whom he knew also to be a very clever and wise Prince, accepted him with pleasure for a son-in-law. The wedding took place the next morning as Riquet with the Tuft had foretold, and, according to the instructions which he had given some time before, a very great feast was served to hundreds of guests. ■

The Lost Camel

In India at the time of Alakapuri's greatest power, there dwelt in it a great king whose name was Alakesa, and he was famous for all the riches which land and sea can yield.

During his reign the cow and the tiger drank side by side from the same pool, and the parrot and the kite, the Indian scavenger bird, laid their eggs in the same nest. Rain refreshed the soil when it was needed, and all King Alakesa's subjects lived like brothers in peace, plenty, and happiness.

Now, there was in Alakapuri a rich merchant who lost his camel one day. He searched for it for a long time without success, until he reached another city, called Mathurapuri, the king of which was named Mathuresa. There were four ministers of that country, called Bodhadita, Bodhachandra, Bodhavyapka, and Bodhavibishana.

For some reason, they had become dissatisfied with their positions at court, and decided to quit the city.

As they journeyed along, they observed the tracks of a camel, and each made some remark about the animal, judging by its footsteps and other indications on the road.

Presently they met the merchant who was searching for his camel.

"Masters," said he, "Have you met a camel anywhere in the direction from which you have come?"

One wise man asked "Was it lame in one of its legs?"

"Yes, indeed," said he.

"And was it not blind in one eye?" asked the second wise man, "the right eye?"

"Yes, it was," said he.

"Was its tail unusually short?" asked the third.

"Yes, yes, then you have seen it?" exclaimed the merchant.

"Was it not suffering from colic, too?" interposed the fourth wise man.

"Yes, yes, it was! But, where is it now?" asked the merchant, in some distress.

"We have not seen it," the first courtier said, "but we have observed its progress along the road."

"Observed it? But please explain," cried the merchant.

"We cannot possibly tell you where it is, we are all now on our way to the court of King Alakesa," replied the traveller, "But if you will come with us we will give

216

you the explanation of our findings."

So, the merchant had no choice but to go with them to the King, Alakesa, and complain that the four men had stolen his beast and hidden it somewhere.

The King was sure that the men must know something about the whereabouts of the camel, since they had given a complete description of it.

"You are all threatened with my displeasure," said he, "If you do not tell me the whole truth. According to what you shall now say, I will make judgment."

The first traveller said, "I noticed, when first seeing the footprints of the camel on the side of the road, that one of the footmarks was deficient, therefore I concluded that the animal was lame."

"Good," said the King, "And you, Bodhachandra, what have you to say?"

"I noticed that the leaves on the left side of the road had been snapped or torn off," said the second courtier, "therefore it was obvious that the camel was blind of his right eye."

The third said "I saw drops of blood on the road which I conjected had fallen from the bites of gnats or flies, therefore I thought the camel's tail was shorter than usual, as it could not brush the pests away."

The fourth said, "I observed that whilst the forefeet of the animal were planted firmly on the ground the hind ones seemed scarcely to have touched it, whence I guessed that they were contracted by pain in the body of the camel."

When the King heard these explanations he was struck by the wisdom of the four men, and the logic of their replies.

"Well spoken," said he, "and I will compensate you, Merchant, for the loss of your camel, as it obviously will not be found easily.

"You four young men from Mathurapuri I beg to remain here and become my counsellors, for I have great need of your intelligence."

And so they came to the court of the great King, becoming ministers of great importance. ∎

The Beggar
and the Gazelle

One of the best-known stories in the English-speaking world is 'Puss in Boots', which came to Britain through the translations of Perrault's 'Le Chat Botté', of 1697. Perrault, writing as he did for the French court, prettyfied this story; and the current story-book form is much distorted. The story is an Eastern one, and appeared in Italy as early as the 16th century. It was known in a French literary translation from Straparola a century before Perrault took it over. The tale has annoyed many people in the West, because they have disliked (as did Madame de Maintenor) its supposed lack of a moral. On the surface, of course, it looks as if a beggar (or a young miller without a penny, as in the 'Puss in Boots' version) has no right to advantages obtained for him by a cat, through trickery. But in the Eastern telling it is easier to see that the animal stands for the fate which constantly gives humanity (in spite of its unworthiness) great opportunities. The ingratitude of the main figure is thus characteristic of man's forgetfulness of a debt. The defection of the Princess symbolises the withdrawal of the advantages which subsist, according to this idea, only when appreciated by a worthwhile person.

The story is well known in the Middle East, where the man is known as Hamadani, and the variant given here is current in substantially similar form in Zanzibar and East Africa, as well as in the Near East.

Once upon a time there was a poor beggar who slept upon the outside oven of a rich man's kitchen. One morning he was awakened by the cries of a vendor who was calling, "Gazelles! Gazelles! Buy my fine miniature gazelles!"

The beggar said, "There is no one awake at this hour in the rich man's house. Cease from your noise until a more civilised hour, brother."

The gazelle-seller, who had several of the poor creatures in a cage on top of a donkey cart, replied,

"Would you like to buy one of these fine gazelles?"

"I have only a handful of coppers," said the beggar. "What would I do with a gazelle, anyway?" And he climbed down off the oven to talk to the gazelle-seller.

At that moment one of the small animals poked its head out of the cage and said in a low voice to the beggar, whose name was Mustapha, "Buy me, and you will not be sorry."

Mustapha was so astonished that he said to the gazelle-seller, "Here is all I have in the world — three copper coins. Can I buy this gazelle with its head out of the cage for that?"

Take it and be blessed!" cried the man, and released the gazelle. "As I shall otherwise only have to feed the thing I shall let it go for whatever you can give me." Then he closed the cage again, took three coppers from Mustapha, and went on his way to the nearest coffee-house.

"Well," said Mustapha to the gazelle, "what about it? I have bought you, and now I have nothing left in the world, until I can get something more sitting on the steps of the mosque at the time of the midday prayer."

"You will not regret buying me," said the gazelle, "for I shall make your fortune."

"How is that?" cried Mustapha, "and what shall I do next?"

"Do nothing, simply stay here until I return," said the gazelle, and it trotted away.

The tattered beggar scratched his head. He would probably never see the wretched animal again, he thought. How did he allow himself to be so deluded as to give his three copper coins for a talking gazelle? Probably the creature was bewitched, and might bring him bad luck. So ruminating, he sat down again on the oven to wait until the rich man's servants woke, hoping that then perhaps they would throw out some food that he could eat.

Meanwhile, the gazelle ran on until it reached the tent of a noble sheikh. It bowed to him and said, "O Sheikh of a Thousand Tents, I am the slave of a great and noble merchant, whose caravan has just been attacked and plundered by thieves. Could you please send some clothes for him to put on, so that he may not have to appear before you completely naked when he comes to pay you a visit?"

"Certainly, good gazelle," said the Sheikh, "My servant shall give you a white linen shirt and a robe of the finest camel-hair to take to your master. And when he has recovered from his shock, let him come here to my encampment, so that I may cause a sheep to be roasted in his honour."

So the gazelle thanked the Sheikh and said, "I was to bring you this emerald in payment of any clothes which you might send, as my master does not wish to accept your kindness for nothing." Thereupon the gazelle placed an emerald without flaw at the feet of the Sheikh, and bounded away with the clothes upon its back.

The Sheikh was delighted at the value of the gift, and resolved that if the man did appear he would offer him the hand of his daughter, for he was apparently a person of great substance.

The gazelle went back to Mustapha and said, "Look, I have brought you clothes from a rich sheikh. Cast off your rags, bathe in the river, and put on these magnificent garments."

The beggar was amazed, and said, "How in the world did you manage to do this? Never in my life have I seen such beautiful clothes."

"Do as I tell you," said the gazelle, "and I shall get you a rich wife as well. Did you not give me back my liberty by buying me from the man who had put me in a cage?"

The long and the short of it was that the clothes transformed the beggar into a man who could sit in a royal court without shame.

"Now, follow me," said the gazelle, and trotted off into a ruined building. "Look under the third brick on the left and you will see a treasure."

Sure enough, as Mustapha lifted the brick he saw the gleam of gold and precious stones in a cavity below. He filled his pockets and his money-belt, until he had as much as he could carry.

"What a piece of luck!" cried the beggar. "I shall never have to go without anything for the rest of my days."

"Not if you marry into the family of the Sheikh of a Thousand Tents," said the gazelle. "Buy yourself a horse, and boots, and we shall set out for the noble Sheikh's oasis at once."

An hour later Mustapha, mounted on a beautiful white horse, followed the gazelle as it sped along like the wind before him. Soon they reached a dip in the sand, and in the distance, beside some tall palm trees, were some black tents.

"Wait here," said the gazelle, "until I come for you; and remember that you are now the Sheikh Abu Zakat, a rich merchant whose caravan has been set upon by thieves and plundered."

"I understand," said Mustapha. "I shall stay here until you return."

The gazelle then descended into the valley of the oasis and, presenting himself to the Sheikh of a Thousand Tents, let fall a priceless ruby without flaw at his feet, saying, "My master, the noble Sheikh Abu Zakat, sends you blessings and peace, and requests that he may call upon you at once, to thank you for the clothes you sent him after his recent misfortune. In the meantime, here is a small token of his regard which he wishes to give to your daughter as a mark of his respect."

"Excellent gazelle!" cried the Sheikh. "Let your master hasten here as fast as he can, for I am eager to meet him, and he should start thinking of himself as my son-in-law from this moment."

The gazelle returned to the Sheikh Abu Zakat and acquainted him of what the Sheikh of a Thousand Tents had said, and soon the one-time beggar and the rich and venerable Sheikh were sitting together drinking coffee like old friends. By nightfall, when the sheep had been roasted and eaten, the Sheikh of a Thousand Tents came to the delicate subject of his daughter. "My son," said he, placing his hand on Sheikh Abu Zakat's arm, "I am glad that I have kept my daughter unmarried until you came along; for I can think of no more suitable match for her. I shall arrange for the marriage rites to be solemnized tomorrow, and she shall come to you with her servants and her finery all complete."

At this news the Sheikh Abu Zakat was delighted and thanked his lucky stars for bringing him such fortune.

Next day, at the wedding, he was congratulated by every member of the tribe, who each piled gifts before the happy pair. The bridal feast went on for twelve hours, and at last they were led to a black tent hung with rare carpets and decorated with lamps of burnished brass set with coral. While they slept the gazelle lay across the threshold, keeping watch.

The months passed, and the tribe moved to another oasis, so the Sheikh of a Thousand Tents gave his daughter and new son-in-law his palace in the desert to live in until his return. There were tinkling fountains in blue-tiled courtyards, carved wooden balconies, vast rooms with painted pillars. The Sheikh Abu Zakat became more and more conceited, and forgot completely what he owed to the gazelle. He spent all day playing knucklebones with his friends.

One day the gazelle went to its mistress and said, "Lady, ask my master if he will give me a bowl of dates and honey, prepared with his own hands, for I am feeling ill, and fear that I may die."

So the girl went to her husband and said, "Peace be upon you, Husband. Please give the gazelle a bowl of dates and honey prepared with your own hands as it is ill and fears that it may die."

And the man answered, "Foolish one, do not worry about the animal. Did I not buy it for only a few pence? Take no notice, and leave me to my game of knucklebones."

Then the girl went back to the gazelle, which was lying on the ground looking very weak and thin, and said, "I cannot get your master to come. Shall I prepare you the mixture myself so that you will get better?"

The gazelle said, "No, mistress, thank you, I would

rather that my master did it. Please go back to him and beg him for my sake to do as I ask, or I shall die."

So she ran back to Sheikh Abu Zakat and said, "Come quickly: the gazelle begs you to do as it asks, or indeed it will die, for it is now so weak and thin, lying on the ground."

But again her husband would not do anything, and told her to go to the gazelle and give it a bowl of milk herself.

When the girl got back to where the gazelle was lying she saw its eyes were very dull, and when she had told it the Sheikh was not coming, it dropped its head and died.

That night, lying in his luxurious palace, the man who had been a beggar said to his wife, "What happened to the gazelle? You did not come back to tell me."

And she answered sadly, "It died, and I am so grieved at the way you disregarded the poor creature's pleas that I have decided when my father comes back I shall return to his tents, for I no longer love you."

"Foolish woman!" cried the Sheikh. "Go to sleep, and in the morning you will have forgotten all about this matter." Within a few moments he was snoring.

In the middle of the night he had a dream. He thought he saw the gazelle again, and its eyes were very sad. "Why did you not bring me a bowl of dates and honey when I begged you to do so? Had you forgotten that you owed all your good fortune to me? I was grateful because you bought my liberty back for me, why could you not show me one act of kindness when I was in need?"

"I asked my wife to take you a bowl of milk!" cried the Sheikh Abu Zakat, feeling suddenly very ashamed of himself.

"It was not the same thing," said the gazelle, faintly, and it disappeared.

In a great fright the Sheikh Abu Zakat sat up, and found himself Mustapha the beggar again, dressed in tatters, sitting against the outdoor oven of a rich man's house in the moonlight. ■

William Tell is said, in 1296, to have shot an apple from the head of his son when an enraged Governor challenged him to do so for refusing to salute his hat, symbol of alien authority. The story, however, is not related of Tell until 1499 A.D., two centuries after the incident. But it does appear in the Old Norse **Vilkina Saga** and, three hundred years before William Tell, in the Saga of Saint Olof. A hundred years ago the Swiss themselves decided that the story was legendary, though a man named Freudenberger had been burned alive by the Canton of Uri in the early eighteenth century for claiming the legend to be of Danish origin. Tradition indeed ascribes the arrow incident to Palnatoki, bodyguard of Harold Bluetooth, in 950 A.D. Some discomfort has been occasioned by the statement (in the Icelandic Saga) that the original apple-target idea was suggested by a Christian saint who wished to convert the heathen hero Eindridi.

Apart from these considerations, the tale itself might well be seen to highlight the problems of category definitions in the field of tales. Is it, for instance, a myth, relating to the Nordic gods, said to be of Hodr in the Edda? Is it a legend, of William of Cloudisley of Britain, as it appears in the 'Ballad of Adam Bell?' As a 'fairy tale', it belongs among the marchen, to amuse; but as a didactic fable, it would inculcate principles. Some, on the other hand, see it as an allegory, that is 'fabulous, but indicating some history.'

It does not help matters that this fascinating idea is very common to others than (as Sir George Dasent has claimed) 'the whole Aryan race'. The Turks, Mongols and Samoyeds all attribute it to their own heroes. I was last told it as a true local story by a Cypriot taxi-driver in Paphos, the legendary birthplace of Venus. As the Swiss William Tell variety is easily found and known to many people, here for comparison is the version from the **Vilkina Saga;** three centuries before Tell's time.

The Apple on the Boy's Head

A certain Palnatoki, for some time among King Harold's bodyguard, had made his bravery odious to very many of his fellow-soldiers by the zeal with which he surpassed them in the discharge of his duty.

This man once, when talking tipsily over his cups, had boasted that he was so skilled an archer that he could hit the smallest apple placed a long way off on a stick, at the first shot; which talk, caught up at first by the ears of backbiters, soon came to the hearing of the King.

Now mark how the wickedness of the King turned the confidence of the father to the peril of the son, by commanding that this dearest pledge of his life should be placed, instead of the stick; with a threat that, unless the author of this promise could strike off the apple at the first flight of the arrow, he should pay the penalty of his empty boasting by the loss of his head.

The King's command forced the soldier to perform more than he had promised, and what he had said, reported by the tongue of slanderers, bound him to accomplish what he had not said.

Nor did his sterling courage, though caught in the snare of slander, suffer him to lay aside his firmness of heart; nay, he accepted the trial the more readily because it was hard. So Palnatoki warned the boy urgently, when he took his stand, to await the coming of the hurtling arrow with calm ears and unbent head; lest by a slight turn of his body he should defeat the practised skill of the bowman. And, taking further counsel to prevent his fear, he turned away his face, lest he should be scared at the sight of the weapon. Then, taking three arrows from the quiver, he struck the mark given him with the first he fitted to the string. But, if chance had brought the head of the boy before the shaft, no doubt the penalty of the son would have recoiled to the peril of the father, and the swerving of the shaft that struck the boy would have linked them both in common ruin.

I am in doubt, then, whether to admire more the courage of the father or the temper of the son, of whom the one by skill in his art avoided being the slayer of his child, while the other by patience of mind and quietness of body saved himself alive, and spared the natural affection of his father. Nay, the youthful frame strengthened the aged heart, and showed as much courage in awaiting the arrow as the father skill in launching it.

But Palnatoki, when asked by the King why he had taken more arrows from the quiver, when it had been settled that he should only try the fortune of the bow *once*, made answer:

"That I might avenge on thee the swerving of the first by the points of the rest, lest perchance my innocence might have been punished, while your violence escaped scotfree." ■

*There is a Middle Eastern proverb, 'The boots of Hunain',
referring to something which is not such a bargain as it seems
to be. This story, in its essentials and with remarkable fidelity of
incident, is found all over the world. There is a Hebrew version,
in which a Jewish cobbler outsmarts a desert Arab who has
been rude to him; a Gaelic one from the Highlands of Scotland,
and a Norwegian tale featuring a master-thief. The modern
Greek and German tales with this plot closely resemble the one
from Bangladesh, while in England the tale is positively stated
to have happened to 'A butcher in Lewes, Essex' (though
Lewes is in the county of Sussex). The following is the
presentation found in Ibn Khallikan's monumental* **Wafayat,**
*written in the thirteenth century, the first Arabian dictionary of
biography. Its author himself came from a Central Asian family,
where the story may have been current.*

The Boots of Hunain

There was once a desert Arab who rode into town
and saw a pair of boots offered for sale in the market.
He went into the shop and made an offer for them,
but Hunain the shoemaker stuck to his price, and in
the end the infuriated beduin stamped out of the
shop. "The price you ask is equal to the value of my
camel," he snorted.

Now the shoemaker was deeply affronted by the
behaviour and language of this Arab, and decided that
he would not let him get away with such insults. The
Arab had mounted his camel and started along the
trail towards the tents of his tribe. The shoemaker,
knowing from where his would-be customer had come,
picked up the boots and went by short-cuts to a point
which the Arab would have to pass eventually. There
he placed one boot on the sand.

Then the shoemaker went a mile or more further
along the road and dropped the other boot, hiding
himself to watch what happened, for he had a plan.

Presently the Arab came along, and saw the first
boot lying on the ground. He said to himself, "That is
one of the boots of Hunain, the cobbler; if only it was a
pair, I would be able to get down and take them away
for nothing." And he went on his way. After all, what
was the use of one boot?

Soon afterwards, of course, the Arab came upon
the second boot. He thought, "What a pity I did not

take up the first one—then I would have had a pair."
Then it occurred to him that he might go back for the
first boot, then he would have them both.

The beduin was some way from his own tents, and
did not want to tire his camel, so he hobbled it and ran
back to the place where he had seen the first boot.

The shoemaker came out of hiding and, leaving the
second boot where it was, he made off with the Arab's
camel.

When the Arab arrived back to the place where he
had left his camel, he found it missing. Thinking it
must have strayed, he made his way back to the tents
of his people.

"What have you brought back from town?" his
fellow-beduins asked, as he limped into the settlement.

"Only the boots of Hunain" said the miserable man.

■

Believed to have been compiled in England at the end of the 13th century, the **Gesta Romanorum** *— 'Deeds of the Romans' was its title, for no obvious reason — is an extraordinary jumble. It was the basis for another Latin book, with the same title, published in continental Europe soon after. Designed for the use of priests wishing to ram home morals by means of tales, some of its 'teachings' are extremely thin. The* **Gesta** *adopted stories from any source: from the Bible, the Koran, the Talmud, the Buddhist scriptures, Hinduism, and previous devout writings. Few among the audiences who were regaled with this material for four hundred years as they sat in church, however, could have suspected that many of the apologues being advanced to bolster their faith originated from several despised 'infidel' civilizations.*

Schiller, Fridolin, Shakespeare, William Morris, Parnell, and a host of other writers whose work is still well known, are indebted to the collection. Shakespeare found in it the plot of his **Pericles;** *Chaucer raided it for his* **History of Constance;** *Walpole for the* **Mysterious Mother,** *and Boccaccio for his* **Two Friends** *— and innumerable others have followed their example.*

Although the manner in which its lessons are put generally seems dispiritingly pedestrian to the modern reader, this English translation of the original of Shakespeare's 'Three Caskets' sequence in **The Merchant of Venice** *gives a fair impression of the* **Gesta** *at its best.*

The Three Caskets

At one time there dwelt in Rome a mighty emperor, named Anselm, who had married the King's daughter of Jerusalem, a fair lady, and gracious in the sight of every man. But she was long with the Emperor ere she bare him any child; wherefore the nobles of the empire were very sorrowful, because their lord had no heir of his own body begotten. At last it befell, that this Anselm walked after supper, one evening, into his garden, and bethought himself that he had no heir, and how the King of Ampluy warred on him continually, for so much as he had no son to make defence in his absence. Therefore he was sorrowful, and went to his chamber and slept.

Then he thought he saw a vision in his sleep, that the morning was more clear than it was wont to be, and that the moon was much paler on the one side than on the other. And after he saw a bird of two colours, and by that bird stood two beasts, which fed that little bird with their heat. And after that came more beasts, and bowing their breasts toward the bird, went their way. Then came there divers birds that sung sweetly and pleasantly. With that, the Emperor awaked.

In the morning early this Anselm remembered his vision, and wondered much what it might signify; wherefore he called to him his philosophers, and all the states of the empire, and told them his dream, charging them to tell him the signification thereof on pain of death, and if they told him the true interpretation, he promised them good reward. Then said they, "Dear lord, tell us your dream, and we shall declare to you what it betokens." Then the Emperor told them from the beginning to the ending, as is aforesaid. When the philosophers heard this, with glad cheer they answered, and said, "Sir, the vision that you saw betokeneth good, for the empire shall be clearer than it is.

"The moon that is more pale on the one side than on the other, betokeneth the Empress, that hath lost part of her colour, through the conception of a son that she hath conceived. The little bird betokeneth the son that she shall bear. The two beasts that fed this bird betoken the wise and rich men of the empire which shall obey the son. These other beasts that bowed their breasts to the bird betoken many other nations that shall do him homage. The bird that sang so sweetly to this little bird betokeneth the Romans, who shall rejoice and sing because of his birth. This is the very interpretation of your dream."

When the Emperor heard this, he was right joyful. Soon after that, the Empress travailed in childbirth, and was delivered of a fair son, at whose birth there was great and wonderful joy made.

When the King of Ampluy heard this, he thought to himself thus: "Lo, I have warred against the Emperor all the days of my life, and now he hath a son who, when he cometh to full age, will revenge the wrong I have done against his father; therefore it is better that I send to the Emperor and beseech him of truce and peace, that the son may have nothing against me when he cometh to manhood."

When he had thus said to himself, he wrote to the Emperor, beseeching him to have peace. When the Emperor saw that the King of Ampluy wrote to him more for fear than for love, he wrote again to him, that if he would find good and sufficient sureties to keep the peace, and bind himself all the days of his life to do him service and homage, he would receive him in peace.

When the King had read the tenor of the Emperor's letter, he called his council, praying them to give him counsel how he best might do, as touching this matter. Then said they, "It is good that ye obey the Emperor's will and commandment in all things. For first, in that he desired of you surety for the peace; to this we answer thus: Ye have but one daughter, and the Emperor one son, wherefore let a marriage be made between them, and that may be a perpetual covenant of peace. Also he asketh homage and tribute, which it is good to fulfil."

Then the King sent his messengers to the Emperor, saying that he would fulfil his desire in all things, if it might please his highness that his son and the King's daughter might be married together. All this well pleased the Emperor, yet he sent again, saying, "If his daughter were a pure maid from her birth unto that day, he would consent to that marriage." Then was the King right glad, for his daughter was a pure maid.

Therefore, when the letters of covenant and compact were sealed, the King furnished a fair ship, wherein he might send his daughter, with many noble knights,

ladies, and great riches, unto the Emperor, for to have his son in marriage.

And when they were sailing in the sea, towards Rome, a storm arose so extremely and so horribly that the ship broke against a rock. They were all drowned save only the young lady, who fixed her hope and heart so greatly on God, that she was saved. About three of the clock the tempest ceased, and the lady drove forth over the waves in that broken ship, which was cast up again. But a huge whale followed after, ready to devour both the ship and her. Wherefore this young lady, when night came, smote fire with a stone, wherewith the ship was greatly lightened, and then the whale dared not adventure towards the ship for fear of that light.

At the cock-crowing, this young lady was so weary of the great tempest and trouble of the sea, that she slept. Within a little while after the fire ceased, and the whale came and devoured the virgin. And when she awaked and found herself swallowed up in the whale's belly, she smote fire, and with a knife wounded the whale in many places, and when the whale felt himself wounded, according to his nature he began to swim to land.

There was dwelling at that time in a country nearby a noble Earl named Pirris, who for his recreation was walking on the sea-shore. He saw the whale coming towards the land; wherefore he turned home again, and gathered a great many of men and women, and came thither again, and fought with the whale, and wounded him very sore, and as they smote, the maiden that was in his belly cried with a high voice, and said: "O gentle friends, have mercy and compassion on me, for I am a King's daughter, and a true maid from the hour of my birth unto this day." When the Earl heard this he wondered greatly, and opened the side of the whale, and found the young lady, and took her out.

And when she was thus delivered, she told him forthwith whose daughter she was, and how she had lost all her goods in the sea, and how she should have been married unto the Emperor's son. And when the Earl heard this, he was very glad, and comforted her the more and kept her with him till she was well refreshed. And in the meantime he sent messengers to the Emperor, letting him know how the King's daughter was saved.

Then was the Emperor right glad of her safety, and coming, had great compassion on her, saying, "Ah, good maiden, for the love of my son thou hast suffered much woe; nevertheless, if thou be worthy to be his

wife, soon shall I prove." And when he had thus said, he caused three vessels to be brought forth. The first was made of pure gold, well beset with precious stones without, and within full of dead men's bones, and thereupon was engraven this: *"Whoso Chooseth Me, Shall Find What He Deserveth."* The second vessel was made of fine silver, filled with earth and worms, the superscription was thus: *"Whoso Chooseth Me, Shall Find What His Nature Desireth."* The third vessel was made of lead, full within of precious stones, and thereupon was insculpt this: *"Whoso Chooseth Me, Shall Find That God Hath Disposed For Him."* These three vessels the Emperor showed the maiden, and said: "Lo, here daughter, these be rich vessels. If thou choose one of these, wherein is profit to thee and to others, then shalt thou have my son. And if thou choose that wherein is no profit to thee, nor to any other, in truth thou shalt not marry him."

When the maiden heard this, she lifted up her hands to God, and said, "Thou Lord, that knowest all things, grant me grace this hour so to choose, that I may receive the Emperor's son." And with that she beheld the first vessel of gold, which was engraven royally, and read the superscription, *"Whoso Chooseth Me, Shall Find What He Deserveth;"* saying thus, "Though this vessel be full precious, and made of pure gold, nevertheless I know not what is within, therefore, my dear lord, this vessel will I not choose."

And then she beheld the second vessel, that was of pure silver, and read the superscription, *"Whoso Chooseth Me, Shall Find What His Nature Desireth."* Thinking thus within herself, "If I choose this vessel, *what* is within I know not, but well I know, there shall I find that which nature desireth, and my nature desireth the lust of the flesh, and therefore this vessel will I not choose."

When she had seen these two vessels, and had given an answer about them, she beheld the third vessel of lead, and read the superscription, *"Whoso Chooseth Me, Shall Find That God Hath Disposed."* Thinking within herself, "This vessel is not very rich, nor outwardly precious, yet the superscription saith, *'Whoso Chooseth Me, Shall Find That God Hath Disposed;'* and without doubt God never disposeth any harm, therefore, by the leave of God, this vessel will I choose."

When the Emperor heard this, he said, "O fair maiden, open thy vessel, for it is full of precious stones, and see if thou hast well chosen or no". And when this young lady had opened it, she found it full of fine gold and precious stones, as the Emperor had told her before. Then said the Emperor, "Daughter, because thou hast well chosen, thou shalt marry my son." And then he appointed the wedding-day; and they were married with great solemnity, and with much honour continued to their lives' end. ∎

The Land Where Time Stood Still

Lafcadio Hearn, the scholar who went from the United States to Japan and taught there, noted that the fishing line of Urashima Taro and some strange jewels he is said to have brought back from the land of No Time are to be seen at the seashore Temple of Kanagawa. Urashima's absence, according to the Nihongi (Chronicles of Japan) covered nearly 350 years: his departure is stated to have been in 477 A.D., and his return and sudden death from senility in 825 A.D. This well-known classical story is the subject of much beautiful art.

*The legend itself has travelled far, in terrestrial terms. Katherine M. Briggs reproduces an English version in her excellent **British Folk Tales and Legends** (London: Routledge, 1977)—where the hero is King Herla of the ancient Britons. When he gets home after two hundred years, the Saxons have overrun his country and people hardly understand his Celtic speech. But even closer to Urashima's tale, often in matters of detail, is the variant chosen here. It was related by a Gypsy in Romania and published by Francis Hindes Groom in 1899. He thought it unique; but since then the theme has been found in many different places. Yet exactly how Urashima of Mizunoe became Herla of England, an unnamed bridegroom of Italy, or even Peterkin of Romania, may never be established.*

This narration gives a good idea, too, of the directness and vigour of the best Gypsy folktelling.

There was once a monarch, called the Red King. He found that food disappeared from a closet, even though it was locked and guards were placed upon it through the night. The food simply was not there in the morning.

He made a proclamation:

"I will give half my kingdom to anyone who can so guard this closet that the food shall not vanish from it!"

Now the King had three sons. The eldest thought to himself, "Half the kingdom should not go to a stranger who might answer this plea! It would be best for me to keep watch."

He went to his father and offered to stay up on guard.

The King said:

"As you wish, but do not be frightened by anything you may see."

The Prince went to the closet and lay down to stay beside it for the night. But, as soon as he put his head on the pillow, he fell asleep, and stayed asleep until dawn, for a warm, sleepy breeze arose and lulled him into a deep slumber.

While he was asleep, his small sister, only a tiny child, got up and turned a somersault. Instantly her nails became like an axe and her teeth like a shovel: she opened the closet and devoured everything in it. Then she reverted to the appearance of an ordinary small child, and returned to her cradle: for she was in fact both a witch and a babe unweaned.

The Prince got up in the morning, and told his father that he had seen nothing. The King went to the closet and found it completely bare: everything had gone. He said to his son:

"It would take a better man than you to solve this, even he might be able to do nothing."

Then the middle son said to the King:

"Father, I shall keep watch tonight."

The King agreed, warning him to be brave.

The second son lay down beside the closet in the palace. At ten o'clock the warm breeze came and cast him into a deep sleep.

The tiny Princess who was a witch arose from her cradle and unwrapped herself from her swaddling-clothes. She turned a somersault and her nails and teeth were transformed as before. Again she went to the closet and opened it and ate up all the food which it contained. And, as before, she rotated herself and went back to her usual place, in the cradle.

When day broke the young Prince went to his father to confess that he had seen and heard nothing, and the King told him that it would take a better man than he to unravel the mystery.

It was now the turn of the youngest Prince, and he asked, and was given, permission by the King to watch the closet that night.

This young man, however, did not at once lay himself down to rest like his brothers. He took four needles and stuck them in four places. When he began to feel tired, he pricked himself with a needle: and so he stayed awake until ten o'clock.

When the tiny witch rose from her cradle, her brother saw her. He watched while she turned a somersault, and as her nails and teeth became transformed, and as she devoured the food, and when she returned to her cradle. The Prince was terrified; he trembled with fear, and it seemed to him, as he lay quietly there, that ten years passed before the dawn.

When it was light, his father sought him out and said:

"Did you see anything?"

"What did I see, what did I not see?" answered the youth: and he would say no more about his terrible experience. He asked the King to give him some money and a horse, and to let him travel, for he had decided to go away and get married.

His father gave him two sacks of money and a horse, and he went to the outskirts of the city and dug a hole. He left the coins buried there, in a stone box, and put a stone cross on top to mark the place. Then he set off on his travels.

He journeyed for eight years, and then he came to the place of the Queen of all the Birds that Fly. She asked him, "Where are you going?"

He said: "I am going yonder, where there is neither death nor old age, to get married."

The Queen said to him, "There is neither death nor old age here."

The Prince asked her how that was.

The Queen said, "Death and old age will not come to take me away until I have broken the last twig of this huge forest."

But the Prince realized that that time would in fact come one day, and so he started off again on his way.

After another eight years, he arrived at a palace of copper. Out of it came a maiden, who took him in her arms and kissed him. She said, "I have waited a very long time for you."

She took the Prince and the horse in her charge and he spent the night there. In the morning he placed the saddle on his horse. Then the maiden began to weep and asked, "Where are you going?"

"I am going further, to where there is neither death nor old age."

She told him that there was neither of those things where they now were, and the Prince asked her how that could be.

"Death will not come here until these mountains are levelled and these forests have disappeared."

"That is not good enough for me," he said, and he went on his way.

Now, of all things, his horse said to him: "Master, whip me four times, and yourself twice: for you have come to the Plain of Regret. And Regret can seize you and throw you down, horse and all! So spur your horse and escape, and do not linger here!"

He did as he was told, and crossed the Plain of Regret; and then came to a hut. A lad came out and asked, "Where are you going and what do you want?"

The Prince told him of his quest.

The lad said: "There is neither death nor old age here, for I am the Wind."

At last the Prince thought he could rest. He stayed there for a hundred years, and he did not age at all.

He used to go hunting, and always found so much game that he could hardly carry it home. The Wind had said to him, "Go, by all means, into the Mountains of Gold and the Mountains of Silver: but do not go into the Mountain of Regret or to the Valley of Grief."

But, one day the Prince did go to the Mountain of Regret and into the Valley of Grief. And that was how Grief cast him down, until his eyes were full of tears. He remembered his home and went to the Wind in sadness, saying, "I am going home to my father, for I cannot stay here any longer."

The Wind told him: "Do not go, for your father is dead, and you have no brothers either. A million years have come and gone since the times you recall at the Palace. Even the place where the building stood is not remembered—melons have been planted on it. I know, for I passed that way no more than an hour ago."

But the Prince took no notice of the Wind, and started on his way back to his home. As he arrived at the Palace of Copper, he saw that the mountains were flat, and that the maiden had cut the last stick of the forest, and that she had died. He buried her and continued his journey.

Presently, he came to the Queen of all the Birds that Fly. When she saw him, she said, "You are still young!" Then she broke through the very last branch in her forest, and she fell and died.

At long last the Prince came to the place where his father's palace had stood, and looked around him. It was practically a wilderness. All he could see, as he exclaimed, "God, Thou art wonderful!" was the well of his father. He went towards it and suddenly his sister, the witch, rushed at him crying, "I have waited long for you, dog!" She was trying to devour him when he made the sign of the cross at her, and she perished.

As he was walking away from the place, he came across an old man, with a beard down to his belt. He said, "Father, where is the Palace of the Red King? I am his son."

"What is that you say, my child?" asked the ancient one. "You say that you are his son! *My grandfather* told me about the Red King. But his palace is gone; his very city has vanished timeless ages ago: and you say that you are his *son!*"

"It is not twenty years, old man," said the Prince, "that I left my father's presence. Follow me, if you do not believe me."

In fact, it was a million years that had passed . . .

The Prince found the cross of stone, now almost completely covered with earth. He struggled for two days to get to the stone box with the money in it. When he lifted the box and opened it, Death sat in one of the corners, and Old Age in another.

Old Age said, "Seize him, Death."

Death said, "Get him yourself!"

Old Age took him in front, and Death from behind, and so he died.

The old man took him and gave him a decent burial, and then took for himself the money and the horse. ■

The Man Turned Into A Mule

This story popular in Spain — and known in Spanish-speaking countries throughout the world — has, in fact, far greater point in the Oriental lands of its origin, where the transforming element is a magician. There is no record of representatives of the Catholic Church having the alleged power to change a man into a mule, whether as a punishment or otherwise. This, of course, is the kind of internal evidence which folklorists look for in plotting the derivations of a tale. And yet, in anti-clerical periods, the narrative has been used to imply that illiberal clergy may keep peasants in such ignorance that they are considered near-magicians. In the Far East, people who feel that human reincarnation into animal form is absurd have used the tale to mock transmigrationists; in other areas, townspeople have been regaled with it to pander to an appetite for 'foolish peasant' jokes. In both the literary and oral forms, it lends itself well to emphasis of whichever of these elements it is desired to point up; and it is also widely regarded as a 'trickster' joke. This multiple potential may account for its durability and popularity. But it also means that those who try to categorize tales (into Humour, Peasant, Reincarnation, Trickster, Anti-Clerical and so on) tend to leave it alone when advancing theories that all stories may be slotted into neat systems.

Once there was a student, who — being extremely poor — began to think of some way of adding to his very small store of silver coins. He gathered together his student friends, and they talked about it all night, each of them being in the same position. Soon, Juan Rivas, for that was his name, thought of a plan. "Friends," said he, "You look upon one tonight who tomorrow shall be the son of one of the first Grandees of Spain!" When the laughter had died down, he looked very wise, but refused to tell them any more. "I assure you that if you will bear with me for a day, by this time tomorrow night I shall be back with a story which will give us all a merry time together."

Putting his plan into action, Juan Rivas, with his friend Carlos, went along the road next morning, looking for a man with a string of mules. Sure enough, after a while he came upon such a man, sitting on the first mule, and leading his string towards the next town.

Juan Rivas let the five mules pass, then, as the last one came by him, he seized it, and handed it over to Carlos, who was hidden behind the hedge. "Take this mule and sell it in the market," he whispered, "Give me the money later when we all meet at the cafe." So saying, he placed the mule's saddle-cloth over his back, and followed the other mules as if he in fact was one of them.

The day was very warm and the muleteer was half-asleep, sitting cross-legged on the biggest animal. Nothing worried him for about half an hour, when he became aware that all the mules had come to a halt. This was the work of Juan Rivas, who was getting to the second stage of his plan.

"Hola!" shouted the muleteer, "Get going, you stupid beasts, I haven't got all day to waste!" and he administered hefty kicks to the sides of the animal he was sitting upon.

Still the creatures could not start, as Juan Rivas was holding on to the reins of the fourth mule, so the muleteer got off his animal, and saw a human being, saddled and bridled, at the back.

"What in the world are you doing there, young man?" he bellowed with many a curse, as muleteers, owing to the nature of their calling, are extremely bad-tempered.

"It is no freak you see, my friend," said Juan Rivas, sadly, "But reality. I am no longer your fifth mule, whom you have beaten so unmercifully in the past, but have now returned to my own shape."

"B-but . . . what do you mean? Explain the matter, as soon as you may," said the puzzled muleteer, scratching his head.

"Well, my friend, I offended Holy Mother Church, many times, I am sorry to say, for which misdeeds I was turned into a mule for several years. That time I have faithfully served, and my period of imprisonment being over, I am now, by the dispensation of Providence, back to normal, as you might say, on this very day."

"But where is my mule, which cost me one hundred pieces of silver not many years ago?" asked the man.

"It may not have been many years to you, my friend, but it has been eternity to me!" cried Juan Rivas. "Do understand me, please, I was that mule! The mule was me! Now I am back in human form, able to speak in a human voice. Would that I could have told you how I felt about it over the years, when you abused me and beat me so much. But that was my punishment, and I have served you faithfully. Now you speak to all that remains of your mule. Do you understand me?"

"Scarcely," mumbled the rustic, "but I am not usually faced with this sort of thing. It appears to me, now, that you must have been that animal . . . I always thought there was something funny about that mule!"

"Well, be quick about it," said the student, "and get this saddle and saddle-cloth off me, and take your uncomfortable bridle, too. I've had enough of it, and I'm bruised from neck to ankle as well. However, all that is now over, and you will always be able to say that the son of one of the first Grandees of Spain served you as a beast of burden, and is now restored to wealth and rank."

"Are you a man of power and money, then?" gasped the man, "O sir, I beg you, forgive me for all I did to you when you were a mule! I hope that you will not have me imprisoned for the kicks I aimed at your excellency, I am a ruined man!"

"No, no, dear fellow," said Juan Rivas kindly, "You were not to know that I was not a mule. Heavens, that is not your fault at all. I am a charitable man; I did

wrong and was punished, it will not in any way help me in my case with Heaven if now I were to take vengeance on you. Think nothing of this, and forget it."

"Then I am forgiven? Your excellency will not hold it against me? Oh, God bless you, noble sir!"

"It will be a great consolation to me that none of my highly-born friends will know what has been happening to me for so many wretched years," said the student, piously, "and I would indeed esteem it a favour if you do not divulge this to a living soul. Give me your word as an honest man upon it."

"I promise your honour that torture would not drag the true state of affairs from me," cried the poor bewildered fellow. "Goodbye, dear exalted sir, and may you never again incur the dissatisfaction of Holy Mother Church!"

Thus they parted, the muleteer pondering over the strange mysteries of life, and the great secret with which he had been entrusted by one of the family of a Grandee of Spain, and Juan Rivas to his rendezvous with his friend Carlos, who, he hoped, had got a good price for the mule.

The pleasure of a grand feast with those young people to whom he had promised hospitality and entertainment the night before made Juan Rivas whistle joyfully as he walked back into the town. As it fell out, they enjoyed good food and wine, telling and retelling the story to all and sundry, till dawn broke.

Some weeks later, there was a cattle market in the town, and the muleteer who had lost his fifth mule was looking for a new animal. The auctioneer, who knew him, asked what had happened to the other one. "I parted with it for personal and private reasons," was all he could get out of the muleteer, "and I cannot discuss those reasons with you."

"Oh, well, why you did it is your own business, of course," said the auctioneer, "but if I were you I would just buy it back, for it stands over there; you will recognise it at once. I did, for have you not been coming in every Friday on it for more years than I care to mention?"

"By the saints," murmured the muleteer to himself, "So it is." Walking over to the animal he said to it "Well, your excellency, I can't imagine what you must have been doing to incur the wrath of the Church so soon again, but terrible indeed, as we know, are the Ways of Providence. Have no fear, I will buy you, and this time I promise to treat you as one born to your station!" ■

The Fox and the Hedgehog

This fable has the distinction of being the very earliest one attributed to Aesop which is on record; it is found in the philosopher Aristotle's **Rhetoric.** *It refers there to people embezzling from the state.*

Quite detailed and conflicting biographies of Aesop exist—but there is no assurance that any of the material in them is at all accurate. He is said to have been black (which is what his name means) and to have been born in Greece or Asia about 620 B.C. Eight hundred years or so later, his fables were published by Caxton in England—they had been printed around the same time in Greek and Latin. The Greeks, Hindus and Egyptians have all been credited with the invention of the fable, and very many of those ascribed to Aesop are from other sources. Some people think that the first ever was the Parable of Jotham in the Bible (Judges, IX, 7-15); and the supposedly Aesopian fable of the Lion and the Mouse is found in an ancient Egyptian papyrus.

Aesop was certainly famous enough for Aristophanes to feature his teachings as being part of oral learning, and Socrates himself is said to have versified some of the stories.

Incidents from the supposed life of the fabulist have been grafted upon a wide variety of people. They adhere to the name of the Dominican monk Etienne of Bourbon, who presented them for preachers in the 14th century. They are in the Arab **Book of Sindibad;** *in the Old English Tale of Beryn, they are credited to Till Eulenspiegel, the German rascal—and they are even found in China as national traditions.*

A fox, while crossing a river, was driven by the stream into a narrow creek, and lay there for a long time, trapped.

He was covered with a multitude of horseflies, which had fastened themselves upon him.

It so happened that a hedgehog, wandering in the area, saw the unhappy condition of the fox, and called out to him:

"Would you like me to drive away those flies, which are tormenting you so much?"

But the fox begged the hedgehog to do nothing of the sort.

The hedgehog was surprised. "Why not?" it asked.

"Because," replied the fox, "the flies which are sticking on to me now are already full, and are not drawing very much more blood. If you were to remove them, a swarm of fresh and hungry ones would descend—and they would not leave a drop of blood in my body!" ■

From Japan to South America, from the Smith Sound Eskimos to the reciters of the **Thousand and One Nights,** the theme of the maiden who becomes a bird through wearing a magical costume—and how she can be trapped by stealing it—is a part of folklore, defying all attempts at tracing it to a single source. There are few myths in which so many of the details accord with such mysterious consistency: the maiden alights from the sky, usually to have a bath; she puts off her bird-cloak and is seen to be wondrously beautiful. The young man steals her dress, courts her, and she marries him. Many of the subsequent adventures of the couple are also similar, especially her flight escape and return to her human home.

The greatest German epic, the **Niebelungenlied,** of the 13th century, features the swan-maidens, both magical and wise, later the subject of the mighty Wagnerian epic, **The Ring.** Once again, at the very heart of a national literature, we find the humble folktale: read and studied as a classic, admired as a great literary and artistic work: yet still recited by Swedish hunters, Japanese fishermen and American Indians.

Race, religion, customs, social organization, and almost every mental attitude may differ among the world's peoples, but the odds are that they will know the Bird-Maiden tale. You may not speak Swahili, Magyar, Tamil or Russian, Persian or the Erse of Ireland but the people who do, and who know nothing of each other, know this story. According to the best anthropology, many of them have not been in cultural contact, at least for many thousands of years.

In a number of versions, the magical instruments of the cloak of invisibility, the cap of knowledge, and the shoes of swiftness are included in the saga. The maiden is very often supernatural: though she may be, as in the Syrian cognate, merely the possessor of a magical (green silk) robe. Varieties also have her transforming herself by means of a wolf-skin, as in Croatia; a sealskin, as in the Shetland Islands; or with white robes, as in Sweden.

In Kurdistan, the daughter of the magical bird Simurgh is the heroine; in Greece it is the Nereids; in Bulgaria, the Samodivas, and in Hungary, Fairy Elizabeth. The mysterious maiden is often the daughter of a king of spirits, and comes from the skies. She may be disguised merely as an unspecified, beautiful bird. Sometimes, as in Russia, she is a swan; sometimes, as in Finland, a goose; in both the Celebes and Bohemia, she is a dove: to the Magyars, a pigeon.

Our version is the famous one of Hasan of Basra, from the Arabian Nights. Perhaps one of its oddest coincidences is that the home of the mysterious lady is in the Islands of Wak-Wak: which does not sound totally unlike "Arawak", the name of the widespread community of South American Indians—who have a legend of a strangely similar sort. In this, there is a magical bird-maiden, daughter of the King of supernatural beings, flying warrior birds who accept the young man who finds them as one of themselves. Is there a relationship between the medieval Arabian story and the very ancient and at that time undiscovered Arawak people of America? If not, how do they come to share the same tale, even if the Wak-Wak/Arawak similarity is a coincidence?

The Bird Maiden

Once upon a time there lived, in the city of Basra, a young jeweller who had inherited enough from his father to set himself up in a good way of business. He was sitting in his shop one day, looking at a book, when a stranger entered. Hasan did not know it, but this man was a magician, and he had a deep plot in his mind.

First he gained Hasan's friendship by praising the workmanship of the jewellery on display. Then, looking at Hasan's book, he said: "I have another book here, something which will be of great interest to you as a goldsmith."

He took out an ancient tome, with a silver clasp and gold edges to the pages.

"What does it contain?" asked the jeweller.

"The secret of how to make gold!" said the magician.

"Could you teach me how to make it?" asked Hasan, who, of course, was by now deeply impressed and interested.

The magician put his fingers to his lips and said:

"Hasan, as I like you, and I have no son of my own, I shall teach you. I will come tomorrow, and we can talk again."

The young man could hardly believe his ears, and he could scarcely sleep for thinking about the magician. He seemed such a venerable old man, surely there could be no harm in just seeing whether he could make gold or not, Hasan asked himself.

The following day, when it was time for him to open his shop, Hasan saw the magician standing outside. Hasan let him in and sent his servant for tea. Then the magician whispered: "Start a fire and put a crucible on it, and we will start the goldmaking."

Hasan did as he was told, and the magician asked him for some copper. He heated and then melted the metal in the crucible; then he took a small paper packet from his turban and sprinkled powder from it onto the liquid copper. This powder was a golden yellow, and Hasan worked the bellows with all his might and main to keep the fire's heat strong enough to maintain the liquid nature of the alloy.

As he watched, it turned into the colour of pure gold.

As soon as it was cold, the magician said:

"Now for the test. Take this lump of gold to the market and see what an independent goldsmith will give you for it, after he has applied all the necessary tests. Then you will know whether I tell the truth or not. Sell the gold, and bring the money back here."

Hasan took the gold, and received twenty thousand pieces of silver for it, such was its great mass and purity. When he went back to the shop, the magician said: "Keep the money, and do what you will with it."

Hasan, overjoyed, took the money and gave it to his mother, who, however, warned him:

"Foolish boy! Have you not remembered what I have always told you about greed and trusting total strangers who say they have something to give you?"

But Hasan would not listen, and he rushed back to his shop, where the magician was sitting.

Hasan and the magician became great friends, and the old man again demonstrated, this time at Hasan's house, how the gold was made. Eagerly, Hasan asked him for a supply of the powder.

"Alas!" said the magician, "that is the last of the powder. But I will give you the list of ingredients."

He recited a number of names of chemicals and herbs, and Hasan memorized them. Then the magician gave Hasan a piece of drugged sweetmeat—and he fell, insensible, to the floor.

As soon as he saw that Hasan was unconscious, the magician filled some empty chests with everything he could lay hands on in the room, and cried out: "Dog of an Arab! At long last I have found you and now you will do my will!"

He called porters and they removed the chests containing the valuables—and one with Hasan inside—to the docks, where a chartered ship lay at anchor.

"Captain!" shouted the magician, "Up anchor and away! We have attained our desire." Before long they were far away from the port of Basra.

When Hasan's mother returned and found the house empty of valuables and her son gone, she knew it was something to do with the magician. When neighbours came in to console her, for she was weeping and wailing, she said "I shall never see my son again, I will make a tomb here in the courtyard, with his name upon it, and mourn him the rest of my life." She tore her clothes, lamenting continually.

On board the magician's ship, Hasan slowly came to his senses.

He was kicked and cuffed by the crew, scarcely knowing where he was. Suddenly the magician appeared before him, shouting excitedly, "By the moon and the stars! I have wonderful work for you to do when we reach land! Now, have no fear, for you are as my son."

"Where are we going?" asked Hasan, but he was given no reply.

Hasan was fed on bread and water, and after a few more days at sea, felt no fear, but waited for what fate had in store.

The voyage lasted for several months; Hasan knew that by the waning and waxing of the moon, and finally they all disembarked in a beautiful green harbour.

"My son," said the magician, "forgive me for abducting you. It was for your own good." The captain and crew were paid off, and sailed away. Only Hasan and the magician were left on the shore. The old man played a tattoo on a small drum; and at once, from a cloud of dust, three she-camels appeared.

"Mount", cried the magician, "We have far yet to ride." Then with Hasan on one camel, the old man on another, and the third loaded with provisions, they set off.

After days of hard riding, they dismounted at a stream to water the camels, and Hasan saw a fine palace with gold cupolas.

"What is that place?" asked Hasan, as he and the old man ate.

"Do not ask me, it is the home of an enemy of mine. Come, we must go," said the magician shortly, and soon they were travelling again.

For seven more days they rode, and at last reached a towering mountain, crested with snow.

"Here we are, the Mountain of the Clouds" said the magician, "There, on the mountain, grows something which helps me to make gold. I need some of that, and you will get it for me. Together we shall make enough gold to fulfill all our desires."

"Yes," agreed Hasan, for now he had fallen completely under the old man's spell.

There was a place on the mountainside, and the magician said "See that place, it is the home of spirits: the Jaan, Ghools, and Devils!"

The old man then killed one of the camels and wrapping Hasan in its skin, commanded him to stand on the open mountainside.

"But what will become of me?" Hasan asked, with a tremor of fear.

"The Rukhs will come, and carry you up to the top of the mountain, to a great nest, and you can cut your way out of the camel-skin with this knife. Frighten the Rukhs, and you can then do as I will tell you."

"What are the Rukhs?" Hasan wanted to know.

"Enormous birds, who can easily bear you up there, they will think you are a camel, and wish to feed on you. However, scare them off when you get there by waving your arms and shouting, and throw me down some of that wood in the great nest so that we can make gold again," said the magician, then he hid behind a boulder. "Remember! I am depending on you, my dear son!"

When Hasan was apprehensively waiting, a great bird flapped down: and carried him to its nest on top of the mountain, as easily as if he had been a mouse.

He cut himself out of the skin, and drove off the bird. The voice of the magician came to him, "Throw down the wood! Throw all you can!"

Soon Hasan had thrown down all there was in the gigantic nest. "Good, that is all I need," shouted the magician, "I will go now, and you can rot up there, for all I care!" His mocking laughter echoed in Hasan's ears.

Mounting his camel, the magician rode off, leading the second camel with panniers of the precious wood on its sides.

Hasan was horrified. How was he to get down the mountain, and would the great bird attack him if he did? He made his way painfully down before the Rukhs came back, and at last found himself beside the wonderful palace where the magician had said there were Jaan, Ghools, and Devils. If they were enemies of the magician, perhaps they would help him. The great gates were open, and Hasan made his way from one courtyard to another, until he finally arrived at a room where two beautiful maidens were playing chess.

They did not seem the least bit alarmed by his appearance.

"Who are you?" asked one, while the other smiled at him pleasantly.

"Hasan of Basra, a jeweller," he replied, and told them his story.

"You must stay here with us and be our brother," said the second girl, "We rejoice that you are safe, for did you not pass here a short time ago with that dreadful magician who is our enemy?"

"Yes," said he, "He left me on the mountain to die." Then said the youngest girl to him:

"Let us tell you our history, for we are not demons or devils, but the daughters of a king.

"Our father is one of the Kings of the Jaan, who are good spirits; he has troops, servants and guards without number. We are seven sisters, and five others are at

the moment out hunting. Here in this place, which is in one of the loveliest parts of the world, we live in complete security, placed here by our father, who wants us to meet no humans nor jinn, for he loves us too much to let us get married."

"Are you all happy here?" asked Hasan.

"Of course, for we have everything which our hearts desire, and when there are weddings or festivals of the Jaan we are taken there and brought back here in all pomp and ceremony, as befits our position and birth." they answered. Then the other sisters, each more lovely than the last, returned, and they accepted him as a brother, begging him to live with them for a while.

The days were wonderful for Hasan after that, and he began to feel he had never lived anywhere else. Each day he walked and talked with the Princesses, and they gave him a secret room for himself. One day, to his horror, he saw the magician approaching (along the same road he himself had been brought) this time dragging a young man. The seven maidens dressed Hasan in armour, and he set out to do battle with the magician. The old man was too busy skinning a camel to notice him until Hasan cried "Villainous wretch! I am alive and will avenge myself!" With one blow of his sword he cut off the magician's head.

The young man, who was shackled to the Magician's second camel, was amazed at Hasan's appearance. "How can I thank you enough?" he asked, as Hasan released him. "Go home in peace, brother," said Hasan, and gave the young man the camels, bidding him make speed to his own country as fast as he could.

The maidens were delighted with Hasan's bravery, and they all returned to feast at the palace. But while the meal was at its height, a cloud was seen on the horizon.

"Hide, Hasan, hide," cried the maidens, "The troops of our father the King have come to take us on a visit!"

So he hid himself in the private room, and for three days and nights the troops of the King of the Jaan feasted in the hall of the palace.

On the third day, the youngest princess came to Hasan and said, "Brother, now we must go to a wedding at our father's command, and we shall be away for two months. During that time, treat this as your home and enjoy all its pleasures. But—and be careful of this or great misfortune will occur—do not open *that* door," and she pointed to a small door set in the wall of the secret room.

After the princesses and the troops had gone, Hasan felt lonely. But, after a while he hunted, and caught game, making himself his own meals. But, the forbidden door again and again caught his eye, until he was no longer able to ignore it. He turned the key in the golden lock, and opened it. There was a dark passageway beyond the door.

He went up some dark steps, and then came out onto a fine balcony at the top of the palace.

He looked out upon beautiful fields, flowers and fruit-trees, with singing birds the like of which he had never heard before.

It was such a wonderful place that he felt the exotic flower scents going to his head. There was a great silver lake, like a sheet of glass, and upon it he saw ten elegant birds alighting.

He watched with bated breath, from behind a shrub, as the exquisite birds drank and preened themselves, and sang. They uttered strange and wonderful cries, and flew onto the grass, plucking at their shimmering feathers with their talons. And Hasan, to his great amazement, saw them turn into beautiful women before his eyes. Nine birds were beautiful beyond belief, but the tenth bird-woman made Hasan mad with desire. Then, leaving their feather cloaks behind, they leapt into the lake and swam like swans.

Hasan watched, his heart in his mouth, and they came out of the water, drying themselves on their feather robes, the loveliest of them all taking great care to dry herself delicately with the feather-robe, like a wild bird that has always been free.

After they had talked and laughed a while, the chief damsel said "O daughters of kings, we have spent enough time here, let us fly away, for we are late indeed."

Then they became birds and rose in the air. The swishing of their wings was all that Hasan heard as he looked to see them circle, then they were gone.

Hasan returned to the inner rooms of the palace. His heart was stricken with love such as he had never known before, and he could neither eat nor sleep. He wandered about for days, not caring if he lived or died.

Each day he unlocked the door which had been forbidden to him, to gaze at the lake and wait for the sound of the bird-maiden's wings, but they did not come.

Beautiful small wild birds sang in the acacias, but they could not soothe the pain in his heart.

Then from the roof he saw the dust-cloud approaching, which told him the princesses were returning from the wedding surrounded by the troops of the King of the Jaan.

Hasan hid himself again till the soldiers rode away and the youngest princess came to tell him he could feast with them again. Hasan's eyes were lacklustre with grief as she looked into his face, and the youngest princess cried "Hasan, are you unwell? What has happened to you? You know that we are never ill here, for the water which flows from that river heals every ailment!"

Hasan said "I am dying of love for the leader of the Bird-Maidens; forgive me, I opened the door, and now I have to pay for that deed."

"Please do not tell my sisters," she said, "For they might punish you terribly!"

"I cannot be punished worse than I am now," murmured Hasan, lying back on his bed.

So the youngest maiden went and told the others that Hasan had pined for them while they were gone, and would soon be better now they had come home.

But day by day, Hasan seemed to get weaker.

Soon it was time for the sisters to go hunting, so they left Hasan in the care of the youngest, promising to bring him some fine game to tempt him. "Look after the Human" they told her, "For he is our beloved brother."

No sooner had they gone than the youngest princess came to Hasan and said "Come, show me where you saw the bird women. I would dearly like to see them myself," and Hasan managed to raise himself up. Leaning on the girl, he at last arrived with her at the top of the palace.

"There they landed," he said, "and there they divested themselves of their feathers, and there I saw *her* in all her great beauty, and fell hopelessly, utterly in love, sister."

Then the princess became very pale and said:

"Brother, you have fallen in love with one of the daughters of a King of the Jaan who is like our father; and, like him, immensely powerful.

"The eldest, whom you have described, is distinguished above all of us in magical guile and wisdom. You are in great trouble if you love her, for you can never have her. Her father is the most powerful of all our Kings."

"But I must have her, or I will die." said Hasan.

"Then," said the youngest princess, "This is what you must do: if you would have her, you must wait till she puts off her feather robe, and possess yourself of it. You must keep it somewhere safe, hidden, and then you can marry her."

"I shall come every day until she is here again!"

Hasan cried, "She *shall* be my wife, for I can never love any other in the world!"

The girl told him: "Remember, never give her back that dress once you have taken it, or she will take wing and escape. When you catch her, hold onto her by her long black hair, and her sisters will fly away. Then you will have gained possession of her."

Day after day, Hasan returned secretly to the spot where he had first seen the bird-maidens.

He ate and drank with the youngest sister, for now he had something to live for, and he daily grew stronger.

At last, when he had almost despaired of seeing them the air was full of the rush of wings, and the bird-maidens landed on the lake. They came to the bank, and began to take off their feather robes. The one princess of whom Hasan was so enamoured left hers within a few feet of him, as he stood hidden behind a flowering shrub. With a little cry of joy she joined the rest in the water.

Hasan snatched the robe and put it inside his shirt. After they had swum around for some time, the maidens returned to the bank and began to dress. All except Hasan's beloved. She searched in the grass for her robe and her face was very close to his. He caught her by the hair and held her, in spite of her weeping. The others dressed quickly and flew up into the air, and soon they were gone. Hasan begged the beautiful maiden to forgive him, saying, "I love you, dearest lady, with a pure and true love, come with me and be my wife!" She kicked and bit, but he put his arms around her, and wrapping her in his cloak, carried her gently to his private room.

After a while, she quietened and he opened the door to the youngest sister of his hostesses.

"I have found her," he cried, "I have caught her!"

Then the youngest damsel bowed herself down before the beautiful Bird-Maiden, and kissed the ground in front of her, and blessed her.

The daughter of the Jaan King said icily:

"Is this how a daughter of a King of the Jaan is treated here in your domain? Do you either of you realise how mighty and powerful is my father? Come, give me back my feather robe, and I shall be back home before my sisters have missed me!"

But the youngest Princess talked long and soothingly to the Bird-Maiden, and told her how Hasan loved her, and how he had been their dear brother for many months, never being other than kind and thoughtful to them.

The Princess of the Jaan began to be more at ease,

and ate and drank with Hasan when food was brought to the room.

At last she actually smiled, and Hasan, dressed now in his finest clothes, bowed low over her hand and said "Oh Lady of Loveliness, be my wife and I will love you for ever, and you will never regret one moment of our life together!"

Then the other sisters returned from hunting, and sent for Hasan to eat with them.

He went to the eldest and kissed her brow, saying: "Dear sister, while you were away I opened the door which is forbidden; but I found the loveliest woman in the world to be my wife. Please forgive me for disobeying your command, and let me enjoy life with she whom I adore!"

At first the sisters were most angry and said "Ah, so you are like all the sons of Adam, after all! You people can never be trusted!"

"Sisters," said the youngest damsel, "Can you blame him, after we left him completely and utterly alone so far away from anywhere? Let us be glad he has caught his beloved, and now has become well again, for he was wasting away!"

"What is she like?" asked the other sisters, full of curiosity, not so displeased with Hasan now that they scented a true romance.

Then, the Bird-Maiden came to them, in the main hall, and they were amazed at her beauty and dignity.

"O daughter of the Supreme King of the Jaan!" said the eldest sister, "Take this human being, and be happy together, for we can vouch for his character. He has told us he has burned the dress of feathers, and we beg you to forget your native land."

Then, one of the damsels deputised for her in the matter of the marriage-contract, and she and Hasan became man and wife.

For forty days and nights they celebrated the wedding in the palace, and at last, Hasan and the Bird-Maiden set out for Basra so that they could live together for the rest of their lives.

"Visit us sometimes," said the seven princesses of the Jaan, as they said goodbye to the newly married pair, now at the head of a vast caravan of laden camels carrying gifts of great price, "and let us not wonder what happens to you, Hasan, for you will always be our dear brother."

Then they threw flower petals on the couple, and Hasan and his bride agreed that they would never forget them or neglect them in the years ahead.

At last, Hasan arrived in the courtyard of his old home, his camels were tethered to the posts outside, and he knocked loudly on the door.

When the mother of Hasan opened it, she could scarcely believe her eyes. "My son, I had given you up for dead," she wept, "But now I am happier than I ever have been in my life."

"This is my beautiful wife from a far land," said Hasan, "Let us come in and we will show you many rich presents which we have been given."

So the mother of Hasan was enchanted by the beautiful young wife, and took her to her heart.

But soon, the mother-in-law said to her son: "Hasan, we must go to the great city of Baghdad so that you may have a big shop befitting your new dignity; let us leave Basra and become important in Baghdad!"

So Hasan moved his belongings and established himself in a new shop which sold fine gold ornaments, and his wife and mother were both pleased.

The house of a minister of the Royal court was to be sold, as the minister needed a larger one, and Hasan bought it. After one year of happily married life, Hasan's wife bore him a son, Nasir, and again a year later, another son, Mansoor.

Hasan's happiness was complete. Never, he felt, had a human being had so much joy on earth.

Three years had passed since the damsels of the Jaan had begged Hasan not to forget them, and one day he said to his wife: "My dear, I will go now and see my seven sisters again, and tell them how things have prospered for us."

Sweetly, his wife agreed to his going, and he loved her even more.

Then he went to his mother and told her the secret of his wife's feather-cloak, and bade his mother keep it safely in the chest buried in the courtyard. "For," he said, "if my wife were ever to find that she would fly away and leave me, and I could never get her back."

His mother agreed to keep the cloak safely hidden, and Hasan rode away, with many presents for the seven damsels.

For the first three days after Hasan's going, the Bird-Maiden showed her mother-in-law great respect, and they exchanged all sorts of confidences.

Then, wheedlingly, the young wife said:

"Mother, let us go to the Baths today. All the time I have been in Baghdad I have never been. Will you take me and the children? I have always wanted to go."

So, they went.

After an hour, the older woman wanted to return

home, but the younger one was enjoying it so much that she asked if she could stay on longer. The mother of Hasan gave permission, and left.

Now, a favourite of the Commander of the Faithful happened to be in the Baths that day, and took back to the Princess Zubeydeh all the gossip from the Baths. She mentioned that a beautiful woman, with two children as lovely as moons, were at the Baths, and the Princess wanted to know who she could be.

"Ah, Princess, I went home with her to find out," said the favourite, "And she lives in the house of the minister of my lord's court, which now belongs to a goldsmith from Basra. But, my Lady Zubeydeh, if my lord could only see her, I am sure he would want her to grace the harem!"

"As beautiful as that?" said the princess reflectively; "I would like to see her. Send a message that she must come to me, and bring the children, too." The Princess Zubeydeh was always looking for suitable slaves as presents for her lord, and this strange woman seemed to have possibilities.

So, Mesroor, a trusted eunuch of the royal harem, was sent to the house of Hasan the Goldsmith of Basra.

"The Lady Zubeydeh, wife of the Commander of the Faithful, sends an invitation for the lady of the house to visit her," said the eunuch when the mother of Hasan opened the door, "and she should bring her two children with her also," he added.

Hasan's mother was greatly worried, as she felt they should not go in the absence of her son, but the eunuch smoothly explained that it was a courtesy extended as a great favour, and so the Bird-Maiden and her children went to the Royal harem.

The Princess Zubeydeh was delighted with the looks of the fair stranger and her children, and showed her many of her finest garments. "Have you any to match these in your country?" she asked, as priceless silks and brocades were paraded before her.

"Yes, I have a feather robe so fine and so delicate it has all the colours of the sun and the moon!" said the Bird-Maiden with much pride.

"Indeed!" said the Princess Zubeydeh, "I should like to see that—a robe made of feathers! Show it to me!"

"My husband's mother keeps it hidden, and will not let me have it," replied the Bird-Maiden. She had overheard her husband telling his mother to keep it safe before he left. "You, dear Lady, ask her to give it to me, and I will show it to you with great joy."

"No, no, there is no such thing as a feather robe!"

said the mother-in-law. "She exaggerates; why, how could there be a robe of feathers all the colours of the sun and moon?"

But the Princess felt that the girl was telling the truth, and sent the eunuch Mesroor to find it. Find it he did, after a short delay, and soon the beautiful robe, with not one feather missing, was once more in the young wife's hands.

She took it with trembling fingers from the eunuch, while the mother-in-law bit her lip, and put it on. It fitted just as it had three years before, and she put her sons inside the robe, singing like a bird, walking like a bird, fastening the feathers around her. She preened and pirouetted before the ladies of the court, and the Princess especially was delighted at the sight of so much loveliness. "Truly it is a wonderful dress," said the Princess Zubeydeh, "Can you show us how to fly in it?"

No sooner were the words out of her mouth than the Bird-Maiden shook out her wings and flew away, taking her children with her. She called to her mother-in-law as she went: "If my husband wants to find me, tell him I am going to the Islands of Wak-Wak!" Then she was lost from sight.

When Hasan returned, his mother was not long in telling him the story, ending with the last words of his wife as she flew away.

"The Islands of Wak-Wak!" shouted Hasan in his grief. "Where are they? The only ones who would know are my seven enchanted sisters, I will ask them," so he turned about and returned to them.

They listened to the tale without speaking, even as he cried "Where are the islands of Wak-Wak, for find her I must, even if I lose my life in the attempt!"

But the seven sisters would not tell him, saying "Be patient, you will be cured of your love in time, for you cannot go to those islands."

However, the younger sister pleaded, as usual, with the six others, on Hasan's behalf, and at last they told him.

"Your wife must want you," they said, "Or else why should she tell your mother where she had gone?"

Now they had a powerful uncle, and his name was Abdelqoodoos. He loved the eldest damsel best of all, and came to see her once a year, bringing many presents.

They had told him about Hasan the Goldsmith, on his last visit, and he was delighted when they gave him the news that Hasan had cut off the head of the villainous magician.

"If anything evil should ever happen to that young man," he said, "Let someone put a few grains from this pouch on the coals of a brazier, and I will come at once to help."

The eldest damsel said to the youngest "Quickly, get that pouch my uncle gave me, and let us summon him."

As soon as the grains were burning on the coals, a puff of smoke appeared on the horizon. It turned out to be the girls' uncle, riding upon an elephant.

"What do you require, O daughters of my brother?" asked the old man, as soon as they had greeted him.

"Uncle, our interest in Hasan the Goldsmith has prompted us to request your help," was the reply, "Will you kindly assist him?"

"I will," said the uncle, "But no doubt this man is in a very dangerous situation. Is that not so?"

"It is," said they, "But what is he to do?"

"Mount up behind me on the elephant," said he, and after kissing them all goodbye, Hasan did so. The animal took them on for a very long way, until they arrived at a sapphire-blue mountain.

The uncle dismounted, and so did Hasan, and Hasan was given these instructions. "Stay here until I can have some conversation with one within, and come in when you are sent for." The old man then dismissed the elephant with a magical phrase, and it disappeared. Abdelqoodoos knocked three times on the rock, and a gigantic slave with a sword appeared. He kissed the sheikh's hands, and opened the door. The skeikh said to Hasan "I will be as quick as I can, have patience." He went through the door with the apparition, and the door clanged shut.

It seemed an age to Hasan before the sheikh returned, but he was smiling.

He took Hasan by the hand through another door, but this time it opened out onto a vast desert. Outside that door stood an Arab steed, saddled and bridled.

"Take this horse," said the old man, "And ride as far as it will let you. When it stops, knock upon the door of brass, and there will come out to you a sheikh all in black.

"Here is a letter; give it to him. He will take it away. If he comes back himself, you may proceed further. If one of his young men comes, sword in hand, you will know your mission has failed. Here is the letter. If you need to escape, call upon the elephant—his name is Fil. He will take you back to safety with the daughters of my brother, and you shall have a better wife than this one which has flown from you now."

"By all that is Holy!" cried Hasan, "I shall never love another! How can I go to these Islands of Wak-Wak that I may see her and my children again?"

"The Islands of Wak-Wak are seven islands, and the inhabitants of those islands are many thousands of virgins, like a great army," replied the skeikh, "I do not know how you can find the island where your wife is now hidden, but if you must go on, then you must. Farewell!"

Before Hasan could thank him, he thrust a letter into his hand, and disappeared. Hasan drove his own steed forward.

Finally Hasan, in great anguish and uncertainty, arrived at the place of which the sheikh had spoken. The horse stopped, neighed, and pawed the ground with its front right hoof.

Hasan dismounted, placed the reins on the pommel, and the horse kicked the sand. Hasan knocked at a great brass door, and the sound echoed strangely.

After a few moments, an old sheikh dressed all in black came to the door and opened it. Hasan saluted him. "Father, please will you read this letter and tell me if I am allowed to proceed further?" said he.

The old man bowed his head and smiled, taking the letter. "Wait here," he said in a low voice. The door opened again. It was the sheikh himself, all dressed in white, instead of the young man to kill him. Hasan felt jubilant, and his heart soared.

Inside the cave, Hasan looked around him. It was as large as any palace hall he had ever imagined, gleaming like purest crystal. Everywhere, great lamps of brass hung from the roof of the cave.

They went through this area, and at last came out to an open garden, where fruits and flowers grew in profusion. Birds sang, and the sound of water gushing from fountains was everywhere.

The skeikh signed to Hasan to sit with him on a seat of marble, and four sheikhs similar to himself approached.

"Recite the tale of your doings to these sheikhs and myself," said the man in white, "and take your own time about it. There is no hurry."

So Hasan told his story.

"Is that the vile magician who caused you to be taken to the top of the mountain, whom you have slain?" one cried.

"Yes, it was," said Hasan.

Then the four sheikhs looked at each other and pursed their lips and said: "O Sheikh of Sheikhs, this young man has suffered enough." They looked at

Hasan and with the kindest expression in their eyes said: "He should be reunited with his wife. O Aburruweysh, for the sake of your brother Abdelqoodoos, give him further help."

Then, the sheikh in white wrote a letter with his own hand, and gave it to Hasan. "Take this, and I shall summon transportation for you." He clapped his hands, and a gigantic Jinn appeared, one of the Flyers, who stood before the sheikh with an expression of the deepest respect.

"You are Dahnash?" asked the sheikh.

"Yes, master, Dahnash, son of Faktash," he replied.

" Take this human being to the Land of Camphor, so that he may give this letter to its King," said the sheikh.

Hasan then was lifted up onto the broad shoulders of Dahnash the Flyer. "One last word," said the old man, "When you are taken into the heavens, on the shoulders of this efrit, and you hear the praises of the angels, utter not a word, or you will fall."

"I promise," said Hasan, and thanked the old man from the depth of his heart.

"Whatever the King of the Camphor Land asks you to do, you should do," said the sheikh, "and may your affairs prosper!"

As he spoke the efrit rose high into the air, and Hasan heard the angels at their prayers, but he kept his mouth shut, and remained safe on the shoulders of Dahnash.

A night and a day they flew, and then came to a land that was as white as snow, the Land of Camphor.

Hasan dismissed the efrit, and took the letter to the King's palace.

Now, the King of the Land of Camphor was a magnificent ruler, called Haroon, and he received Hasan kindly. "Come to me tomorrow morning," he said, "now go and rest."

A court official took Hasan to the house reserved for guests, and he slept like the dead all night. At the early morning court of the magnificent King, Hasan was the first admitted. The King was reading the letter, and shaking his head over it.

"What is your condition?" the King asked Hasan. "Ill," replied Hasan, "But I seek to remedy that."

"I send ships to the Islands of Wak-Wak, and sometimes they send ships to me," said the King.

"Tomorrow one of their ships will come here," he continued, "and you shall embark upon it, I will have you placed on board under my protection."

"King, may you live for ever!" said Hasan, fervently, "I would give my life for even one glimpse of my wife!"

"Take great care, or you may be in danger beyond estimation," warned the King, "You are lucky that you arrived at this time; I hope that your luck will hold."

So, next day, Hasan was sent on board one of the ships bound for the Islands of Wak-Wak, under the King's protection, and the ship set sail.

For the next ten days the ship went on, through shark-infested seas, till its anchor was thrown out, and Hasan stepped ashore.

On the dockside there were a thousand or more beautiful divans, with cushions and fine cloths draped on them, as if a huge concourse of people were in the habit of using them to rest.

He hid behind one of the divans, and waited silently. When evening came, there arrived a great company of female soldiers, converging upon the place where the divans were arranged.

Each soldier threw herself upon one divan, and discoursed with her neighbour. They were dressed in chain-mail, with swords in their hands. Hasan saw they were all tall and most beautifully formed, notwithstanding their rough attire and warlike equipment.

They wore steel helmets, with intricate designs, and had thongs binding their legs.

Hasan waited until he saw one approach his divan, and called to her in a low voice, "O help me, I beg you not to kill me!"

She looked at him with great blue eyes full of fire, her sword in her hand ready for action.

"Who are you?" she asked.

"My name is Hasan," he answered, "Take under your protection one who has lost his wife and children, and does not want to lose his life in search of them without putting up a fight!"

She was intrigued, and he heard her say "Hasan my son, you are fortunate you have chosen an old woman, for I fear one of my young officers would have killed you! Hide under this divan, and wait; what is to be, will be."

Hasan concealed himself, and the time passed with stories of war and battles far too bloodthirsty for his tender heart. The female army desported themselves, and told tales and laughed loudly like the soldiers they were.

Now, the woman he had spoken to appeared in the darkness and handed him coat of mail and chain-mail trousers just like those which the women wore, and signed to him to put them on over his own clothes. She then gave him a steel helmet and beckoned him

to follow her.

He did so, and she led him to a tent which was obviously that of the commander, from the pennants fluttering outside.

He saw her, now that she was without her armour, to be old and hideous, pockmarked with smallpox, grizzled of head, and bold of face. The only thing good about her was her candid blue gaze.

Appealing to her humorous eyes, Hasan begged for sanctuary. She asked him "How in the world did you get here, and why and how long do you expect to live, now that you have arrived?" and she slapped her hip, laughing.

Hasan answered as best he could; and she was so impressed by his replies that she promised him her protection as commander of the army. Hasan thanked his lucky stars that he had chosen her.

The commander then sent instructions to her officers to take the army out in battle order, and to rehearse for their next foray. None was to remain in the camp, under pain of death.

As soon as they had all marched away, the old woman told Hasan that she was called Shawahee, and that she was in possession of news for him.

"Your wife, of whom I have heard, is on the seventh island of the Islands of the Wak-Wak. The distance from here is very far, and fraught with danger," she said.

"I must go, whatever the perils," said Hasan. She nodded approvingly. "You must go past the island of the hyenas, the place where the lions roar; the Island of Birds, where terrible birds of prey utter horrible cries continually; then you must pass over the Land of the Jinn, where the flames rise from the ground, and no man can live in peace. But I will take you, and we shall pass all these places, and more, till we come to a great river, and this river extends to the Islands of Wak-Wak. Do you understand the dangers?"

"I do, but I would go to the ends of the world," said Hasan fervently, "For I love my wife, and I believe she loves me."

"Do you realise that you may lose your life?" asked the female commander.

"Yes," said Hasan stoutly, "And if you will help me, I am ready to go now."

"Those islands get their name from the trees which have heads fixed upon their branches, which continually raise their eyes to Heaven and cry "Wak-Wak!" she told him, "I will make all arrangements, and we shall go when my soldiers return."

"So be it," said Hasan, and prayed to Allah that he might be successful.

By dawn, the entire army returned, and Hasan heard the commander address them, and tell them that she was leading them on an expedition to the dreaded Islands of Wak-Wak. Each woman raised her spear in the air and cheered. The Commander was a popular one with the troops. Dressed in mail, Hasan left at the side of the female chief, full of courage and strength of purpose. The jingling of the harness, neighing of horses, the rattle of swords in their scabbards was music to his ears.

Sometimes they travelled by road, sometimes by sea, suffice it to tell that at long last Hasan looked upon the green Islands of Wak-Wak, where the heads, impaled upon the branches of trees, continually cried out "Wak-Wak!" and those pitiful cries pierced the hearts of whoever heard them.

"Now, Hasan," said the commander, pointing to a wondrous palace, "there lies the place where your wife lives. Wear this cap of invisibility. It will take you safely into the very midst of her father's guards.

"Go, and blessings upon you." Then she turned her troops about and departed.

Lean as a greyhound, sunburned as dark as a Moor, still as strong as when he began his search, Hasan went to the palace. It was guarded by heavily armed men, soldiers of the King of the Jaan.

But, with the magic cap, he was able to enter the gate, and penetrate to the room where, on a bed covered with a cover of gold brocade, his wife lay asleep.

After the long campaign, his gruelling marches and long rides on horseback, voyages by sea and land, Hasan felt he could have shouted aloud at seeing at long last that beautiful face.

But, having a care for his safety, he bent over the bed, and whispered in her ear "I am here, my Beauty of Beauties, here is Hasan, come to take you away!"

When she woke, and looked around, he took off the cap of invisibility, and she saw him.

The Bird-Maiden cried out "Hasan! It is not safe for you to be here! You will be killed if you are seen!"

"I have got so far without being killed, my love, and I shall get you away safely, too," he said. He quickly told her the story of the last few months' journey.

"I never thought to see you again," she murmured, "It has been so long since I returned here."

"Is it not enough that I have come?" he answered, "I shall take you and the children away with me."

"You cannot! It is impossible," she said, "You do not know how well-guarded we are. My father would never let me escape. Go now, and save yourself, forget about me."

"You cannot take from me the spoils of my victory!" answered Hasan, boldly, "I have won my way to you, and as you are my wife, I shall take you!"

"You must know what we would have to face, on the way back, and it may be death for you any moment now!" cried the Bird-Maiden.

Then his two sons came into the room, and knew their father, and he played with them a while.

The Queen, the Bird-Maiden's mother, then knocked on her daughter's door saying "What is this I hear, a man's voice? Open to me that I may punish you, for no one of the human sort may be allowed in this holiest island of all our Islands!"

So Hasan straightaway put on his cap of invisibility, and hid from the Queen's sight, and she went away satisfied that there was no one there.

That evening, as dusk came, Hasan came out of the closet of his wife's room, and said to her:

"Come, my love, you take one child and I will take the other, and we will go from here, for I am strong, and you must go with me."

So, they each took a child in their arms, and Hasan with his cap of invisibility, led her through the guards, who lay on the palace floors, in twos and threes, like sleeping dogs.

Just as they got to the palace grounds, they met an old woman.

"Let me help you," she said, "O daughter of the Jann, I see your husband, who is human, though he has a cap of invisibility on his head. Take this reed, and strike it three times upon the ground, and Efrits will come to bear you away."

The Bird-Maiden thanked her, and gave her a jewel from her finger. The Bird-Maiden struck the reed three times upon the ground, and two gigantic efrits came, bowing low in homage.

"We obey the owner of the Magic Reed," they said, "Give us your orders and we shall perform our duty."

"What distance is there between here and Baghdad?" asked Hasan.

"Not far, if we take you upon our shoulders," said the efrits, and Hasan said:

"Then let us go to Baghdad, now!"

One efrit took the Bird-Maiden and one child, and Hasan was lifted upon the shoulder of the second, his younger son in his arms.

The air was filled with a strange rushing sound, the night became black, without a star in the sky, and Hasan felt himself being carried at great speed through the air.

In less time than it takes to tell, the two efrits landed safely in Hasan's garden in Baghdad, and placed Hasan, his wife and the children safely on the ground.

Dismissing the efrits, Hasan loudly knocked on his own door, calling his mother with joyful anticipation. His wife, standing beside him, looked at him with her eyes shining with love.

In a few moments he heard the bolts being drawn, and his mother opened the door.

The moment she saw them, the old woman shrieked with happiness. Then she clasped them in her arms, one by one. Hasan vowed to himself that never again would he ever leave his home, or his family. His wife went to her own apartments, and dressed herself and the children in their finest clothes.

"Husband," said she, when Hasan went in to her, "I swear I have learned by being parted from you that I love you with all my heart, and will never leave you again. Light the fire," she continued and when he did so, she dropped the feather robe into the flames. Then she returned shyly to Hasan's arms.

Within a few weeks, Hasan once more became the Goldsmith of Basra, and they lived happily the rest of their lives. ∎

The Slowest May Win The Race

The hare and the tortoise, according to Aesop, ran a race because the hare boasted about his speed, but the tortoise won because of his steady plodding. But the theme of the animal race in which the slower wins has been presented among all manner of people to illustrate a variety of supposed truths. In a Sinhalese tale it is a lion and a tortoise, and the latter arranges with his brother to appear at the opposite side of a river bearing a flower in token of identity. Far from there being a virtue in plodding, the slower creature here uses only his wits. In Madagascar, a chameleon actually makes a wild hog carry him in its mane. Every time the unwitting hog stopped, the chameleon leapt upon the grass a little way ahead and seemed to be in front.

The story has even travelled as far as Fiji, where a crane and a crab are in competition. This time the crane stops every now and then at a crab-hole and hears the buzzing which he takes for that of his challenger. The message is that anything may be accomplished by trusting to the co-operation of relatives.

Here is the Siamese presentation, collected in Thailand by Adolf Bastien.

The Garuda — magical bird of Vishnu — was hungry as, one day, he flew over a lake and saw a tortoise in it. The tortoise diverted his interest by suggesting that, before being eaten up, they should run a race to see who was the faster.

The magnificent bird agreed, and rose high into the air, ready to fly. While he was doing that, the tortoise collected all his friends and relatives — all the living tortoises — and placed them in rows of 100, of 1,000, of 10,000, of 100,000, of a million and of ten million, so that they covered every inch of the ground.

When he was ready, the tortoise called out:

"I am ready to start. Your Highness may go through the air, while I shall move by water, and we shall see who is the winner. The wager is that if I lose, you will be able to eat me up."

Now the Garuda flew with all his might, and then stopped and called to the tortoise. And, whichever direction he flew, a tortoise always answered him, from somewhere ahead. He even flew as far as the great mountain, the Himaphan. At last he had to tell the tortoise that he had been outraced, and he returned, baffled, to his home, the *rathal* tree, to rest. ∎

The
Three Imposters

One hundred years before the European invention of printing, Prince Manuel, nephew of the Spanish King Alfonso the Wise, wrote 'The Fifty Pleasant Stories', one of the real gems of early Spanish literature. He died in 1347, and the book was not printed until over two hundred years afterwards, when it appeared in Seville. It lay forgotten until the Madrid edition of 1642, and these two impressions are today among the rarest books in the world. After nearly another two centuries it came out in Stuttgart (1839) and then in Paris the following year. This story, 'A King and Three Imposters', is said by Prince Manuel to come from a Moorish source. It is, of course, undoubtedly the basis of Hans Christian Andersen's 'The Emperor's New Clothes.'

Three imposters came to a king and told him that they were weavers, and could produce a cloth of such a strange kind that a legitimate son of his father could see it, but nobody else could, even if they were believed to be legitimate.

Now the King was much pleased at this, thinking that by this means he would be able to distinguish those who were the sons of their supposed fathers from those who were not. So he ordered a palace to be set aside for the making of this cloth. The three men, to convince him that they were genuine and sincere, agreed to be shut up in this building until the cloth had been made; and this satisfied the King.

The weavers were given a large quantity of gold, silver and silk and many other things to work with. They set up their looms in the palace and pretended that they were working all day at the cloth.

After some days, one of the men went to the King and told him that the cloth had been started, and he told him all kinds of things about it, and asked him to visit them, but asked that he should come alone.

The King was very pleased, but thought that he would get another opinion of the magical fabric first, so he sent the Lord Chamberlain to have a look. The Lord Chamberlain duly went and could see nothing, but he dared not admit that the wonderful cloth was invisible to him, so he returned to the King and said that he had really seen it.

The King then sent someone else, and received the same report. Now the King decided to see for himself.

When he entered the Palace, the King found the men there, and they described the cloth in detail, including its design. They all agreed on these details,

and even the origin and method of making of the cloth. The King could not see anything at all, for there was no cloth there. But he began to feel very uneasy, fearing that he might not be the true son of the King who was supposed to be his father. "If *I* cannot see it," he thought, "I might have to lose my kingdom, which depends upon inheritance". So he started to praise the cloth, and repeated the details which the imposters had outlined.

When he returned to his own palace, the King continued to speak of the cloth as if it were real, though at the same time he inwardly suspected that something was wrong.

After a few days, the monarch asked his Wakil, the officer of justice, to go and see the cloth. Exactly the same thing happened to the Wakil. He went into the palace of the weavers, who described the pattern, though he could see nothing of any cloth of any kind. Naturally the unhappy Wakil immediately imagined that he could not be the true son of his father, and that that must be the cause of the material remaining invisible to him. Fearing that the discovery of this fact about him would mean the loss of his important position, the Wakil set about praising the non-existent cloth in even more extravagant terms than the King and the Lord Chamberlain.

He went back to the King, and told him that he had, indeed, viewed the cloth, and that it was the most extraordinary tissue in the world. The King was deeply distressed: there could now, he thought, be no doubt that he himself was not the offspring of his father. But he hastened to agree with the rapturous descriptions of the wondrous fabric brought him by the law officer. And he did not forget to add unstinted praise for the inspired workmen who were weaving it.

The King continued to send people to see the cloth, and they, not unnaturally, all came back to him with the same impressions as everyone else.

This tale continued in just the same way until the King was told that the cloth was finished. He ordered that a great feast be prepared, where everyone should be dressed in clothes made from the miraculous material. The weavers thereupon presented themselves, with 'some of the cloth' rolled in fine linen, and asked his Majesty how much would be required; and the King told them the quantity and what kind of clothes were to be made.

The feast day arrived, and the clothes were reported to be complete. The weavers came to the King with the magic robe which he himself was to wear. The King, of course, did not dare to say that he could not see it, or even feel it.

Now the imposters pretended to dress the King in his new clothes; and he mounted his horse and rode into the city. Luckily it was summer time! People who saw the King pass were very surprised at what they beheld. But word had got around that only the illegitimate were unable to see the cloth, so people kept their distress and amazement to themselves.

All of them did, in fact, except a black man who was among those lining the streets. He immediately approached the King and said:

"Sire, it is of no interest to me whose son I am. So I can tell you that in fact you are riding about without any clothes on!"

At first the King struck the black a blow, saying that he must be illegitimate and that was why the cloth was invisible to him. But other people, once the spell of silence and fear had been broken, saw that it was true, and said the same. Even the King and his court now realized that they had been tricked.

The false weavers, of course, when they were sought, were found to have fled with the things which the King had given them 'to make the cloth from'. ■

It is often claimed that folk-tales represent survivals of ancient religious beliefs. This story either gives the lie to that suggestion — since it has no identifiable Christian message — or else it supports it: if it represents some other, more ancient belief-system. How the individual can prevail over and dominate a spiritual power, upon which he is shown in the tale itself to depend for the benefits of the Hereafter, is justified, can perhaps only be explained by the wish-fulfillment factor.

This account, although not the only example of its kind, is taken from Sicilian folklore.

Occasion

There was once an orphan, named "Occasion", who was taken in, from pity, by a certain couple. When he was grown up, the foster-parents said:

"Well, Occasion, is it not time that you supported yourself, as you are now a man?"

Occasion set off on his travels, and journeyed until he became completely exhausted and ragged. He arrived at an inn, where he asked to become a servant, in exchange for nothing more than a piece of bread for wages.

The innkeeper and his wife, Rosella, took him in, and he worked so well that they adopted him. When they died he inherited the inn.

When Occasion took over the establishment he announced: "Whoever should come to Occasion's Inn can have food for nothing."

Jesus and St. Thomas heard about this, and the latter said that he did not believe it, and would only credit it if he touched it with his hands. They went and ate and drank and were well entertained by Occasion.

Before leaving, St. Thomas asked whether Occasion would like a favour from the Master. Occasion said that he could not get any figs from his tree, as boys climbed up it and stole them. "I would like this favour" he asked, "that whenever anyone climbs this tree, he just stays there until I allow him down."

The request was granted. Occasion found that all the boys who climbed the tree were stuck fast, and he punished them when they tried to steal his fruit, and they stole no more.

Occasion's money was coming to an end as time passed. So he called a carpenter and had him make a bottle from the wood of the fig-tree. The power of this bottle was that whoever was shut in it could not get out.

Then Death came to Occasion, for he was now very old.

Occasion said:

"I am ready to go, but do me a favour. There is a fly in this wine bottle. Get it out for me before I drink, and then I will come with you."

Death went into the bottle, and Occasion put it in his wallet, saying "Stay a while with me."

Now, since Death was imprisoned, nobody died: there were old men with long white beards everywhere.

The disciples came to hear of this and went to the Master again and again. Eventually he visited Occasion and complained.

Occasion said:

"If you give me a place in paradise, I will let Death out."

The Lord thought: "If I do not agree, he will give us no peace." So he granted the request.

So people were allowed to die, and Occasion had some years of his own life left.

This is why there is a saying: "There is no death without Occasion." ■

World Tales was designed by Ivan Tyrrell and Alan Tunbridge of Carver Tyrrell & Tunbridge Ltd., Brighton, England.

The typeface used for this book is a film version of Souvenir. The tales are set in 12-point Souvenir Medium, and the introduction to each tale is set in 10-point Medium Italic. The Souvenir face was originally drawn in 1914 by Morris Fuller Benton.

The text was typeset by Origin, Ltd., Brighton, England.

Colour separations of the illustrations were prepared by Offset Separations/Mondadori, Milan, Italy.

The paper used for **World Tales** is 80-pound Warren's Patina.

The book was printed and bound by W. A. Krueger Co., New Berlin, Wisconsin.